Printed in Great Britain
by Amazon

53615704R00147

The Vault
of Walt

VOLUME NINE

Halloween Edition

Spooky Stories of Disney Films,
Theme Parks, and Things
That Go Bump In the Night

Jim Korkis

Theme Park Press
The Happiest Books on Earth
www.ThemeParkPress.com

Theme Park Press is not associated with the Walt Disney Company.

The views expressed in this book are those of the author and do not necessarily reflect the views of Theme Park Press.

Theme Park Press publishes its books in a variety of print and electronic formats. Some content that appears in one format may not appear in another.

Editor: Bob McLain
Layout: Artisanal Text

ISBN 978-1-68390-274-4
Printed in the United States of America

Theme Park Press | www.ThemeParkPress.com

Address queries to bob@themeparkpress.com

Dedicated to Jack Hannah, the director of the Disney Halloween short Trick or Treat, *who was the first Disney animator I ever interviewed and who always gave me little treats of information.*

Like me, he loved that particular cartoon and, of course, the lesson that was in its theme song: "Trick or Treat. Trick or Treat for Halloween. When ghosts and goblins by the score ring the bell on your front door, better not be stingy or your nightmares will come true."

Contents

Introduction

I always wanted to write a book filled with the stories of Disney and Christmas that I had collected over the decades. When I started to review the material, I was surprised and pleased that it all easily aligned with the format that I had established for the *Vault of Walt* series of books.

It was a no-brainer when it was all finally gathered together to just release it as Volume 7 in the series. The book was well received and my publisher asked if I might be able to do a similar book themed to Halloween.

The challenge was not to write just another book about Disney villains or Disney films that had some supernatural element but to tell stories specifically connected to Disney and Halloween.

I was intrigued and felt that I might be able to do something in a year. Over two years later, I finally finished. It always takes longer to write something than you expect especially when there is no previously existing material about so many of the chapter topics.

I was amazed at how much material I was eventually able to find that related to Halloween and was often guided by things that Disney included in its own Halloween compilations.

I grew up as a "Famous Monsters" kid. I eagerly read issues of *Famous Monsters* magazine and its many imitators. In the days before video recording, I had to schedule my Saturdays so I could watch in black-and-white the horror matinee movie on my local television channel and for films I loved like *King Kong* (1933) to try to catch the repeat showing later that day.

At Halloween, my family had limited means but my mother always found time to sew handmade costumes for me and my brothers using her sewing machine. One year I was attired as Robin Hood and the next year with some alterations it became

my Peter Pan costume. I also recall being a cowboy several times and Zorro twice.

In those days, no one worried about anyone tampering with Halloween candy. The big fear was not getting the "good" candy when approaching the houses of complete strangers and hearing stories the next day from friends who had better luck in a different neighborhood.

When I grew older, I assisted in the creation and operation of homemade backyard haunted houses for the holiday. I worked at Six Flags Magic Mountain for its first "Haunted Mountain" Halloween promotion where I helped design and build a not-so-scary Fun House with happy ghosts and funny black cats for children at the front of the park and performed as the wild Dr. Electric (looking very much like Doc Brown from *Back to the Future*) with his sparking electric chair for the amusement of adult guests up in Spillikin Corners.

I do believe in the supernatural and over the decades have had some brief encounters that had no other logical explanation but none at Disneyland or Walt Disney World.

Disney's approach to Halloween has the underlying elements of humor and safety. In only one Disney animated film, *The Legend of Sleepy Hollow*, does the villain actually win at the end although some may argue that Foxy Loxy in the 1943 animated short *Chicken Little* might be considered the only other example.

This book is my version, as that great showman Orson Welles said at the end of his 1938 CBS radio broadcast of *War of the Worlds*, "of dressing up in a sheet and jumping out of a bush and saying Boo!"

May all your Halloweens be happy Disney ones!

Jim Korkis
Disney Historian
July 2020

DISNEY ANIMATION

As a kid, I was terrified at the climax of the Disney animated feature film *Sleeping Beauty* (1959), where the evil fairy Maleficent, frustrated by all her previous failed attempts to stop Prince Phillip, conjures her dark powers to transform into a massive, fire-breathing dragon.

Artist Marc Davis has stated that the horns on her headdress were meant to represent the horns of the devil.

Having previously described herself as "the mistress of all evil", she cries out, "Now, shall you deal with ME, O' Prince—and all the powers of HELL!" However, the sound in the background partially obscures the end of the word "hell" although it is clearly obvious that is what Maleficent is saying.

I once wrote to former Disney Archivist Dave Smith if the Disney Archives had any record of complaint from audiences about the use of that word in a Disney animated film either on the film's initial release or subsequent re-releases. He responded that there was no record of any complaints.

The fact that the prince was finally able to kill the dragon with the Sword of Truth brought me some comfort but not enough to assuage the fear that Maleficent had engendered in the rest of the film or the fact that she could call on all the powers of Hell. As a kid, animation was as real to me as live action.

To create the sound of the dragon's fiery breath, Disney sound effects expert Jimmy MacDonald (also the voice of Mickey Mouse) contacted the United States Army for some training films on flame throwing. Castanets were used for the sound of the dragon's snapping jaws.

Of course, Disney had gone to Hell as early as the fourth Silly Symphony, *Hell's Bells* (1929).

Ub Iwerks is credited as the director and did much of the animation along with Les Clark and Wilfred Jackson on this five minute black-and-white cartoon. The Symphonies were intended to have no recurring characters and usually ended up having little or no real plotline. Primarily, they were intended for experimentation that would later be used in Disney's first animated feature film.

Most of the Symphonies tended to be dance numbers (as in the first Symphony, *The Skeleton Dance*) or lyrical, pastoral works (as in *The Old Mill* that also had some horrific scenes). In this cartoon, an imp band and dancers entertain the Devil.

The hooded Grim Reaper enters and then departs. A huge spider swings back and forth towards the audience (literally blacking out the entire screen for a moment) and then is consumed by flames. A snake-like dragon swallows a bat, sprouts the bat's wings, and flies off.

Satan's demons play instruments made from skeletons and skulls. Demons milk a goofy-looking, smiling "dragon-cow" and serve the flaming milk to Satan. Satan feeds one of the demons to Cerberus, his three-headed dog drawn to be comical rather than frightening. Satan chases another demon who refuses to be fed to Satan's hound. That demon ends up kicking Satan off a cliff ledge and Satan is consumed in a pit of flames as the film ends.

It certainly is a cartoon filled with disturbing images but is merely an excuse for unconnected gags timed to music that included Mendelssohn's *Spring Song*, Gounod's *Funeral March of a Marionette* (best remembered as the theme song for the *Alfred Hitchcock Presents* television show), Mendelssohn's *Fingal's Cave* and Grieg's *In the Hall of the Mountain King*.

The following chapters contain information on animation that was very closely tied to Halloween and still retains its powerful impact today.

The Skeleton Dance (1929)

Almost every Halloween, the Walt Disney Company seems to showcase one of its earliest black-and-white cartoons, *The Skeleton Dance* (1929), the very first Silly Symphony.

While not specifically stated to be Halloween, merely a supernatural frolic during the midnight hour, this five-and-a-half minute innovative short cartoon certainly encapsulates the imagery and spirit of the spooky holiday.

The cartoon starts with flashes of lightning and a close-up of an owl's eyes with a full moon in the background. The owl hoots in time with the music while the wind causes a branch, shaped like skeletal bones of a hand, to reach out to grab the bird. The clock strikes twelve and bats come flying from the belfry of the nearby church in the background. They fly towards the viewer as a spider pops down from seemingly nowhere.

A dog howls. Two cats on opposite gravestones meow at each other in syncopation and tug on each other's noses. They are scared away when the first skeleton appears from behind a tombstone between them. He springs forward toward the audience and then tiptoes through the graveyard.

He takes off his skull and flings it at the owl, knocking the feathers off the animal. Four skeletons appear and start their dancing and there are a series of gags from stretching taller and shorter, playing the ribcages of skeletons with leg bones, and grabbing a cat's tail to play like a cello string.

When the rooster crows as dawn approaches, the skeletons scramble back into a single casket. Unlike the Mickey Mouse cartoons, there is no storyline or focus on a single character. The dance sequence is full of variety from the skulls remaining still but the bodies swaying to performing a dainty pirouette to hopping on each other like a pogo stick.

The working title for the film was *The Spook Dance* although other suggested titles included *Mysterious Melodies* and *Haunted Harmonies*.

While working with Walt Disney on the scores for the first Mickey Mouse cartoons, Carl Stalling, who was basically the Disney Studios' first music director, had an idea for a new series of cartoons with the drawings made to fit the music that he suggested in late 1928.

He and Walt would get into arguments about the music for the Mickey Mouse cartoons. Stalling wanted the music to be more prominent and not have to force it to fit the action on the screen, a musical technique that would later be called "Mickey Mousing".

Walt wanted the music to more closely emphasize each action for comic effect and to be able to lengthen or shorten a sequence and have the music adapt to the changes.

Finally the disagreements got so intense that Walt told Stalling they would do a second series of cartoons because it would allow him to do some experimentation, not be restricted by the formula of the Mickey cartoons and generate an additional stream of revenue. In the new series, the score and the animation work together perfectly, completely in syncopation.

Initially, Walt thought that Stalling was envisioning something along the lines of the sing-a-long reels that had been done by studios like the Fleischers and had some popularity.

As Stalling told reseachers Michael Barrier, Milton Gray and Bill Spicer during a June 1969 interview: "He thought I meant illustrated songs, but I didn't have that in mind at all. When I told him that I was thinking of inanimate figures, like skeletons, trees, flowers, etc., coming to life and dancing and doing other animated actions fitted to music more or less in a humorous and rhythmic mood, he became very much interested. I gave him the idea of using the four seasons, and he made a cartoon on each one of those."

Walt wrote to his brother Roy and Ub Iwerks on September 25, 1928, that "Carl's idea of a skeleton dance for a musical novelty has been growing on me."

The subject for the first Silly Symphony had an interesting origin.

Stalling recalled:

> The Skeleton Dance goes way back to my kid days. When I was eight or ten years old, I saw an ad in The American Boy

magazine of a dancing skeleton, and I got my dad to give me a quarter so I could send for it. It turned out to be a pasteboard cut-out of a loose-jointed skeleton, slung over a six-foot cord under the arm pits. It would 'dance' when kids pulled and jerked at each end of the string.

As historians Russell Merrit and J.B. Kaufman have pointed out in their book about the Silly Symponies:

> (*The Skeleton Dance*) roots are labyrinthine, stretching back at least to the nineteenth century phosphorous skeleton marionettes and *danses macabres*. One of the first films ever made (in 1898) was a sixty second Eidson documentary called *Skeleton Dance, Marionettes* featuring Gray's Royal Marionettes; and seven years later Melies interpolated a skeleton dance into *Les Palais des Milles et une Nuits*.

> By the 1920s, skeleton dancing acts, like comic skeleton and ghost songs were staple as novelty entertainments.

Stalling said:

> Ever since I was a kid, I had wanted to see real skeletons dancing and had always enjoyed seeing skelton dancing acts in vaudeville.

The idea was given to Ub Iwerks who was the primary animator working for Walt and the two of them developed the ideas for gags as they did on previous cartoons with Stalling contributing some ideas as well.

Stalling used a bit of Edvard Grieg's *March of the Dwarfs* (1893) but primarily composed an original fox-trot piece so it seemed lively and a little jazzy in keeping with the times.

Stalling recalled:

> It wasn't Saint-Saens' *Danse Macabre*, although some writers have said it was. Walt couldn't get copyright clearance so he asked me to compose something similar, but my music wasn't similar at all to the *Danse Macabre*. It was mostly a fox trot, in a minor key.

> Walt never wanted to pay for music; he wanted me to just make up something. In one picture, he wanted to use the song *School Days*, but he would have had to pay for it. So he said, "Carl, can't you write something that sounds like *School Days* but isn't?"

> For a name or title for the series, I suggested not using the word 'music' or 'musical', as it sounded too commonplace, but

to use the word 'symphony' together with a humorous word. At the next gag meeting, I don't know who suggested it, but Walt asked me: "Carl, how would Silly Symphony sound to you?" I said, "Perfect!"

Iwerks went to the local library for inspiration. He found pictures drawn by the English cartoonist Rowlandson of skeletons dancing. In other books, he found photographs of skeleton dances depicted upon the walls of Etruscan tombs.

It was Iwerks who came up with the idea of the skeletons not rising from their graves to threaten people but just have a playful night of partying with each other. They would socialize, not terrorize. Iwerks experimented with different perspectives as well to provide an experience not previously seen by movie audiences.

Animation under Iwerks began in January 1929 with it taking almost six weeks to finish. The soundtrack was recorded at Pat Powers' Cinephone studio in New York in February 1929 along with the fifth Mickey Mouse short cartoon *The Opry House*. According to Roy O. Disney's records, the total cost for the film was $5,485.40.

Walt wrote to Ub from New York where he was meeting with theater exhibitors on February 9:

> I am glad the spook dance is progessing so nicely—give her hell, Ubbe. Make it funny and I feel sure we will be able to place it in a good way. I have them all worked up and raring to see it—so we can't disappoint them.
>
> We have a score to it. The music sounds like a little symphony. I feel positive everything will fit the picture properly. If it doesn't, it is possible we might fix the cartoon action to fit, judging by the way *The Opry House* fit. I feel positive it will be great.

On February 10, Walt wrote to his wife Lillian:

> I feel positive the 'Spook Dance' will make a real hit when shown. Everyone praises Ubbe's art work and jokes at his funny name.

The Skeleton Dance was completed in March 1929 and a preview was held on March 20.

Stalling remembered:

> It was a late show at the Vista Theater down on Hillhurst and Sunset in Hollywood; a small theater. Walt was disappointed

in it. There were very few people there, no house. We saw *Steamboat Willie* in New York at eight or nine o'clock, with a full house. But here in Hollywood, at eleven o'clock, there were only a few stragglers.

There wasn't any reaction, and Walt didn't think it went over at all. He said, "What the hell's the matter with the damned thing?"

In a June 12, 1929 letter to Powers company, Walt wrote:

It's hard to explain just what we have in mind for this series but I feel myself that it will be something unusual and should have a wide appeal.

As Walt's daughter Diane Disney Miller recalled:

Father wasn't easily discouraged. He took *The Skeleton Dance* to a friend who ran the United Artists Theater in Los Angeles and asked him to look at it. "We're looking at some other things this morning," the man said, "and I'll have my assistant look at it. You go with him."

Father sat beside the assistant while the film was run. It was just before the first morning show; a few customers had drifted in and it was obvious they liked *The Skeleton Dance* but the assistant didn't listen to them. "Can't recommend it," he said. "Too gruesome."

Father got a hold of another friend and asked him if he could put him in touch with Fred Miller who managed the Carthay Circle, one of the biggest and most important theaters in town. Father's friend sent him to a salesman on Film Row. "Maybe he can get him to look at your skeleton film."

Father found the salesman in a pool hall shooting a little Kelly (a game played on a standard pool table with sixteen pool balls where each player draws one of fifteen numbered markers called peas or pills at random from a shake bottle which assigns to them the correspondingly numbered pool ball, kept secret from their opponents, but which they must pocket in order to win the game). "Leave your picture here, Disney," the Kelly player said. "I'll look at it. If I like it, I'll get in touch with you."

It sounded like a stall but he actually did look at the film. When he looked he said, "I think Fred will like this. I'll take it over to him myself." As a result, Miller showed *The Skeleton Dance* with a feature picture he was running. It went over big.

Father clipped the local press notices and mailed them to Powers with a note: 'If you can get this to Roxy (the nickname of Broadway showman Samuel L. Rothafel who ran New York's prestigious Roxy Theater), he'll go for it the way Miller did. Powers got a print to Roxy and Roxy liked it. He ran it in his huge New York theater.

It ran at the Carthay Circle theater along with the feature *Four Devils* starting on June 10, 1929. It was the first cartoon ever programmed there and the theater would later host the Hollywood premieres of *Snow White and the Seven Dwarfs* and *Fantasia*. Walt attended the screening with Iwerks and scratched his head. "Are they laughing at us or with us?" he asked Iwerks.

Walt and Roy also arranged for it to be shown at the Fox theater in San Francisco on June 28, 1929 with the feature film *Behind the Curtain* starring Boris Karloff.

It ran at the Roxy theater on July 16, 1929 with *Pleasure Crazed*. Rothafel wrote, "without exception, one of the cleverest things I have seen and as you know the audience enjoyed every moment of it."

In early August, Columbia Pictures signed a contract to distribute the Silly Symphonies nationally and made the short available in late August. Its first playdate was at the Roxy on September 7 shown with *Big Time*. It was the first time in history that a cartoon had had a second engagement at the theater.

The review in the July 17, 1929, issue of *Variety* stated:

> Title tells the story, but not the number of laughs included in this sounded cartoon short. The number is high. Peak is reached when one skeleton plays the spine of another in xylophone fashion, using a pair of thigh bones as hammers. Perfectly times xylo accompaniment completes the effect. The skeletons hoof and frolic.
>
> One throws his skull at a hooting owl and knocks the latter's feathers off. Four bones brothers do a unison routine that's a howl. To set the finish, a rooster crows at the dawn. The skeletons, through for the night, dive into a nearby grave, pulling the lid down after them. Along comes a pair of feet, somehow left behind. They kick on the slab and a bony arm reaches out to pull them in. All takes place in a graveyard. Don't bring your children.

The review in the July 21, 1929 issue of *The Film Daily* stated:

> Here is one of the most novel cartoon subjects ever shown
> on a screen. Here we have a bunch of skeletons knocking out
> the laughs on their own bones, and how. They do a xylophone
> number with one playing the tune on the others spine. All
> takes place in a graveyard, and it is a howl from start to finish,
> with an owl and a rooster brought in for atmosphere.

It had an effect on animators as well. Art Babbitt who had
been working at the Paul Terry animation studio told an interviewer that when he saw *The Skeleton Dance* "I knew that was
the place I wanted to work" and quit immediately and left New
York to go to Los Angeles.

Joseph Barbera who would later go on to worldwide fame
with his partner William Hanna recalled that he saw the film
from the third balcony at the Roxy Theater:

> I saw it about seventy miles from the screen, but the impact
> on me was tremendous nevertheless. I saw these skeletons
> dancing in a row and in unison, and I asked myself: How do
> you do that? How do you make that happen?

Les Clark recalls that Ub animated all of *The Skeleton Dance*
except for the first scene which Clark animated. Year later Clark
claimed he had done a scene with a pair of skeletons playing the
spines of other skeletons like xylophones. Wilfred Jackson supposedly animated the crowing rooster at the end of the cartoon.

At the time Jackson and Clark were members of the Disney
staff but were still considered in-betweeners and clean-up artists
working with Iwerks. Iwerks was a mentor to the new animators
and also served as a "go-between" for the animators and Walt.

The title card for the cartoon says "Drawn by Ub Iwerks,"
which is a bit different than the Mickey cartoons which said
only "A Walt Disney Comic By Ub Iwerks."

Iwerks started having minor run-ins with Walt in 1929.
Walt would take Ub's drawings at night and prepare exposure
sheets for them, timing them the way he wanted but sometimes it was not the timing that Iwerks visualized. On *The
Skeleton Dance*, Walt relented and deferred to Iwerks' timing.
Timing is very important to an animator so this was not considered a casual intrusion.

Iwerks yelled at Walt:

Don't you ever touch my drawings! These are my drawings and this is how I solve the problems. Keep your hands off them!

In addition, during work on *The Skeleton Dance*, Iwerks worked on every drawing sometimes drawing the skeletons "in rough" letting Jackson and Clark fill in the ribs and other black areas like the eyes and noses.

Walt felt having Iwerks do all that work was a waste of his valuable time. He wanted Iwerks to just draw the key drawings/poses and allow the other animators to fill in the between action but Ub argued that he would lose the flow of the action and the rhythm if he did it that way.

He preferred animating "straight ahead" as it was called, leaving only minor details to be filled in. He felt he would lose control over the movement if he only drew some static poses for reference. Walt was trying to streamline the process to save time and money but Iwerks knew what worked best for him.

Animator Mark Kausler told Iwerks' granddaughter:

[Iwerks] created more of a dance. The characters move their arms....and they move across and around in perspective. He really figured out how to give a dance-like rhythmic quality to his animation.

In an interview done years later, Iwerks stated:

[*The Skeleton Dance*] was a different type of film from the Mickeys. I did all the animation but I did it rough, in line form. Other guys put in the rib cages and teeth and eyes and bones.

Walt sent a print to New York for his film distributor to promote the new series. But after getting poor reactions from exhibitors who felt the film was grotesque, Pat Powers wrote back tersely: "They don't want this. MORE MICE." As a compromise, Walt added the title "Mickey Mouse Presents a Silly Symphony". Walt said:

The whole idea of the Symphonies was to give me another street to work on, you know. Getting away from a set pattern of a character. Each Symphony, the idea would be a different story based on music with comedy and things.

Iwerks was attracting more attention because of getting credit on the title cards of the theatrical cartoons and a byline on the Mickey Mouse comic strip. Walt felt it was diverting attention

away from the Disney brand he was trying to create. As a result, Walt became more insistent and critical of Iwerks' work.

Ub finally went in to see Roy O. Disney on the morning of January 21, 1930 while Walt was in New York. He told Roy he was leaving the studio and gave as his reason the personal differences between himself and Walt. He went on to set up his own animation studio, Celebrity Productions, financed by Pat Powers who had distributed the early Disney cartoons.

Released in December 1929, the Mickey Mouse cartoon *The Haunted House* has Mickey hiding from a storm in a deserted house. Actually, the house is filled with skeletons who force him to play an organ while they dance.

Some of the animation from *The Skeleton Dance* was reused, especially the skeletons dancing in a circle holding hands and moving in a line back and forth across the screen. However, there is a new punchline as near the end of a dance cycle, wind from an open window blows away the upper bodies but the legs and feet keep dancing.

Iwerks himself revisited the concept when he directed The Columbia Color Rhapsody entitled *Skeleton Frolic* (1937). It is very similar to *The Skeleton Dance* in tone and action but in full, rich color and with much more use of extreme perspective and detail. There is an owl, a spider, pumpkins, bats from a belfry and more.

In the dark of night in a cemetary, a gnarled, tiptoeing tree knocks on a gravestone and wakes up some skeletons. A yowling black cat frightens them and they throw their skulls at the animal splitting it into six smaller cats. More skeletons pop out of their graves and with instruments and play music.

One skeleton loses its skull and makes several attempts to steal another skull from another skeleton. A male and female skeleton dance but the female skeleton keeps losing the lower half of her body. There is a similar dance with mulitple skeletons as in *The Skeleton Dance*. A crowing rooster alerts them that night is ending and in a panic they rush back to their graves.

Stalling said:

> If it had not been for Walt Disney then in all probability there would never have been a Mickey Mouse. This makes me wonder sometimes, would there ever have been a Silly Symphony or who would have suggested *The Skeleton Dance*—if...?

Donald Duck's
Trick or Treat (1952)

"Trick or Treat. Trick or Treat. Trick or Treat for Halloween. Better give a treat that's good to eat if you want to keep life serene.

"Trick or Treat. Trick or Treat. Trick or Treat the whole night through. Little scalawags with fiendish gags can make it tough on you.

"So when ghosts and goblins by the score ring the bell on your front door, better not be stingy or your nightmares will come true."

Written by Mack David, Al Hoffman and Jerry Livingston (not Paul Smith as some places state) and sung by the Mellomen (Bill Lee, Thurl Ravenscroft, Bob Hamlin, Max Smith), this catchy tune was the theme to a Donald Duck short cartoon entitled *Trick or Treat* (1952).

It was originally written in May 1948 for the *Legend of Sleepy Hollow* animated featurette. It was titled Tricker Treat. At the time, the songwriters were hard at work on *Cinderella*. It was later replaced during production with *The Headless Horseman* song sung by Bing Crosby.

Early storyboard drawings show Witch Hazel singing her own little Halloween tune but as the short started developing it was felt that a more prominent theme song was necessary for what was considered a special cartoon.

The short was in development as early as 1951 and played a special pre-release engagement in late September 1952 at the prestigious Radio City Music Hall in New York City.

Released October 10, 1952 and directed by Jack Hannah from a story by Ralph Wright, it was nominated for but did not win an Academy Award. Wright who would later go on to do the voice for the gloomy Eeyore the donkey in the early Winnie the Pooh featurettes was renowned for his wild gags that he contributed to the Goofy "How To" series of shorts.

Animation was provided by Bill Justice, Volus Jones, Don Lusk and George Kreisl; effects animation by Dan MacManus; layout and background by Yale Gracey, who would later be the genius behind the illusions in the Haunted Mansion.

In 1953 it was included in *Halloween Hilarities*, a theatrically released feature length compilation of spooky Disney theatrical shorts.

A very mean Donald Duck plays tricks on his nephews Huey, Dewey and Louie instead of giving them treats. The boys are befriended by a real witch named Witch Hazel (voiced by June Foray) who uses some special spells to pry the treats from a reluctant Donald.

She finally enchants his feet with a magic spray so that Donald is involuntarily used as a battering ram to smack into the locked closet of goodies. Witch Hazel flies off as the night comes to a close and the kids enjoy their treats.

Jack Hannah, in an interview I did with him in 1978, said:

> I enjoyed directing *Trick or Treat* because I got a chance to work with a different personality. June Foray, who did such a great job as the voice of the witch, still mentions the film to me whenever I see her.

> The short got a very high ARI rating when the Studio watched it in the sweatbox. Walt said he couldn't understand some of the words; that the dialog was too fast. I heard that Carl Barks later adapted the cartoon into a comic book story, but I never saw it.

ARI refers to the Audience Research Institute that was hired briefly by Disney in the 1940s to test how the public responded to story descriptions and potential titles for animated shorts. It was abandoned because it didn't seem an effective way for testing creative ideas.

The acronym "ARI" survived as a name for test screenings with questionnaires for studio personnel viewing a short cartoon before it was released to the general public in order to make changes.

Rough animation was completed by February 1952. An incomplete version was screened for specially invited Disney Studio personnel not involved in production.

Hannah was there to monitor the audience reaction and review the survey cards.

Calling *Trick or Treat* "a masterpiece of jovial jitters," the press release stated:

> It has just been viewed at the studio in the early phases of production, and even in that state of animation shows the sure signs of another Disney short subject hit.

Two years later, Warner Brothers released a short entitled *Bewtiched Bunny* (1954) directed by Chuck Jones, also featuring a witch named "Witch Hazel" voiced by Bea Benederet. In this cartoon, Bugs Bunny must rescue Hansel and Gretel from a rather naughtier witch.

Jones had tried to get Foray to do the voice but the actress who was doing voice work for Disney had great hesitation about being involved. When the cartoon was released with no adverse reaction from Disney, Foray agreed to do the role.

Jones recruited her to do the voice for the sequel *Broom-Stick Bunny* released in 1956.

She went on to play the character in *A Witch's Tangled Hare* (1959) and *A Haunting We Will Go* (1966), as well as in such television shows as *Sylvester and Tweety Mysteries* and *Pinky & the Brain*.

Foray had just started doing voices for Warners when Jones' initial Witch Hazel cartoon came out, but Bea was still the studio's main female voice artist. That changed both after the re-opening following the six-month shutdown in 1953 of the *Burns & Allen Show* and its changeover from a bi-weekly live show to a weekly filmed one that required more of Bernaderet's time.

With 39 episodes a year to do, Bernaderet focused on her TV career, and by the time *Broomstick Bunny* came out, Foray was doing virtually all the female voices at Warners.

A similar Witch Hazel character voiced by Foray pops up in the 1956 Tom and Jerry cartoon *The Flying Sorceress*. A little girl calling herself Witch Hazel appears in Casper's *Which is Witch?* (1958). Mighty Mouse also fought a Witch Hazel in *Pandora's Box* (1943).

Tress McNeill did Witch Hazel voice in a episode of *Tiny Toon Adventures* as well as Candi Milo doing it in the *Tiny Toons Adventures Halloween Special* "Night Ghoulary".

The character became an official and popular supporting performer in the Warner Brothers cartoon universe.

In a December 1995 interview in *Animation* magazine, Foray said:

> I did Witch Hazel as a short at Disney. She was a very funny character that I created the voice for. Chuck Jones loved it so much that he called me over to Warner Brothers to do her again. I went over there and they said, "You're going to do Witch Hazel."
>
> And I thought, 'how in hell are they going to do that?' Disney owns it and they're so litigious. But we did it. Chuck just went ahead and did it! So I asked him, just a couple of years ago, "How the heck did you ever do that and get away with it, taking a character out from Disney's nose?"
>
> And he said, "Because it was an alcohol rub! He didn't own the name!" So Disney couldn't capitalize on that or stop Chuck because it was already a copyrighted name.

Jones was probably referring to a North American shrub and the herbal medicine derived from it, witch hazel. This is probably the reason that John Stanley was also able to use a Witch Hazel character in his Little Lulu comic book stories. The name seemed natural for the name of a witch much like jiminy cricket, a popular expression, seemed natural as a name for a cricket.

In addition, Disney's version of Witch Hazel was a short, stout blond who spoke in Shakespearian English while the Warner Brothers version was significantly taller, had scraggly black hair and a green complexion. The WB version would often break into hysterical, cackling laughter and when she dashed away suddenly would leave a bunch of hairpins momentarily lingering in the air.

Hannah said:

> We had a lot of fun with (our version of Witch Hazel). She spoke sort of Shakespearean English, full of *thous* and *thees*.

In addition, Disney's Witch Hazel has an anthropomorphic broom named "Beelzebub" that acts as both her servant or familiar as well as her method of flying transportation just like a traditional witch.

Witch Hazel's recipe for the magic brew inspired by the witches in *Macbeth* that was made in a cauldron of swamp

water consisted of the ingredients of eye of needle, tongue of shoe, hand of clock, neck of bottle, tail of coat and whiskers from a billy goat.

The Little Golden Book titled *Donald and the Witch* (1953) with art by Dick Kelsey tells the story of the nephews thinking they saw a witch but Donald doesn't believe them. After some supernatural hi-jinks, Donald becomes a believer and he and the boys enjoy a fall harvest feast with Witch Hazel.

For Disney, Foray went on to voice Grammi Gummi in *Disney's Adventures of the Gummi Bears*, Magica de Spell in *DuckTales*, and Grandmother Fa in *Mulan* (1998).

An RCA Victor Records 45 RPM record entitled *Walt Disney's Trick or Treat* was released in 1952 with June Foray not only doing the voice of Witch Hazel but also the narrator of the story.

Released in 1975 was the Disneyland Records 33 1/3 RPM *Walt Disney's Trick or Treat Stories and Songs of Halloween*. The twelve minute version of *Trick or Treat* was on one side while the flip side had The Haunted Mansion. Written by Jimmy Johnson who also produced the disc, the voice of Witch Hazel and the narrator was Ginny Tyler.

Some excerpts from the original cartoon with Foray doing the voice were also used. Some of Witch Hazel's dialogue in the original cartoon were re-recorded by Tyler. Tyler skillfully matched Foray's vocals.

The LP came complete with two Halloween masks that could be cut out and used. One was of Hazel's face and the other of a pumpkin that might be the jack-o-lantern who pops up to say "Boo!" at the cartoon's conclusion.

The *Trick or Treat* song was performed by Karen Pendleton and Cubby O'Brien for the LP *Holidays with the Mouseketeers* (1958) and was sung by Anne Lloyd and the Sandpipers on Little Golden Records in 1952.

The same time the theatrical cartoon was originally released, Dell comic books produced an adaptation written and drawn by Hannah's old Disney writing partner, Carl Barks.

The story appeared in *Donald Duck* No. 26, November-December 1952

Western Publishing did a lot of seasonal comic books from special Back To School issues to, of course, Christmas

specials. So it was not unusual for them to come up with a comic book themed to Halloween and they did several with non-Disney characters.

Western Publishing comics editor Chase Craig said:

> We wanted to do a Halloween book, and Disney had made this picture *Trick or Treat*, so we got the storyboards on it and turned them over to Carl.

Barks said:

> I was sent the storyboard stats and told to make the stuff into a feature-length story. I soon found that the material wouldn't fill 32 pages that were then the length of a feature. So I ad-libbed some extra stuff. I didn't see the movie until long afterward.

The artwork on the boards that Barks saw was by Ralph Wright.

Some of Barks' changes were minor, like a nephew carrying a pumpkin on a pole instead of balancing it on his head. Other changes were more major. The Donald Duck of the animated cartoons was limited to what he could say since the audience had difficulty understanding Clarence Nash's "duck speak" clearly.

The Donald Duck of Carl Barks' stories was much more eloquent. So this adaptation is atypical of the work that Barks was doing at the time with Donald Duck when it came to dialog since he talks so little.

Barks did borrow some of Witch Hazel's lines from the animated cartoon as well as some of the staging from the storyboards and poses from Witch Hazel's model sheet.

Barks scripting emphasizes the reason for Donald's meanness when it comes to giving out treats. He sees it as an unwelcome violation of his privacy. Barks also reinforces that Witch Hazel's efforts on behalf of the nephews is to remind people that witches do still exist and the nephews belief in witches needs to be rewarded.

Barks included some additions to the story including a short segment with the nephews trying to get the hair from a billy goat that might have been on the original storyboard and another where Hazel disguises herself as a beautiful blonde duck femme fatale to get candy from Donald. Barks also

changed Donald battering open the locked door from using his head to his feet.

However, not all of Barks' changes and additions were welcomed by the editorial staff at Western. To flesh out the thin story, Barks added an episode with Smorgie the Ogre, a six armed Cyclops wearing a derby hat who had been conjured up by Hazel, and that sequence ran for several pages.

Editor Alice Cobb who had seen a preview screening of the short at the Disney Studio felt that Barks' interpretation had deviated so wildly from the original cartoon that those pages were deleted from the original printing of the story and Barks was refused payment for those additional, unwanted drawings.

To replace those missing pages, Barks wrote and illustrated a nine-page story, *Hobblin' Goblins* to fill out the rest of the comic book. The story recounts how the nephews get a "Goblin Foiler" device from Gyro Gearlose that only makes their lives worse when dealing with their Uncle Donald.

Cobb also felt that Barks opening panel of a graveyard in the foreground to Duckburg was too grim and grisly even though it was based on the opening shot of the cartoon itself. Barks replaced that splash panel with a page and a half more clearly explaining why Donald felt he had to lock up the treats from the nephews because they had already made an attempt to steal the goodies.

The ending to the comic book story version is more uplifting that the final pumpkin "Boo!" scare in the animated cartoon with Donald coming to the realization that he enjoys Halloween and will dress up as a goblin next year.

The complete version, including all the missing pages, were pieced back together and re-colored by Marie Severin, and published in the *Carl Barks Library* in 1985 and have since been reprinted multiple times.

One panel remained missing and was recreated from art pulled from elsewhere in the story.

Witch Hazel also appeared in two sequels to the story: "Too Late for Christmas" in *Donald Duck Adventures* (Gladstone Series) #30 in December 1994 and "The Poorest Duck in Duckburg" in *Donald Duck Adventures* (Gladstone Series) #35

in October 1995. She also appeared in the second issue of *The Beagle Boys* comic book (November 1965) but is inexplicably called Wanda Witch.

The character became very popular in Italian comic books where she was nown as Nocciola Vildibranda Crapomena, born in The Witch Country in 817 B.C. These stories were the work of the cartoonist Luciano Bottaro and the writer Carlo Chiedi starting in 1960.

According to the Italian comic book stories, she was a sorceress sent from the Wtich Country to restore the faith in magic among normal people specifically Goofy who refuses to believe that witches and magic are real. Hazel uses every spell in her book to try to convince him but fails every time. These series of stories ended around 2005.

Witch Hazel appeared in "The Mad Hermit of Chimney Butte," broadcast on *Walt Disney Presents* on April 1, 1960, featuring new animation of Witch Hazel directed by Jack Hannah to tie-in with the regular cartoon.

The regular cartoon was frequently shown on television starting with "All About Magic" on January 30, 1957. It was also part of the Disney special *A Disney Halloween* which first aired in 1981 as well as other showings including *The Mouse Factory*.

Witch Hazel makes a brief cameo during the final scene of *Who Framed Roger Rabbit* (1988) where she is standing in the back amongst the crowd of toons. She also appears in a couple of shots in *Mickey's House of Villains* singing along with the others to the song "It's Our House Now!" The appearance is somewhat odd because the character is not really a villain other than the fact that all witches are considered to be bad.

The animated cartoon remains extremely popular and timeless. In the Disney Channel October 2017 special *The Scariest Story Ever: A Mickey Mouse Halloween Spooktacular,* Huey, Dewey and Louie are attired in their same Halloween costumes (a devil, a ghost and a witch) that they wore the classic short.

The Legend of Sleepy Hollow (1949)

The Legend of Sleepy Hollow is a short story by American writer Washington Irving first published in 1820. Based on a German folk tale, Irving transplanted it to upstate New York in 1790.

Sleepy Hollow is actually the name of the valley near a small rural community that was founded in the 17th century by people of Dutch descent. North Tarrytown is located in Westchester County, New York about 25 miles north of midtown Manhattan in New York City. In 1996, the town officially changed its name to Sleepy Hollow. Washington Irving is buried in Sleepy Hollow Cemetary.

An opportunistic, itinerant school teacher named Ichabod Crane who looks like a walking scarecrow takes a position teaching in Sleepy Hollow's one room schoolhouse. He sets his sights on the wealthy Katrina Van Tassel as a marriage prospect that will allow him to inherit her father's considerable fortune and live a life of ease.

His rival for her affections is a rowdy prankster and bully named Abraham Van Brundt whose nickname is Brom Bones for whom thinking is a painful process. He is an athletic young man and is the self-appointed leader of some drunken young ne'er-do-wells who in the Disney film are labeled the Sleepy Hollow Boys. Both Ichabod and Brom are invited to a dinner party at the Van Tassels' home along with other locals.

For the evening entertainment, Bones and others begin to tell ghost stories, primarily about the local legend, the ghost of a Hessian (German) soldier who fought for the British during the American War of Independence. In a battle, his head was shot off by a cannonball and his ghost supposedly rides the night searching for a replacement.

Bones swears he saw the ghost and only escaped by crossing the bridge since ghosts cannot cross over moving water, a popular

superstition of the time. Crane is highly superstitious often spending his time reading books about witches and ghosts and once thinking he saw the devil following him home. The frightening stories of a Headless Horseman seem all too real to him.

On the way home alone from the dinner party, Crane is confronted by the demon presence of the Headless Horseman and in a panic tries to reach the bridge. The Headless Horseman throws a large pumpkin at him and the next morning there is no trace of Crane. His horse is found without a saddle and when the saddle is located, a shattered pumpkin is lying next to it.

Some think that Crane simply decided to relocate to another town to avoid paying for his lost saddle and horse or that he found better martial prospects elsewhere.

Others think that a disguised Bones was the cause for the schoolmaster's departure since according to Irving's story, he "was observed to look exceedingly knowing whenever the story of Ichabod Crane was related and always burst into a hearty laugh at the mention of the pumpkin".

Bones marries Katrina. Most people in Sleepy Hollow believe that Ichabod was carried off by the Headless Horseman. Local children do not dare to go near his old abandoned school house after dark, for fear that the teacher's ghost is still inside it but without a head.

Interestingly, the story itself has a timeless charm even though the three lead characters aren't truly likeable or sympathetic. Katrina is manipulatively pitting Ichabod and Brom against each other for her own vanity; Ichabod is a glutton and is much more in love with her father's wealth than with her; Brom is quite obviously a physical bully with a mean streak.

In fact, even the supporting characters are fairly unappealing. Yet the story has been adapted numerous times for stage, film, television, comic books and other media.

The earliest surviving film version of the story is a 1922 American silent movie called *The Headless Horseman* starring Will Rogers. Two other silent movies based on the story are known to have been made but do not seem to have survived.

The first animated adaptation of the tale was a theatrical cartoon short created by Ub Iwerks and released to theaters in 1934.

Iwerks who left the Disney Studio in early 1930 had formed his own animation studio, Celebrity Productions, and his short cartoons were distributed by Pat Powers who had distributed the early Mickey Mouse cartoons.

Iwerks produced three different series from 1930 to approximately 1936: Flip the Frog, Willie Whopper and the ComiColor cartoon fables filmed in two strip Cinecolor (blue and red). The ComiColor cartoons were adaptations of classic fairytales and folklore like Sinbad the Sailor, Jack and the Beanstalk and, of course, The Legend of Sleepy Hollow.

The Headless Horseman was a roughly eight minute cartoon released October 1, 1934 and was directed by Iwerks with animation by Al Eugster, Shamus Culhane, Grim Natwick, Rudy Zamora and others. The musical score was by Carl Stalling who would later go on to be the musical director for Warner Brothers cartoons.

Except for the music and some sound effects, the cartoon is virtually a silent cartoon since there is no narration or dialog. The animation of the black silhouette of the Headless Horseman riding furiously on his steed is reused countless times during the story as is some other animation. The film makes clear that it is Bones impersonating the horseman.

The final scene is Bones and Katrina getting married but showing up at the ceremony is the Headless Horseman who scares everyone away. Ichabod's red-headed face pops up out of the collar and laughs.

Work on an adaptation of the Washington Irving tale as a possible animated feature started at the Disney Studio in the early 1940s but was put on hold along with other features in development because of World War II. Some of the early concept sketches show a more spectral horror approach to the final scene.

When the war was over, and work resumed on the story, one animator even found that the scene he had been working on before he left for military service was still waiting for him upon his return to the studio.

In December 1946, Walt Disney committed to the project. In late 1947, the studio was still financially struggling from the effects of diminished revenue during World War II so Walt

decided to pair the story with another adaptation being developed, *The Wind in the Willows*.

Neither project seemed to have a story that could be stretched into a feature film and by pairing them together both time and money could be saved. Disney had already released several package animated features like *Fun and Fancy Free* and *Melody Time* that had mulitple segments and celebrity voices who could be used to publicize the movie.

The working title for this new package film was *Two Fabulous Characters* and the intention was that Jiminy Cricket would introduce both stories as he had in *Fun and Fancy Free*. Walt intended the word "fabulous" to mean its traditional definition of "a creature of fable" but he was convinced that an average audience would be unfamiliar with that definition.

Other money and time saving efforts included recyling some animation from *The Old Mill* (1937) like the cattails thumping and the reeds swaying. The character of Katrina Van Tassel used the same model sheet for the character Grace Martin from *The Martins and the Coys* segment from *Make Mine Music* (1946). Even Ichabod's horse, Gunpowder, seemed to resemble Cyril Proudbottom who was Mr. Toad's horse companion.

The Adventures of Ichabod and Mr. Toad (released October 5, 1949) was directed by Jack Kinney, Clyde Geronimi, and James Algar. Story was credited to Erdman Penner, Winston Hibler, Joe Rinaldi, Ted Sears, Homer Brightman and Harry Reeves.

The directing animators were: Frank Thomas, Ollie Johnston, Wolfgang Reitherman, Milt Kahl, John Lounsbery, and Ward Kimball. Character animators included Fred Moore, John Sibley, Marc Davis, Hal Ambro, Harvey Toombs, Hal King, Hugh Fraser, and Don Lusk.

To further increase the possibilities of financial success, Walt decided to have the stories told by celebrity narrators. Actor Basil Rathbone's distinctive British voice would tell the tale of writer Kenneth Grahame's Mr. Toad and his misadventures while singer Bing Crosby would lighten up some of the frightening aspects of Ichabod's story especially with some of his well-known, unscripted ad-libs like nicknaming the lead character "old Icky".

In its first theatrical release, the film grossed $1,200,000 in domestic rentals in the United States and Canada.

In 1948, it was announced that Bing Crosby's four sons would be filmed in live action gathered around a radio listening to their father's voice telling the tale of the Headless Horseman. The Crosby family would receive five percent of the gross revenue from the film up to $200,000 in lieu of a straight salary. That introduction was never filmed.

Crosby recorded 44 different songs, some of them in several takes, between November 8 and December 31, 1947. The reason for the busy recording schedule was that a recording ban was looming, as the musicians' union prepared to go on strike (just as it had in 1942-1944) on January 1, 1948, and Decca Records wanted to stockpile Crosby recordings.

Among those recordings were songs from two upcoming movies, *A Connecticut Yankee in King Arthur's Court* ("Once and for Always," "Busy Doing Nothing," and "If You Stub Your Toe on the Moon") and the songs for the animated Walt Disney featurette *The Adventures of Ichabod and Mr. Toad* ("Katrina," "Ichabod," and "The Headless Horseman") with Jud Conlon's Rhythmaires.

Oliver Wallace was the musical director for the film. When he wrote the score, he recorded himself whistling to show Ichabod trying to keep his composure even as he became more and more scared as he rode through the woods at night.

For the dance sequence, Wallace composed a song that was never used entitled "Whoop-Ta-Doodle-Dey" ("Roll up the carpet, shine the floor and dance like you never danced before. Whoop Ta Doodle Dey!").

For the final film, Ken Darby adapted two pieces of traditional music and added an original melody for the background score that kept pace with the terpsichorean shenanigans between rivals Ichabod and Bones.

At one point, voice artist Thurl Ravenscroft with his deep, frightening voice was going to sing *The Headless Horseman* song instead of Crosby. It was decided that it would make it more consistent to have Crosby do everything except the women's voices. Ravenscroft did record the song which was much creepier than Crosby's interpretation and Disney decades later released it on CD.

Bea Benaderet, who voiced Katrina Van Tassel and Tilda, is best known as the voice of Betty Rubble on Hanna-Barbera's

The Flintstones. She also played in several 1960s television series including *The Beverly Hillbillies* and *Petticoat Junction*

The Headless Horseman as well as the two other songs in the featurette was from composers Don Raye and Gene de Paul. The popular singing trio, the Andrews Sisters, loved Raye's work and he was responsible for such World War II hits as "Scrub Me Mama, with a Boogie Beat", "Boogie Woogie Bugle Boy" and "Beat Me Daddy Eight to the Bar."

Raye received recognition for his skills for clever, dense-ly-worded lyrics that is well demonstrated in the song of the phantom horseman. He became the resident songwriter at Universal Studios and was teamed with Gene de Paul beginning in 1941 on a number of films.

The pair ended up at the Disney Studio in the late 1940s and contributed songs to *So Dear to My Heart* and *The Adventures of Ichabod and Mr. Toad.* The pair wrote the song "Beware the Jabberwock" for *Alice in Wonderland* but it was not used.

The two songwriters incorporated the popular music styles of the mid-20th century into the colonial American setting. It was felt that the Dutch settlers would be less afraid of merriment than their more dour and puritanical New England neighbors. At one point when instructing the students, Ichabod warbles "boo boo ba boo" which was a phrase associated with Crosby's singing as a crooner.

To capture the authentic feeling of the Hudson Valley country, Walt Disney personally visited the region around Tarrytown. The film depicts accurate details of clothing, buildings and landscape. The church shown during the opening narration was drawn to look like the actual Old Dutch Church built in the late 1660s in the Sleepy Hollow area.

Ironically, the Disney animated featurette is considered one of the most faithful adaptations of the Irving story especially depicting Ichabod as an unsympathetic, greedy dandy. However, that doesn't mean that Disney didn't add its own little embellishments to the story but essentially still stayed true to the "spirit" of the original.

For instance, Halloween is never mentioned in the original story but Disney set the Van Tassel party in October and made it a Halloween party with the various guests chiming in about

the various ghastly things that happen on that special night before getting to the Headless Horseman. As the song says, "I'm telling you brother it's a frightful sight, To see what goes on Halloween night."

In the original story, the horseman throws a pumpkin while in the Disney version, it is a flaming jack-o-lantern. In fact, this was the first time that a jack-o-lantern rather than a regular pumpkin was connected to the horseman.

While it is clear that Irving intended Ichabod's encounter with the horseman to be another prank by Brom Bones, the Disney film implies that he became entangled with an actual phantom.

Ichabod looks down into the neck of the horseman and finds nothing there but blackness. The horseman is less robust than Bones and the horse looks a little different from the one Bones rode earlier in the film and does not have a saddle.

However, as animators Frank Thomas and Ollie Johnston wrote, "The dangers in the woods of Sleepy Hollow are actually all in Ichabod's imagination, but the audience was nervous because they saw what *he* saw rather than what was *really* there."

The original character sketches of Ichabod Crane were exaggerated caricatures of humorist Will Rogers who portrayed the role in the 1922 silent film.

Animator Andreas Deja said that his work on the character of Gaston from *Beauty and the Beast*, was influenced by Brom Bones:

> [Brom] is a rich character, full of confidence and full of himself. Milt's (Milt Kahl) animation shows just the right amount of dash and bounce.
>
> Although the style of the film is pretty cartoony, Brom Bones's physique required careful and somewhat realistic draftsmanship in terms of anatomy ... This was great inspiration for myself, when I started work on Gaston in *Beauty and the Beast*.

Disney Legend Blaine Gibson specifically requested to animate on the scene of a scared Ichabod riding his horse into Sleepy Hollow because it reminded him of an incident when he was boy on a farm in eastern Colorado.

Gibson said:

> I can empathize with this guy because I've been on a horse out on the farm at night when I wanted to whistle because I'd heard some noise and I wouldn't know what it was.

Animator Frank Thomas used his own experience from horse riding where he felt either ignored or stymied by the horse for animating Ichabod riding the plowhorse. Thomas said:

> I had suffered from more than my share of miserable experiences in trying to get unresponsive nags to behave like the wonder horse of the cowboy movies.

> Joe Rinaldi did the story sketches for the scene including the outlandish gag that Ichabod's panic was so intense the audience could almost believe his legs could hold a horse as he grabbed and swung around a tree. With the wild comic panic, Ichabod and his horse frantically defied all natural laws of weight and gravity but in a very believable way.

> Joe Rinaldi had done a masterful series of drawings exploring every possible position for a tall, skinny man trying to hide on top of a horse.

Thomas told writer Jim Fanning:

> When I was animating Ichabod, he had the same sort of trouble that I had had. I felt he didn't know anything about horses. The horse didn't care about him. He didn't care that he was in Sleepy Hollow, or whether there were ghosts. But Ichabod had this terrible apprehension about going through Sleepy Hollow and he had to use this horse. He would have been better off without a horse.

The Headless Horseman was primarily animated by Woolie Reitherman who told Fanning:

> I just started with one drawing and kept going to see what would happen. I'm basically action-oriented. I like danger. I think I always enjoyed a fight because it stirred my emotions when I was doing it, and if it stirred my emotions, it would stir the emotions of an audience.

Animator John Sibley also worked on the chase scene. The colors for the Headless Horseman are black, dark scarlet, fierce purples, and livid magentas to heighten the dramatic confrontation.

It was the evocative concept artwork of Mary Blair and John Hench that inspired the overall "look" of the film. The

Zorro television series used the Headless Horseman's laugh in its 1957 fourth episode "The Ghost of the Mission".

Many of the animal sounds were done by Clarence Nash, who was the original voice of Donald Duck, and Ichabod's screams were done by Pinto Colvig, the original voice of Goofy. Billy Bletcher provided the laugh of the Headless Horseman. Bletcher had provided the voices for Pegleg Pete and the Big Bad Wolf.

When *The Legend of Sleepy Hollow* was first run on the weekly television show on October 26th, 1955, to fill out the hour, a new fourteen minute animated segment about the life of Washington Irving was included. Walt Disney said:

> Most of us are well acquainted with Ichabod Crane and the legend of Sleepy Hollow, a story which has entertained and delighted readers for a century and a half.
>
> But some of us may be less familiar with the man who created the legend of Sleepy Hollow and whose literary genius brought him international recognition as America's first professional man of letters.

The new prologue told about Irving's life and adventures as a child in Manhattan, New York, which included visiting old and abandoned houses that were said to be haunted, and even visiting Sleepy Hollow itself. The biography also shows Irving's time as a writer and his trips to different countries of Europe. This prologue has never been released on any form of home media.

The Legend of Sleepy Hollow was released on its own to theaters as a 33-minute featurette in September 1963. This was the same edit presented on the *Disneyland* television series, minus the 14-minute prologue and the Walt Disney live-action host segments. This version was first released on VHS in 1982.

In its first theatrical release, the film grossed $1,200,000 in domestic rentals in the United States and Canada.

The New York Times stated:

> Mr. Disney, abetted by his staff, such perfect narrators as Bing Crosby and Basil Rathbone, and a pair of durable literary works, has fashioned a conclave of cartoon creatures, which, by and large, have the winsome qualities and charm of such noted creations as *Mickey Mouse, Dumbo,* et al.

Time magazine wrote:

> This lighthearted, fast-moving romp has inspired some of Disney's most inventive draftsmanship and satire. The midnight chase through a clutching, echoing forest with the gangling, lily-livered schoolmaster in full flight before the Headless Horseman is a skillful blend of the hilarious and the horrible. It is Disney at his facile best.

The Headless Horseman is such a powerful image that over the decades, there have been mulitple attempts to include him in the Disney theme parks.

On October 16, 1957, Imagineer Ken Anderson submitted to Walt a concept for the haunted house at Disneyland that included this frightening finale with guests looking out a huge window from inside the house:

> Commence with a windy moonlit night with the reflection of the moon in the bayou beyond the graveyard. The clouds will obscure the moon and distant flashes of lightning and sounds of thunder will next be heard. While the sky is darkening, the ghostly apparition of the Headless Horseman will fade into view or appear from behind a distant tree and gallop toward the graveyard and house from right to left foreground.
>
> He will disappear behind some trees to the left, but the sound of his horse's approaching hoof beats will continue to grow louder. Suddenly, he bursts into view in the courtyard just outside the windows and gallops across from left to right... reining to a noisy halt just out of view below the balcony on our right.
>
> His cape is the only part of him we need to see at this last crossing, since the shrubs will obscure the horse. His cape must match in color and value with the previous projected mirage. Next, a bolt of lightning against the sky and a werewolf's howl signal the appearance of the ghosts rising from the tombs, first one, and then two, and more, until ghosts are materializing from the earth around the tombs as well as the tombs themselves.
>
> First part is projection with Ub Iwerks' special loop projector using Kronar based film. Second part is florescent Japanese silk cape on a wire frame and moved by an aluminum arm from above past the windows. Match the color to the projected image.

This concept was abandoned when the attraction ceased being a "walking tour" and became a ride.

When Liberty Square was being built at the Magic Kingdom in 1970, Imagineer Tony Baxter pitched the idea of a dark ride based on *The Legend of Sleepy Hollow* to help the transition of the intersection from Fantasyland to Liberty Square.

Guests would have ridden in hollowed-out spinning jack-o-lanterns through a variety of scenes until the final confrontation with the headless horseman.

However references to the famous Irving story did make it into Liberty Square.

The exterior architecture of the Sleepy Hollow food and beverage location at the entrance to Liberty Square is based on the tiny, two-room cottage that writer Irving purchased on ten acres along the banks of the Hudson River in Tarrytown, New York.

Irving spent many years remodeling and expanding the residence, combining elements of colonial New York architecture and buildings he knew in Scotland and Spain. He named it Sunnyside in 1841, and history shows that it was usually busy with lots of friends and family.

Sunnyside is now a museum in Tarrytown. The Sleepy Hollow food and beverage location offers a souvenir plastic stein with the image of Ichabod on one side and the Headless Horseman on the other.

When the shop building opposite the Hall of Presidents was converted and reopened February 1996 as Ye Olde Christmas Shoppe, one of the new stores was devoted to music.

Outside the music shop was a sign stating "Music & Voice Lessons by appointment, Ichabod Crane, Instructor", a profession that Ichabod did to earn some additional money from his regular teaching assignment.

The spooky Headless Horseman rides from Frontierland to Main Street U.S.A. in advance of each performance of Mickey's "Boo To You" Halloween Parade as part of the separately ticketed Mickey's Not-So Scary Halloween Party.

In addition, during the Halloween season starting in 2017, the Fort Wilderness Resort and Campground offered "Return to Sleepy Hollow" including a group viewing of the 1949 Disney animated film inside the resort's Tri-Circle-D Ranch stables. During event nights, guests got to see galloping ghosts

and experience an up-close and personal encounter with the Headless Horseman.

For several years during the Halloween season, Fort Wilderness offered a roughly fifteen minute Haunted Hayride that was a spooky trip through the swamps down along Bay Lake with the climax being a close encounter with the Headless Horseman. Then it became Haunted Carriage Rides in 2008 and then was completely discontinued after 2012.

The film was the last of the notorious package films Disney produced after the war to save time and money. It remains a popular Halloween film with just the right balance of humor and horror.

As the song states:

> Ghosts are bad but the one that's cursed,
> Is the Headless Horseman; he's the worst.
> They say he's tired of his flaming top,
> He's got a yen to make a swap.
> So he rides one night a year,
> To find a head in the hollow here.
> With a hip, hip and a clippity clop,
> He's out looking for a top to chop.
> So don't stop to figure out a plan,
> You can't reason with a headless man.

Night on Bald Mountain (1940)

Walpurgis Night is the eve of the feast day of Saint Walpurgis, a saint of the Roman Catholic Church. Walpurgis Night falls on April 30th and is a traditional holiday celebrated in northern Europe and Scandinavia with many similarities to Halloween.

Originally, the event had little to do with either Christianity or Saint Walpurgis but was a pagan ritual to welcome spring and ensure the fertility of the land.

On Walpurgis Night witches and other evil entities roamed freely around the land so certain practices were developed to keep them at bay. Thus, in Germany, on Walpurgis Night, people would dress up in costumes, and make loud noises.

Much like offering treats on Halloween, to ward off malevolent forces, people would hang blessed sprigs of foliage from houses or barns, and leave offerings of bread with butter and honey (known as 'ankenschnitt') for phantom hounds.

Another typical activity carried out on Walpurgis Night is the lighting of bonfires, which, according to one tradition, was also a means of warding off witches. With the arrival of Christianity, bishops connected these traditional activities with the saint.

In the Disney animated feature film *Fantasia* (1940), the segment titled "Night on Bald Mountain" recounts the tale of an immense dark demon who awakens on Walpurgis Night to summon a bevy of supernatural spirits from the local graveyard. This living horror also invokes harpies, witches, strange beasts and other unholy beings to join the fearful ceremony.

All these horrible creatures gather on Bald Mountain to pay homage to the huge winged devil who toys with them and tortures them in the fiery gorges and the rough hewn rock strata of the forbidden mountain. His evil reign of terror is only ended by the sounds of church bells and the singing of a holy choir that accompany the light of dawn.

Traditionally, majestic mountains like Bald Mountain thrust themselves upwards from the flat plains surrounding their base. Their craggy, barren peaks pierce the heavens like fingers reaching for the stars.

At the highest levels, it is a different world often devoid of vegetation in the rarified air as well as often unfriendly and dangerous to common people who seek to discover its secrets.

Towering like silent monarchs over the day-to-day activities at their foundation, mountains are mysterious and magical. For countless ages, people have gazed skyward at the tops at those upper regions in the firmament and conjured visions of gods and monsters.

"Night on Bald Mountain" is a musical composition by composer Modest Mussorgsky that is most familiar for its re-orchestration by Rimsky Korsakov in 1886. Leopold Stokowski did his own arrangement of the piece utilizing elements from both of the previous composers for the film *Fantasia*. All versions were meant to depict a Witches' Sabbath held at a foreboding mountain peak.

The word "bald" comes from a literal translation of the original Russian word that was used to indicate that the mountain was barren of trees. Some performances have referred to the piece as "Night on Bare Mountain" instead, which is an alternative translation.

Mussorgsky was inspired by Slavonic mythology of a horned demon named Chernobog. The adjective "cherny" means "black" or "dark" and the word "bog" roughly translates as "god."

So, Chernobog was a dark god who dwelt on a terrifyingly high mountain and who might actually be merely concealed during the daylight as part of that deadly mountain itself.

When animation historian John Culhane asked animator Bill Tytla, who animated the villainous character the film, what was going through his mind when he created this classic sequence, Tytla replied:

> I imagined I was a mountain, you see, and made of stone. But, I could think and feel and move....and I did.

Tytla's forceful sketches made audiences believe that the malignant monster was a natural extension of the rocky

mountaintop with the same unyielding elemental strength to devastate anything in its way.

Jim Algar who was one of the directors of the film said that Tytla's version of the creature "was a deep brooding response to old fears, old folklore, old superstitions existing in the Russian psyche."

Tytla gave Chernabog an alien animal mentality that made the character so fearsome to audiences because it seemed unnatural. Instead of eyes that occasionally flashed, he drew the eyes without pupils and made it seem that fires were burning in the eye sockets.

Those unsettling images were not on the storyboard but came from Tytla's contribution. Walt never expected that the imagery would be so real and menacing but kept it in the film.

Most viewers assumed that the terrifying figure was meant to be Satan, especially since Walt once referred to the character as "the devil himself."

The enormous, heavily veined black wings of Chernobog are easily mistaken for the highest point of Bald Mountain when they are wrapped securely around the evil fire-eyed monster as they are at both the beginning and end of the sequence. The crafty Chernobog is always there, but has merely blended back into the natural outline of the hilly design.

Actor Bela Lugosi, best remembered for his iconic portrayal of Dracula in the 1931 film, did some live-action reference for Chernabog posing while wearing his original Dracula cape for animator Bill Tytla the first week of November 1939. Animator Wilfred Jackson who was going to direct the sequence in the film did the live action filming.

Tytla later found the pictures taken from those sessions unusable for his purpose so he had the skinny Jackson strip to the waist and pose following Tytla's directions who took photos. Jackson later recalled that his hands were also filmed in close-up as reference for Chernabog's hands as he manipulated the flames.

However, for publicity reasons, it was promoted that Lugosi was the model and that little anecdote has appeared for decades.

From *Modern Screen* magazine February 1940:

Versatile Bela

When Bela Lugosi had a call from the Walt Disney studios the other day, he proceeded over there considerably perplexed about what kind of role the cartoonist had dreamed up for him. The actor was met by Disney and Leopold Stokowski. Mr. Stokowski will direct his orchestra in music symbolizing the eruption of a volcano, Disney explained, and will you please interpret the volcano?

Lugosi admitted it was something of a shock to be called on for anything of this nature, but, being of the old school, he launched into the assignment. So successful was his interpretation that moving pictures were taken of him. These will later be used as models by the Disney artists when drawing the erupting volcano for the animated cartoon.

"Guess I'm one actor," said Lugosi, "who doesn't have to worry about being typed."

Lugosi's confusion came from being told he was the top of a mountain and perhaps Tytla encouraged him to make strong dramatic movements like an erupting volcano.

"No one but Tytla could have given Chernabog the odious, predominantly animal mentality which made him so fearsome" wrote fellow animators Frank Thomas and Ollie Johnston.

Tytla himself was Ukrainian so the character was part of his folklore growing up and he was quite familiar with the legends and beliefs surrounding the character.

Artist Thornton Hee recounted the story of going into Tytla's room to ask a question but found the animator hard at work on drawing the character. The room was completely dark except for a fluorescent light under Tytla's animation disc that eerily lit up his face from underneath. Hee quietly backed out of the room without asking his question.

Director Jackson was confronted with a problem because Walt had instructed him to "get it out in a hell of a hurry and be sure not to disturb Stokowski's music because that was sacred." However, Jackson discovered there was a long musical passage that was repeated later so he tried to eliminate the repeat because it was slowing down the action.

No one would help him make the cut. Desperate, Jackson tore the film so the repeat of the music was out and took it to

an assistant editor to splice back together because the film had been "accidentally torn".

The editor with some hesitation made the splice and Jackson showed it to Stokowski. It featured the rough story sketches along with the music. After seeing it, Stokowski had no objections.

In 2015, Disney announced it was developing a live-action feature film starring the character of Chernabog with Matt Sazama and Burk Sharpless writing the script and executive producing the film.

Bald Mountain was inspired by a real life counterpart, Mount Triglav, meaning "three-headed." Mount Triglav is the highest mountain in Slovenia (formerly Yugoslavia) and the highest peak of the Julian Alps.

The name does not come from the topography of its summit, but from the fact that the ancient people of the region felt the massive rock outcropping was the connection between the three elements of the sky, the earth and the underworld. That belief made it a perfect location for supernatural ceremonies.

"Walt wanted this mountain sequence to give audiences the chills...being drawn into an atmosphere of unease and terror and evil," revealed film historian Leonard Maltin.

The initial inspiration for the look of Chernabog came from the work of German artist Heinrich Kley who did a pen and ink drawing of a gigantic demon blocking a chimney to force workers out of a factory. Artist Albert Hurter who worked at the Disney Studios studied this drawing and others by Kley and drew sketches of a winged devil tossing handfuls of souls into a volcano.

It was also Hurter who drew sketches of Chernabog's hands with his tiny minions desperately trying to clamber onto his fingers for safety. However it was artist Kay Nielsen who established the final appearance of Chernabog and his world.

Animation historian John Canemaker said:

> The sequence retains the integrity of Kay Nielsen's work from his sensuous line; the lush coloring he used; and bits of Aubrey Beardsley, Art Nouveau, and Japanese and Chinese woodcuts. It is retained particularly in the designs of the backgrounds like the mountain.

Kay Nielsen was a Danish illustrator who was as popular and successful in the early 20th century as artists like Arthur Rackham and Edmund Dulac. His masterpiece is usually considered to be his twenty-five watercolor paintings for the book *East of the Sun and West of the Moon* composed of fifteen Nordic tales.

By 1939, he was working at the Disney Studios, providing concept artwork for "Night on Bald Mountain" and the "Ave Maria" sequences. He also supplied some designs for a *Fantasia* sequel and for a proposed *The Little Mermaid* animated feature that were never produced during his lifetime.

Animation historian John Culhane stated, "Nielsen provides a real sense of place to the whole thing."

It was rumored that Walt Disney World would be getting a Villains Mountain attraction at the Magic Kingdom (on the former location of the 20,000 Leagues Under the Sea attraction) where guests would have been taken through Bald Mountain that would have towered over Fantasyland.

Inside, evil Disney villains were meeting to take over the Magic Kingdom and arguing over who was the best villain to be put in charge. Once the presence of the guests was detected, there would be a hair-raising escape as the ride vehicle was pursued by these villains that would culminate in a plunge down the outside of the mountain.

During the planning, it was never decided whether the attraction should be a roller coaster or a log flume ride. When discussions arose about having a separate Disney villain theme park (Dark Kingdom) or a section of the Magic Kingdom devoted specifically to Disney villains (Shadowlands), the development of the attraction was put on hiatus until those discussions were resolved.

The Disney version of the demonic Chernabog appears in the games Kingdom Hearts (at the End of the World) and Kingdom Hearts 3D: Dream Drop Distance (in Symphony of Sorcery). In the later game, Chernabog can summon "Fiends" during battle and can control fire and flap his huge wings to create gale force winds.

Having survived the destruction of his homeworld Symphony of Sorcery, he ends up at the End of the World.

Ansem, Sora, Donald Duck and Goofy stumble upon the remnants of Bald Mountain and in so doing awaken Chernabog who attacks them.

The only known historical references for the actual Chernabog are a 12th century Christian chronicle and a 13th century Icelandic legend linking him to darkness and death. In general, he was assumed to be the contrasting counterpart to the good deity Bylebog known as the "white god" who was often depicted as an old man with a long white beard dressed in white.

Chernabog made a single appearance in the thirteenth episode of the fourth season ("Darkness on the Edge of Town") of ABC's television series *Once Upon a Time*. The character Rumplestiltskin explained to Cruella, Maleficent and Ursula, that Chernabog was "an ancient demon that feeds on evil. It seeks out the heart with the greatest potential for darkness and devours it."

He was portrayed as a powerful demon with some physical similarities to a human. Its body was covered in dark scales and it had big, glowing orange eyes as well as a pair of black bison-like horns. Its legs and forearms were covered in thick dark fur and it had large bat-like wings. It possessed fangs and a long pointy tail.

In the series, Chernabog ends up trapped in the Sorcerer's hat and is mistakenly freed but is destroyed when Emma and Regina toss it beyond Storybrooke's town line where magic cannot exist.

In the *House of Mouse* animated television series, the character is voiced by Corey Burton and is sometimes seen in the audience at one of the tables. At one point, he admits to gossip columnist Clarabelle Cow that he is afraid of the dark. The character also appears in *Mickey's House of Villains* where he chats with Maleficent after she has turned into a dragon.

In the theme parks, he is one of the villains seen during the *Fantasmic!* water show during clips from the feature film to indicate him summoning a host of demons against Mickey Mouse.

An amusing cameo appears in the two-minute sequence called *Michael and Mickey* directed by Jerry Rees and shown

at the Disney MGM Studios beginning in 1989 as well as on the opening of the *Best of Disney—50 Years of Magic* (1991) television special.

An animated Mickey Mouse joins a live action Michael Eisner in his office at the Disney Studio and they walk down the hall to the screening room accompanied by staff and animated characters. When they sit down in the theater, Chernabog is sitting in front of Mickey, blocking his view. When Mickey timidly tries to point this out, the character rises up to its full menacing height. Eisner reminds him to sit down and Chernabog apologetically acquises.

The short was made at the Disney Studio in Burbank to introduce a "Coming Attractions" Disney movie reel at the end of the Backstage Magic Tour at the newly opened theme park in 1989. It was shown in the Walt Disney Theater. The animation was done by Mark Kausler, Steve Moore, Bruce W. Smith, David Spafford and Frans Vischer.

Even Chernabog was terrified of Michael Eisner.

Halloween with Winnie the Pooh

Halloween wisdom from *The Book of Boo* (2002):

> Eeyore: "Never been much good at the whole Halloween thing, I guess.
> I got to admit, getting a little spooked does give you a charge, as long as it's with your friends."
> Piglet: "Don't you think g-ghosts are scary, Eeyore?"
> Eeyore: "Ghosts, goblins, gargoyles, ghouls. A bunch of words that start with 'G' as far as I can tell."

Every October over the last thirty years, Disney transforms the fabled and beloved Hundred Acre Wood into the Haunted Acre Wood with Winnie the Pooh and his friends enjoying a very Americanized version of the frightful holiday.

In fact, they have been branded to the holiday as a way of embracing younger children to the celebration who may have some fears.

The Halloween version of Disney's Winnie the Pooh and his friends have been found on almost everything including figurines, pins, buttons, plush figures, trick or treat candy buckets, bags, multiple books, CDs (including *Halloween Songs and Sounds* 1997 from Walt Disney Records), cookie jars, musical snow globe, inflatable figure, beanie babies, light set, night light, mugs and much more.

Winnie himself goes out trick-or-treating outfitted as a bee, pumpkin, skeleton, bat, wizard, witch, black scaredy cat, pirate, rabbit and even one time as Tigger as well as other costumes including as a totem pole with Piglet.

While the holiday of Halloween originated in ancient Britain as the festival of Samhain, British author A.A. Milne never wrote about his creations participating in Halloween. If he had, it would have been an unusual version since the U.K. celebrates the holiday differently.

Brits tend to wear more traditional Halloween costumes, dressing up as ghosts, zombies, and other fearsome creatures rather than the wide variety their American cousins choose from including pirates to princesses to superheroes.

It's rare for people in the UK to put up an excessive amount of Halloween decorations. Spooky sweets might include Nestlé Milkybar Ghosts and Cadbury Pumpkin Patch Cakes that are sold seasonally at the time rather than candy corn.

Guy Fawkes Day celebrated just days later on November fifth with bonfires and fireworks has always been the more significant holiday although in recent years Halloween has gained more and more popularity.

However, once Disney took control of the Winnie the Pooh characters, they became progressively more Americanized so it was natural for them to celebrate the spooky holiday the way it was done in the United States.

When *Snow White and the Seven Dwarfs* was released in 1937 to such success, Walt aggressively and quickly looked to obtain the rights to other fanciful stories, from *Peter Pan* to *Winnie the Pooh*. Walt had a two-fold purpose: To obtain material for future projects and to prevent other studios from producing films based on those stories.

Author A.A. Milne who created the bear of very little brain in 1926 and his friends based on his son Christopher's stuffed toys had admired Walt Disney. He even wrote to Kenneth Grahame's widow about *Toad of Toad Hall* that, "I expect you have heard that Disney is interested in it? It is just the thing for him, of course, and he would do it beautifully."

When Disney released its version of *Wind in the Willows* in 1949, the story reflected Milne's renowned stage adaptation of the tale as much as the original story by Grahame.

Sometimes, the quest for those rights to projects took decades. In the case of *Winnie the Pooh*, Walt made several attempts in the 1940s and 1950s to obtain the rights even though it seemed apparent that Walt had little personal enthusiasm for the characters and the stories.

He first became aware of the stories because in 1938, his young daughter Diane would read the stories and laugh out loud and it made him curious.

On July 16, 1961, the Disney Studios obtained the rights to Winnie the Pooh but it was still years before Walt announced that he was planning an animated feature based on Milne's books.

As Walt continued to discuss the project, he made the decision that American audiences might not fully embrace such a British influenced story as he felt he had learned from the mixed reaction to his version of *Alice in Wonderland* (1951) and that it was best to begin with a "featurette" entitled *Winnie the Pooh and the Honey Tree* (1966) to introduce the characters.

Wolfgang "Woolie" Reitherman was assigned to direct and in an interview from that time period seems to take pride in the fact that he had never heard of Pooh until Walt mentioned it to him in 1961. In fact, Walt purposely wanted people involved who were unfamiliar with the characters. In the film, the characters, including Christopher Robin, seemed to speak in a Midwest American accent instead of a British one.

"The Midwest accent is the generally neutral accent at which we aim as it is acceptable in the whole American market," claimed Reitherman, who had cast his own son, Bruce, in the role of Christopher Robin. "We've got the spirit of Milne and Shepard (the illustrator of the original stories) but it's Disney, too!"

Christopher Robin was physically changed as well. Animator Hal King said, "Christopher Robin came out too sissified. So we gave him a haircut and some decent clothes."

There were complaints about the redesign of Pooh himself. Not realizing the difficulty of animating a stuffed toy (especially in a pre-computer era), complaints were thrown at abandoning the original Shepard design.

Fun was made of Pooh's red T-shirt, even though Pooh bears wearing such a shirt were authorized and sold at F.A.O. Schwarz store in New York in the 1940s and 1950s. From an animation standpoint, the T-shirt helps define the character, much like Mickey Mouse's distinctive shorts.

Despite all the criticisms, the "featurette" was popular in the United States and overseas.

Milne's widow, Daphne, said in an interview:

> Ever since I sold the film rights of the Pooh books to Mr. Walt Disney, I had been wondering with some anxiety what

he would make of them in a cartoon. I had confidence in Mr. Disney's genius for handling imaginative themes yet one never knows whether one is going to agree! On an evening last August, I turned on the television in my London flat to see a brief advance excerpt of the Pooh cartoon being shown in a program of Walt Disney films.

I was nervous. If I did not like this version of Pooh, I would feel deeply disappointed and hurt. Pooh is part of my life, part of my cherished memories. I leaned forward. There was a nursery scene and a glimpse of Christopher Robin as a child in cartoon.

There was the tree in the 100 Aker (sic) Wood with bees buzzing about it, and Pooh, attached to a balloon, sailing upwards in search of honey, his favorite food. I relaxed. It was all right. Nothing jarred. I was very relieved.

Ernest Shepard, who had illustrated the books and was in his 90s, declared that the Disney version was "a complete travesty."

Despite the success of the featurette (certainly better remembered that the live action film it accompanied in theaters, *The Ugly Dachshund*, the Walt Disney Company was sensitive to the criticism from the United Kingdom and in the next featurettes, Piglet returned and Christopher Robin sounded British.

After the turn of the century under the leadership of CEO Robert Iger whose financial model was to buy franchises for the Walt Disney Company, the Pooh Properties Trust licensed additional rights to Disney and accepted a buyout of $350 million of their claims to royalties as defined in a 1991 lawsuit brought by Stephen Slesinger, Inc.

Stephen Slesinger had acquired in 1930 sole and exclusive rights to virtually all uses for Pooh and the other characters outside of the Dutton books as well as rights to any sorts of future uses. Slesinger aggressively licensed the first Pooh doll, board game, puzzle, radio broadcast and more.

By November 1931 Winnie the Pooh was a $50 million business, providing an eye popping return on Slesinger's one thousand dollar upfront payment to Milne. Milne also received 66% of subsequent income from the arrangement.

After Slesinger's death in 1953, his widow licensed the rights to Disney in 1961 in return for regular semi-annual royalties but the family sued the Walt Disney Company in 1991, claiming to have been short-changed by Disney by two billion dollars. Disney was found to have destroyed some forty boxes of documents that were clearly labeled relevant to the case.

In 2008, a judge found misconduct on the part of the Slesinger estate. After a long running dispute between Stephen Slesinger, Inc. and Disney Enterprises over various trademarks derived from the Winnie-the-Pooh works, the Federal Circuit Court of Appeals confirmed a lower ruling that Disney was in fact the owner of Winnie the Pooh and the Pooh characters, and prior rulings prevented Slesinger from arguing that its agreement with Disney was only a license to use the trademarks.

The copyright on Pooh runs out in 2026 but trademarks can last as long as the property is active. Pooh's popularity continues to increase in every country around the world and the flood of Pooh merchandise shows no signs of abating.

In fact, at one point Pooh merchandise was significantly outselling all merchandise featuring Mickey Mouse. Within the last five years, revenue on Pooh has doubled whereas other top characters have only seen an increase of roughly twenty percent.

Within the world of *Winnie the Pooh*, Halloween has been depicted on film a number of different times, including, but not limited to the following:

Because It's Halloween (1984)

Welcome to Pooh Corner was a live action television series that aired on the Disney Channel beginning in 1983. It featured performers in full-sized character costumes using "puppetronics", radio controlled devices that allowed the mouths and eyes to move. The residents of the Hundred Acre Wood (Pooh, Rabbit, Tigger, Owl, Piglet, Kanga and Roo) plan their annual Halloween party at a scary location. Eeyore intends to attend but can't decide on a costume so gets his advice from his friends and tries on different outfits. At the party, everyone is scared of the other costumes but Roo shows up and wins the costume contest.

The Monster FrankenPooh (1989)

The New Adventures of Winnie the Pooh was an a half hour animated television series produced by Disney that aired from 1988 to 1995 first on the Disney Channel and then on ABC.

Tigger, Rabbit, Gopher are telling scary stories on a dark night in the Hundred Acre Wood. Piglet tells a story of a scientist (who looks exactly like Piglet) and under a blanket on a table is the Monster FrankenPooh. With contributions to the story from others, the creature becomes bigger and bigger until it hits its head on the ceiling of the castle.

The scientist Piglet runs for help as FrankenPooh goes looking for honey. After terrorizing Rabbit and Gopher in the story finally a trio of angry villagers (Rabbit, Gopher and Owl) storm the scared scientist's castle. The real Piglet is terrified of this turn in the story and Tigger, Rabbit and Gopher comfort him and counsel him to learn the difference between what is real and what is not.

Boo to You Too! Winnie the Pooh (1996)

This was a twenty minute special produced by Walt Disney Television Animation that aired October 25, 1996 on ABC. It was part of an hour special that also included the short cartoons *Lonesome Ghosts, Pluto's Judgement Day* and *Trick or Treat*. The Pooh segment was later included in *Pooh's Heffalump Halloween Movie* (2006).

For Halloween, the inhabitants of the Hundred Acre Wood are eager to go trick-or-treating but Piglet has never done so because he is too afraid. However, this time, at their urging, he decides to join his friends. While out, Pooh who is dressed in a bee costume tries to get honey from a bee hive but the bees chase the group into Rabbit's garden and destroy his pumpkins in the process.

As night approaches there is a threatening thunderstorm forming and Tigger excitedly talks about the horrors of Halloween that frightens Piglet to run home and boards up his windows.

His friends (Pooh, Eeyore and Tigger) decide to throw Piglet a less scary "Hallo-wasn't" party but when the costumed friends show up at Piglet's house, he mistakes them for monsters and runs away. The friends go search for the missing

Piglet who ironically is looking for them. He finally decides they have been taken by "Spookables".

During the stormy night, Pooh's costume gets stuck on a tree branch and Eeyore and Tigger try to help the bear who is crying for help. Piglet believes that two "Spookables"are attacking his friend and he summons his courage to rescue his friend. They commend Piglet for his bravery and they all go trick-or-treaing together.

The Book of Boo (2002)

The Book of Pooh is a half hour television show that ran on Playhouse Disney starting in 2001 done in a style of puppetry based on Japanese bunraku puppetry. With the cut-out-styled computer 3-D backgrounds, the show has the look of a pop-up book.

On the evening of Halloween, everyone gathers at Owl's house to hear the story of "The Goose Who Hated Halloween". Everyone loves the story except Eeyore who finds the story boring because nothing much scares him. He heads for home.

The others go to Kanga's house for a Halloween party where they dress up in costumes. Eeyore decides to move to The Scary Woods because nobody goes there and he won't be bothered. In addition, his house of sticks would be safe from being knocked over so he would feel safe. Piglet goes searching for Eeyore but ends up scaring him when his costume becomes covered in leaves and resembles ragweed. Piglet wins the Halloween costume contest. Eeyore decides to join in celebrating Halloween.

Pooh's Heffalump Halloween Movie (2005)

This sixty-seven minute direct-to-video movie was produced by Disney Toon Studios.

It is Lumpy the young Heffalump's first Halloween in the Hundred Acre Wood with his best friend Roo, Winnie the Pooh and the other inhabitants. They discuss their plans for trick-or-treating but Tigger warns them all about the Gobloon that he saw in the woods earlier. The Gobloon comes out every Halloween and captures someone to turn into a "jaggedy lantern".

However, if the Gobloon is captured, it will grant its captors one wish. Roo and Lumpy set out to capture the Gobloon to wish for some Halloween candy since Pooh has eaten it all. They journey past the Creepy Cave, the Slimy Slide and the Tree of Terror. As they get closer to the Gobloon's lair, Lumpy loses his courage so Roo tells him the story from *Boo To You Winnie the Pooh* (1996) when Piglet was afraid at Halloween.

Lumpy and Roo set a trap but end up running away with Lumpy getting stuck in the trap. Roo finds a Jack-o-lantern that looks like Lumpy so he thinks the Gobloon has captured his friend and transformed him. Roo asks Pooh, Piglet, Tigger, Eeyore and Rabbit to help him capture the Gobloon and save Lumpy.

Lumpy breaks free from his trap when he hears them coming. The group finally go trick-or-treating. It turns out that Tigger mistook Kanga for the Gobloon because she had carved jack-o-lanterns in the likenesses of the friends but somehow accidentally dropped the one of Lumpy. Everyone ends up enjoying the Halloween party.

Darby's Halloween Case (2009)

My Friends Tigger & Pooh was a computer animated television series that first aired in 2007 on Playhouse Disney. Instead of Christopher Robin, the series featured a six year old red-headed girl named Darby and her dog Buster. Darby is the younger best friend of Christopher Robin who went off to college.

She is the leader of the Super Sleuths composed of Darby, Buster, Pooh and Tigger. They wear outfits with question marks on them and they solve mysterious activities in the Hundred Acre Wood.

When Turtle hosts a Halloween party in his cave, everyone hears strange noises and things start moving on their own. They decide that the cave must be haunted by ghosts so Piglet calls the Super Sleuths to find out what is happening.

Winnie the Pooh's Spookable Fun (aka Spookable Pooh) featuring "scary" animated episodes first came on television in 1990 and then to VHS in 1996. It was re-released on VHS again in 2000. The third time it came out on VHS was in 2002. There was also a DVD that came out in 2003 that included *Boo To You*.

Multiple books have been released over the years with Disney's version of Winnie the Pooh celebrating Halloween but they are all geared to the youngest readers. Here is a listing of some of them:

Disney's Winnie the Pooh's Halloween (1995)

This thirty-two page book written by Bruce Talkington has Christopher Robin explaining to his animal friends some of the mysteries of Halloween. Pooh, Tigger, Eeyore and others don their costumes to go out but Piglet decides to remain at home to hide from spooks.

Pooh Trick or Treat (1997)

This twenty-four page Golden Book was written by Ann Braybrooks with illustrations by Arkadia with Pooh and Piglet wearing a joint costume of a totem pole while Tigger wears a sheet.

Disney's Pooh Says Boo (1998)

This ten page "Lift the Flap" book written by Nancy Parent has Pooh and his friends ready to trick-or-treat but Piglet too scared to join them. The short page length leads to some confusion with both Pooh and Tigger changing costumes without explanation and fearful lightning bolts discovered under one flap. Apparently inspired in part by the straight-to-video movie *Boo to You Winnie the Pooh*.

Winnie the Pooh's Spookable Halloween (1998)

This ten page giant "Lift the Flap" board book was written by Nancy Parent. Pooh and his friends dress up in costumes, carve pumpkins, and head off on a Halloween exploration through the Hundred Acre Wood.

Pooh's Halloween Parade (1999)

This thirty-seven page book written by Isabel Gaines tells the story of Pooh and his friends gathering together for their annual Halloween parade when they discover a scary and noisy rock in the back of the room.

Winnie the Pooh Happy Halloween Coloring Book (1999)

Seventy pages from Golden Books

Pooh's Happy Halloween (1999)

Seventy page Random House children's storybook.

Disney's Trick or Treat, Pooh (2000)

This twelve page "Lift the Flap" book tells the tale of Winnie-the-Pooh, dressed as a honey pot, and Piglet and Roo, dressed as each other, going trick-or-treating but can't seem to find anybody at home at Halloween to give them treats.

Pooh's Halloween Pumpkin (2003)

This thirty-two page "Step Into Reading" book written by Isabel Gaines and illustrated by Josie Yee has Pooh planting pumpkin seeds in hopes of having a big pumpkin by Halloween. The story goes through the process of planting in the spring and harvesting in the fall. While he waits, Pooh eats and eats and eats.

Winnie the Pooh's Halloween Pumpkin (2013)

This ten page board book is shaped like a pumpkin shaped trick-or-treat bucket with a braided cord handle. While walking through the Hundred Acre Wood, Pooh stumbles upon a giant orange pumpkin. With the help of his friends, Pooh comes up with a perfect plan for the pumpkin which is to make it a jack-o-lantern for the holiday.

Disney Winnie the Pooh—Happy Halloween (2018)

This eighteen page publication by is a "Look and Find" board book that is themed to Pooh and his friends at Halloween. Readers search seven vividly illustrated scenes for hidden characters and objects. While there is text, no reading is required for younger children to participate.

Boo to You Winnie the Pooh (2019)

This eighteen page board book is the rough storybook adaptation of the straight-to-video film of the same name where Pooh and his friends have to find a way to help Piglet overcome his fears of trick-or-treating.

DISNEY FILMS

While the Disney brand seems to focus on magic and happy endings, many of the films even during Walt Disney's lifetime have some darker elements even if they never veer into the blood, slashing, gore and frightening terror common in most horror films.

After Walt Disney's death, the Disney Studios produced several films that invoked images of dark magic and the devil including *The Devil and Max Devlin* (1981) where ironically, comedian Bill Cosby plays Satan's chief henchman, Barney Satin.

Something Wicked This Way Comes (1983) featured author Ray Bradbury's Mr. Dark's Pandemonium Carnival that wanted to claim innocent souls for damnation. The fact that it takes place in Autumn and has supernatural aspects makes it feel like a Halloween film.

"Nowhere else can the drama of fantasy be so excitingly projected as on the movie screen. Nowhere else can the legitimate love of fantasy be more appealingly entered into," wrote Walt in his essay "Children Love Fantasy" in the magazine *The Instructor* (January 1955).

While Disney animation has certainly provided some strikingly horrific images that have given young children nightmares, Disney live action films have certainly done so as well.

The horrific banshee in *Darby O'Gill and the Little People* (1959) made many hide their eyes and haunted their dreams despite the limits of special effects in those days that used a simple Chroma Key technique.

The banshee effect was achieved by shooting in black-and-white against a black background while the banshee was entirely white. The negative was then printed, enlarged

and kept out of focus. It was then added into film using the optical printer and an eerie green tint.

A banshee is a female Irish spirit who is always wailing to signal the death of a family member. In the film, she is portrayed by an uncredited Joanne Genthon whose haunting keening sound has been used elsewhere including the Haunted Mansion attraction.

One of the scariest Disney films could have been *The Watcher in the Woods* (1980). It is a supernatural ghost story about an American family that moves into an old English manor where the teen daughter and her sister discovers a ghostly secret.

It was marketed as a straight horror film that was not suitable for young children. The film received such a negative response when it was first shown that Disney eliminated a pre-credits sequence and filmed an entirely new ending. The project had been pitched to Disney executive Ron Miller as "This could be our *Exorcist* (1973)!"

Of course, Disney has delved into lighter movies for television that still had creepy moments like *Mr. Boogedy* (1986) about a ghost who back in Colonial times in the town of Lucifer Falls sold his soul to Satan for a cloak that gives him magical powers. It even sparked a sequel *Bride of Boogedy* (1987).

Originally, it had been planned as a horror movie parody in the style of the movie *Airplane!* called *Cheap Thrills* and to star Cheech & Chong but Disney bought it and intended it for a possible television series. Disney had the horror elements toned down into a more family friendly approach. Boogedy's memorable makeup was done by Emmy award winning Rick Stratton.

Over the decades, Disney produced films that flirted with Halloween-related themes like *Under Wraps* (1997), *Don't Look Under the Bed* (1999), *Mom's Got a Date with a Vampire* (2000), *Scream Team* (2002), and even films like *Zombies* (2018).

However, the following chapters are devoted to films that are specifically about Halloween.

Tim Burton's The Nightmare Before Christmas (1993)

Talking about *Tim Burton's The Nightmare Before Christmas* (1993), creator Burton said, "This film is special for me. The characters are very personal to me. This film has all the elements I wanted for it: the holidays (I love both Halloween and Christmas), beautiful but misunderstood characters, drama, sadness, optimism. When I watch it now, after having had it in me for so long...I love it."

Burton grew up near the Disney Studio in Burbank, California and for him drawing was a sanctuary from his perceived horrors of everyday life and school. Burton explained that his childhood in ever-sunny Burbank, California was not marked by the usual visual seasonal changes elsewhere in the country like the changing color of leaves, so holiday decorations were an especially important factor for him in determining the time of year.

He recalled that local merchants were so eager to increase sales that there was sometimes a melding of Halloween and Christmas decorations and advertisements in some stores to lengthen the shopping season.

As a result, in his mind, it seemed natural for Halloween to intrude on Christmas and become a combination of his two favorite holidays. For him, the city of Burbank looked as bland as any other small town but during the holidays, the lights and decorations made it seem a place of wonder.

"I loved Halloween," said Burton. "I wanted to do a story that would put (Halloween and Christmas) together. Somehow I thought of a Halloween Town to match the North Pole and took images and just sort of twisted them together."

To get the look of Halloween Town the production design team utilized a film technique that was used in days of German Expressionist film, painting graphic textures right

on the sets and then combining the 2D illustration with the modern art of 3D.

Director Henry Selick explained that they'd smear sets in plaster or clay, then scratch lines into this material "to give it that sort of etched texture or feel to make it look like a living illustration." He tried to capture the unique cross-hatching design style of Burton's drawings and thought of the characters performing as if they were in a giant pop-up book.

Selick said:

> I wanted Halloween Town to feel prickly; if you could rub your hand across the skyline, you'd bleed. Color was limited to black and orange, with some greens and greys, the lighting spooky, especially at night.
>
> In Christmas Town, I pushed for soft and friendly (Dr.) Seuss, buildings like gingerbread, landscapes like soft serve ice cream—rub your hand across the skyline and it would feel pleasant and smooth. We used Christmas colors and warm, friendly lighting.

Burton got an artistic scholarship to attend California Institute of the Arts in 1976. In 1979, the Walt Disney Company reviewed the students' year end projects and were impressed with his short animated horror film about a creepy dentist entitled *Stalk of the Celery Monster*.

He was offered an apprenticeship at the studio and teamed with veteran animator Glen Keane to work on the animated feature *The Fox and the Hound* (1981). Burton found that he couldn't adapt to the approved "Disney-style" of drawing.

Burton became visibly depressed at work, demonstrating erratic behavior including sleeping in a closet, and was finally assigned to the animated feature *The Black Cauldron* that the studio hoped would more closely align with his drawing style.

Burton's work caught the attention of producer Julie Hickson and the head of creative development at Disney at the time, Tom Wilhite. They sensed that Burton's originality might be worth exploring on non-traditional Disney projects and got funding to make an animated short written and directed by Burton. It was entitled *Vincent* (1982) about a boy who wanted to grow up to be the Vincent Price he had seen in horror films.

Burton worked on several other projects including a live action version of "Hansel and Gretel" and for another project titled *Trick or Treat* that would have dealt with kids on Halloween and a haunted house.

Before he left Disney, Burton also directed a black and white live action short titled *Frankenweenie* (1984), a twist on the classic *Frankenstein* horror film, where a young boy brings his stitched-together dead dog, Sparky, back to life through electricity.

In 1982, while still at Disney, Burton worked on another poem story like *Vincent* but this time about a Halloweenland. It was three pages long and featured Jack Skellington, his ghost dog Zero who had a tiny glowing orange jack-o-lantern as a nose and Santa Claus. It was called *The Nightmare Before Christmas* as a take-off on the famous Christmas poem, *A Visit from St. Nicholas* that is commonly known as *The Night Before Christmas*.

Burton proposed it as a half hour television holiday special, perhaps narrated by Vincent Price. Burton also proposed it as a possible children's book but again, Disney was uninterested.

Burton said:

> I took it around the networks, did storyboards and sketches and Rick Heinrichs did a little model of Jack. Everybody said they liked it, but not enough to do it at that time. I guess that was my first real taste of show business mentality—a nice big smile and an "Oh, yeah, we're going to do this." But as you proceed it becomes less and less of a reality.
>
> There was even some talk about doing it as a feature film but as drawn cel animation. But I didn't want to do that. I decided to try to hide it away but always with that feeling that I would do it some time but do it right.

With the arrival of Michael Eisner and Frank Wells at Disney in 1984, some people were let go including Burton who was fine with leaving since he had been so frustrated.

He went into directing live action films and his first four were critically and financially successful live action feature films in a row that grossed over four hundred million dollars: *Pee-Wee's Big Adventure* (1985*), Beetlejuice* (1988), *Batman* (1989) and *Edward Scissorhands* (1990).

Instead of enjoying this notoriety, Burton was overwhelmed and wanted to return to a more personal project about which he was truly passionate. Burton had his agent quietly check into the status of *The Nightmare Before Christmas*, hoping he might be able to get it back but wasn't really surprised to discover that Disney owned it completely and had no intention of releasing it.

David Hoberman, then president of Disney/Touchstone, said that he "sent researchers down into the files to see what we had and they came back with *The Nightmare Before Christmas* material."

Disney Chairman Jeffrey Katzenberg had become the executive who had spearheaded the renaissance of animation at Disney with *The Little Mermaid* (1989). He saw the request as being an opportunity to get into business with Burton and continue to reinforce Disney's domination of feature animation.

Burton himself had expressed concern that all of his feature films were being done at Warner Brothers and he didn't want to align himself too closely with just one studio but he didn't want his film, as Burton said, "to fit in to the same type of cartoon movies Disney have been having so much success with."

Disney offered Burton a contractual promise of creative autonomy but insisted that the film be officially titled *Tim Burton's The Nightmare Before Christmas* to capitalize on his name recognition as well as to distance it from a standard Disney film.

Of course, Burton was unable to direct the film himself because he was already committed to the feature film *Batman Returns* (1992) that was going into production at the same time and he was already doing pre-production for *Ed Wood* (1994).

In addition, Burton did not want to be involved with the pain-staking and time-consuming process of doing stop-motion animation where maybe a minute's worth of footage could be produced in a single week.

However, Burton was adamant that the film would be done in stop motion just like the Rankin-Bass holiday specials he loved:

> In so many ways, drawn animation is easier because you can draw anything. Three-dimensional animation has limitations

because you're moving puppets around but for me, it is more effective because it feels like it is actually there.

It's the handmade aspect of things, part of an energy you can't explain. When the animators move the figures, there's an energy that is captured. It's something that computers will never be able to replace because they are missing that one element.

The initial impulse for doing it was the love of Dr. Seuss and those holiday specials that I grew up watching like *How the Grinch Stole Christmas* (1966) and *Rudolph the Red-Nosed Reindeer* (1964).

Those crude stop-motion animation holiday things (done by Rankin-Bass) that were on year in, year out make an impact on you early and stay with you. I had grown up with those and had a real feeling for them, and I think, without being too direct, the impulse was to do something like that and with somebody like a Grinch who is perceived as scary but isn't.

One of the few friendships that Burton had made at Disney was with Henry Selick who had carved out a niche for himself after leaving Disney with his stop motion animation for MTV and some short films.

In addition he had done some storyboarding for the Will Vinton claymation scenes in Disney's *Return to Oz* (1985). Burton and Selick shared a similar artistic sensibility.

He had been an early supporter for the *Nightmare* idea a decade earlier and Burton offered him a huge measure of creative freedom to direct the film. Visual consultant Rich Heinrichs originally recommended Selick to Burton as the on set director.

Selick realized it was his opportunity to direct his first feature length film but didn't suspect how much he would be overshadowed by Burton's celebrity not only in the title itself but during the publicity during the release for the finished film.

Burton served as producer, had created the original idea and came up with initial designs for the film and some of its main characters. Even twenty-five years after it was first released, people still consider it an official part of Burton's impressive filmography with Selick's significant work often forgotten.

Selick said:

It was my job to make it look like 'a Tim Burton film', which is not so different from my own films. We can collaborate because we often think of the same solution to a problem. It's why we hit it off at Disney.

I don't want to take away from Tim, but he was not in San Francisco when we made it. He came up five times over two years, and spent no more than eight or ten days in total. We did communicate while he was filming in Los Angeles and he offered suggestions. It's more like he wrote a children's book and gave it to us and we went from there. But the bottom line was that Tim Burton's name before the title was going to bring in more people than mine would.

Selick was even responsible for the final design of Jack's suit. Burton's original design was that Jack was dressed all in black but Selick saw that would be a major concern because the one color suit would blend into the dark backgrounds and disappear. He added the white stripes to make it a pinstripe suit that helped the figure stand out.

The film is filled with many of Burton's ideas including having the different Holiday Doors in the forest. These doors were the iconic images of a pumpkin (for Halloween), a decorated Christmas Tree (for Christmas), a turkey (for Thanksgiving), a brightly colored egg (for Easter), a green four leafed clover (for St. Patrick's Day), a red heart (for Valentine's Day), and a red and white firework (for July 4).

To his credit, Burton was always effusive in giving Selick credit:

Henry is a real artist. He's truly the best. When I wasn't shooting (*Batman Returns*), I would go up there (to the studio) because I loved it, but most of the time, Henry would just send me stuff—there'd be a few shots during the week—and so over the period of a couple of years, it all came together.

Anyway, I would get a reel and I had an editing room and I would edit some shots. It was the hardest thing I ever worked on, in a way, because it just took so long, and there were a lot of people involved, a lot of artists. I would try to keep it all on a certain track.

I could still affect things as I needed to. When I saw the first shots, I knew that Halloween Town had to be darker and blacker. I felt very comfortable with my role and I knew Henry and how talented he is. I knew what was going on.

It is more beautiful than I imagined it would be thanks to Henry and his talented crew of artists, animators and designers.

The songs were written before the final script. Burton brought in composer Danny Elfman. The former member of the band Oingo Boingo had already provided the scores for *Pee-Wee's Big Adventure, Beetlejuice, Batman* and *Edward Scissorhands*.

In *USA Today* newspaper and *Adweek* magazine in October 1993, Elfman stated:

Tim and I would just start to talk through a scene and I'd start to hear a melody in my head. Then I'd shoo him out of the room because I didn't want to lose it. I'd call him three days later and play him the new songs.

Nightmare could never work by trying to squeeze it into the *Beauty and the Beast* framework—you know, a six-song, contemporary Broadway-ish Disney musical. None of us had done a musical. Tim sent me a whole series of color drawings of Jack Skellington, the sleigh and the reindeer. The drawings really got me going.

Elfman at that point had collected skeleton imagery for twenty-two years. His home was adorned with Day of the Dead artifacts and images, as well as a real shrunken head from Ecuador.

"So it was not like a major stretch for me to relate to Jack Skellington," said Elfman.

Burton remembered::

Danny and I would go through my little outline and I'd say "Jack does this and then he does that and then he falls into Christmastown." We'd worked together so much that it didn't matter that we didn't know what we were doing. We just took a stab at it.

We worked very quickly which was good because we needed the songs so we could do the script. There's Henry. There's me. There's Danny. There's Caroline (scripter Caroline Thompson) and that's a lot to deal with.

In a way, Elfman was responsible for much of the story. When writer Caroline Thompson who had written *Edward Scissorhands* was brought in to write the screenplay, the

already almost completed ten songs took up most of the plot and running time of the film.

One of the reasons that Thompson was brought in was not just her previous collaboration with Burton but that at the time she was living with Elfman and had heard the songs over and over even before Burton had heard them so she was quite familiar with the story and the characters.

Thompson said:

> I never even saw the original script. "They just gave me Danny's lyrics. I remember saying to Tim 'Just let me take it away for a week and I'll see what I can bring back'. So I went up north for a week, rented a house on the beach, wrote fifty pages, came back, and he was happy.
>
> The script would go to the storyboard artists, and they would basically tear it apart. Then I would see the drawings they had done and incorporate it and wing it back. Even with all the changes, the basic structure of the script remained what I gave them after that initial week of work.

Storyboard artist Joe Ranft said:

> Caroline would rewrite based on our drawings and we would re-board from her latest draft. Or we'd have an idea and do some drawings and fax them to her, and she'd write it into the script. It was a fun collaboration.
>
> We'd do thumbnails (small, quick drawings) and pin these up in rough order and Henry would come back and say 'This is great' or 'This isn't what I wanted at all' or 'Just make a couple of changes here and there.'

One of Thompson's significant contributions was with the fuller development of the character of Sally, resulting in Elfman writing a song for the character. Thompson never saw the first unfinished adaptation done by writer Michael McDowell, who had written *Beetlejuice* but was let go because Burton decided it was best to work on the songs first.

Skellington Productions (named after the main character) opened up in a warehouse in San Francisco's South of Market district in July 1991 and filming began the following October even though there was no final script. They began with animating the song *What's This?*

Selick lived and worked in the San Francisco area previously but it was primarily chosen as the location because it was so far removed from Burbank that it was felt there would be less tampering by the Disney Studio.

A number of special effects and commercial production companies with experience in stop motion like Industrial Light and Magic (ILM) already existed in the San Francisco area as well as a veteran talent pool and those were also factors in the final choice.

The goal was to produce roughly seventy seconds of usable animation every week so it took a crew of nearly 120 workers utilizing twenty individual sound stages close to three years of constant working to create over 100,000 single frames for the final seventy-four minute film.

If something was off even just a fraction of an inch, the entire shot was ruined and had to be re-shot. There were fifteen animators manipulating the character figures.

Nightmare ended up being the most complex and longest stop-motion project in history up to that point in time. Many scenes required numerous characters, special lighting effects and it was approached as if it were a live action film.

The film utilized a motion-control camera (known as a "mocon") technology controlled by a computer that allowed elaborate crane and tracking shots. The biggest and most awkward one was dubbed Luxo Sr. as a tribute to John Lasseter's Luxo Jr. character from the Pixar films.

One of the most challenging scenes was when Jack reaches for the shiny doorknob on the Christmas door in the forest. Its golden knob reflects not only Jack but the rest of the forest behind him in an odd oval shape.

Selick recalled:

> I'll put it this way: there were no easy scenes in *Nightmare*, just hard, hard and almost impossible. Jack heading out on Christmas Eve in his coffin sled with skeleton reindeer was difficult because virtually every character in Halloween Town was there to send him off.

To allow animators easy access to the puppets, the sets had pathways behind and beneath them so that the armatures inside puppets could always be manipulated by the puppeteers or allow them to swap out faces for a wide range of expressions.

Jack Skellington had over 700 different replacement heads for mouth and eye shapes. Only his nostrils remained unchanged on each face to maintain some consistency. Supervising animator Eric Leighton stated:

> On this film, the animators and camera crews constantly found themselves having to crawl around just to reach the puppet. The physical labor aspect of this project challenged even the best of our animators. We went through kneepads quickly. A masseuse came weekly to rub sore backs, cramped necks and arching shoulders. An on-set ping pong table and punching bag helped keep hands and wrists limber.

The film contains 74 characters, requiring several hundred fully armatured puppets. Oogie Boogie needed 173 separate parts. They all had to be built strong enough to withstand the long shooting and hold a pose.

Most of the puppets were built 12-15 inches tall with Oogie Boogie being two feet tall. That made the puppets larger and heavier than in other stop-motion animation films and required the sets to be reinforced.

Joe Ranft who would later become legendary for his story work on Pixar animated feature films and was the storyboard supervisor on the film is caricatured in the film as Igor, Dr. Finkelstein's assistant, and supplies the character's only line in the film.

Burton himself was to appear briefly in another cameo. When the ice-skating vampires are playing hockey, originally they were batting around a decapitated pale head with spiky black hair and bags under its eyes that resembled Burton. It was considered a little too gruesome and was replaced in the final film with a jack-o-lantern.

Danny Elfman provided the singing voice for Jack Skellington. He remarked:

> I had a lot in common with Jack. I felt with Jack's character that I had nailed it and no one else would be able to do a better job than I had.

He also provided the voices for Barrel, one of the mischievous trio, and the Clown with the Tear-Away Face. He was also given a caricature cameo as the redheaded corpse face tucked in the upright bass of the Halloween Town band.

However, it was felt that it might be better to have a professional actor to do the speaking voice, one of the things that caused a rift between Elfman and Burton for a while. "We basically had to find an actor who matched my voice," recalled Elfman. "Normally, it is the other way around but this is the reverse. Jack sings more than he speaks. Usually they'd find the actor and then someone to match their voice to sing."

The actor who speaks Jack's lines was Chris Sarandon who had already played the vampire in *Fright Night* (1985) and Prince Humperdinck in *The Princess Bride* (1987) among many other memorable roles. Sarandon went on to reprise the role of Jack in video games like *Kingdom Hearts, Oogie's Revenge* and for several Disneyland Halloween projects like Halloween Screams, Frightfully Fun Parade and Haunted Mansion Holiday.

For casting, Burton relied on actors with whom he had worked previously like Glenn Shadix (as the two-faced mayor), Catherine O'Hara (as Sally and Shock) and Paul Reubens (as Lock).

The character of Oogie Boogie was problematic for Disney because while he was not black in color or had any design aspects to suggest a particular race, he was perceived as possibly racist.

Selick remarked:

> In some parts of the world, like in Alabama where my mother is from, a 'boogie man' is a monstrous black person, so the name had racial connotations. The character really came from (the Fleischer Studio) Betty Boop cartoons though, which would have Cab Calloway, the (black) jazz band leader and a great singer serve as the basis of what they would call 'specialty numbers.'
>
> He would dance his inimitable jazz dance and sing *Minnie the Moocher* or *Old Man of the Mountain* and they would rotoscope him, trace him, turn him into a cartoon character like a walrus. I think those were some of the most inventive moments in cartoon history, in no way racist, even though he was sometimes a villain.
>
> In the end we went with Ken Page, who is a black singer, because he was the best guy to sing the song. He had no problems with it.

The last sequence to be shot in August 1993 was Oogie Boogie coming apart at the seams and it was one of the most complicated because of the numerous moving insects.

At one point, instead of Oogie Boogie being torn up and reduced to bugs, it was discussed that he be unmasked as the evil scientist Dr. Finkelstein who was in disguise. His whole scheme was revenge because Sally loved Jack, even though Finkelstein made her to be his mate. Burton rejected the idea.

The film includes many tributes that a general audience usually misses like the two children attacked by one of Skellington's toys has the girl wearing a Mickey Mouse print nightgown, while her brother's pajamas are covered in Donald Duck faces.

The snake looks exactly like a Sandworm from *Beetlejuice* and a shrunken head resembles one from the waiting room in the same film. There is a duck that resembles one in the film *Batman Returns*.

While the film has become a beloved holiday classic, when it was first released, the reviews were decidedly mixed even from executives at the Disney Studio. Looking at the final film, Disney decided it was too far removed from its family friendly brand and decided to release it through its more adult Touchstone Pictures branch.

The film certainly never became the blockbuster that the Disney Studio hoped but it grossed nearly forty-nine million dollars during its first sixteen weeks of domestic release on an initial budge of eighteen million for the film.

That profit increased with foreign distribution and video sales which were all strong as well as with further re-releases. In addition, the film generated huge merchandise sales and continues to do so.

Selick said:

> A long time ago, we joked about Jack Skellington taking over Valentine's Day or President's Day or St. Patrick's. And I've certainly wondered what Jack and Sally's children might look like. But I don't think there will be a sequel.
>
> Why mess with a good thing? *Nightmare* never seems to get old; people never seem to get tired of it and they keep selling merchandise.

Burton agreed:

> I was always very protective of the film not to do sequels or things of that kind. You know, 'Jack visits Thanksgiving world' or other kinds of things, just because I felt the movie had a purity to it. Because it's not a mass-market kind of thing, it was important to kind of keep that purity of it. I try to respect people and keep the purity of the project as much as possible.

Hocus Pocus (1993)

Eight year old Emily Binx died in Salem, Massachusetts on Halloween October 31, 1693.

She had her life force drained from her by the Sanderson sisters, a coven of three evil witches, who were hanged to death on that same date for that foul deed. The trio returned three hundred years later on Halloween October 31, 1993 thanks to the lighting of a black flame candle by a virgin so they could plague the town once more for one frightening night.

That is the basic premise for the 1993 Disney movie *Hocus Pocus* but there is so much more to the story that has become a cult favorite.

Director Kenny Ortega described it as "Three outlandishly wild witches—Bette Midler, Sarah Jessica Parker, and Kathy Najimy—return from 17th century Salem after they are accidentally conjured up! It's a Halloween night full of zany fun and comic chaos once the tricky trio sets out to cast a spell on the town and reclaim their youth—but first they must outwit three kids, a 300 year old zombie and a talking cat!"

The film was released in July 1993 to take advantage of the young audience that was off on summer vacation from school and also so it wouldn't compete with the Halloween-themed *The Nightmare Before Christmas* (1993) that Disney was releasing during the upcoming holiday season.

While the film made a modest profit, it received mixed reviews and continues to do so today. On its initial release, *Entertainment Weekly* called *Hocus Pocus* "acceptable scary-silly kid fodder that adults will find only mildly insulting. Unless they're Bette Midler fans. In which case it's depressing as hell."

Film critic Roger Ebert wrote that it was like "attending a party you weren't invited to, and where you don't know anybody, and they're all in on a joke but won't explain it to you." He gave the film one star.

Actress Bette Midler who portrayed Winifred Sanderson said in 2013:

> We made (*Hocus Pocus*) before the tidal wave of Halloween happened. In the old days, it was 'Oh, Halloween is Halloween. And the kids will go out.' But now it's huge. The kids, grown-ups, everybody takes part in it.
>
> And this movie was kind of the beginning of the wave. Kathy, Sarah Jessica and I have talked about it. We are totally thrilled to death. Because when it came out, it laid a tiny little bit of an egg, so we didn't expect much. And now look at it!

Doug Jones ,who was Billy the Zombie, stated:

> It didn't perform very well at the box office. So, I thought that was the end of it. Then when it began airing on TV every Halloween and grew in popularity to the point where it's a bigger hit of a movie now 25 years later than it ever was. That did come in a slow-building, very pleasant surprise.

The film was the brainchild of David Kirschner.

Kirschner was the producer of all the films in the *Child's Play* film series featuring the Chucky doll. He also developed the 1986 animated feature *An Americal Tail* where he established a good relationship with filmmaker Steven Spielberg.

The *Hocus Pocus* story started as a bedtime story Kirschner would tell his two young daughters based on the neighbor's black cat who would sometimes stray on to their back porch.

In addition, when he was younger, Kirschner had found and taken in a black cat and named it "Inks", because of its inky black coloring, which helped inspire the name "Binx" for the boy in the story who had been changed into a cat by witches.

Binx was actually played by nine different black cats that each had a certain skill like jumping on command or moving a paw. Treats and clickers were used every time a new cat was brought out to the set and it took time for each of the cats to get adjusted to the children. In addition, there were floppy cats, pose-able stand-in cats, and inflatable versions of Binx.

Actress Thora Birch who played the youngest girl Dani remembered:

> There were a number of live cats, animatronics cats [too]— the thing with the cat was a toss-up. You never knew what would happen.

Rhythm and Hues, who created the CGI Binx, went to great lengths to make sure that the facial features were authentic to an actual cat. However, Disney found the teeth a little too realistic and scary. To make the cat appear friendlier, Rhythm and Hues had to make the fangs smaller and less pointed. The acrylic teeth on the animatronics cat also had to be filed down which was difficult because of its small mouth.

In addition to voicing Binx when he was eighteen years old, actor Jason Marsden played Eric's best friend on *Boy Meets World*, D.J.'s rich boyfriend on *Full House*, and J.T.'s friend on *Step By Step*. He also voiced Goofy's son Max in *A Goofy Movie*.

He had auditioned for the role in the film of Max Dennison that went to Omri Katz although a young Leonardo DiCaprio was brought in for that role but turned it down to do another film, *What's Eating Gilbert Grape* (1993). In later years, DiCaprio said he had no regrets about making that decision.

Katz actually hung out on the set while it was filming because he was working on a television series that was in production nearby. He was not cast as the voice of Binx until after the film finishing shooting, doing two or three days in ADR sessions dubbing the dialog.

Marsden told writer Kevin Fallon in 2017:

> Sean Murray, who plays the human version of Thackery Binx in the film, was the voice first. They were using him first and animating his performance.
>
> Sean has a very contemporary sound. After it was all said and done, they—and I'm sure they worked with him on this—after the movie evolved they thought it would be more realistic, since the witches come from this time period, that Binx should also have an affected accent. Not only did I have to do Binx, I had to lip sync Sean as well for consistency. (Laughs.) I'm sure he loved that when he saw the final film.

Kirschner first turned the legend of the Sanderson Sisters into a short story for *Muppet Magazine* and then decided to develop his Halloween-themed tale into a full-fledged film script.

During the original pitch for Disney in 1984, Kirschner came a half hour early and had a Halloween decorated grocery bag filled with about twenty pounds of candy corn that he tore

open to create a serpent-like shape of the treats on the conference table "so that the whole room smelled like Halloween".

He also hung props on the wall like child-drawn pictures of black cats and suspended from the ceiling two brooms and a Hoover stand-up vacuum cleaner, the mode of transportation for the Sanderson Sisters in modern times, and darkened the room.

The executives loved the pitch and gave Kirschner approval to develop the idea as an original movie for the newly launched Disney Channel that was desperately in need of material.

Mick Garris, who had already produced and directed several documentaries about horror films, was working as a story editor and writer on the *Amazing Stories* television series being produced by Spielberg. Because of Kirschner's previous working relationship with Spielberg, he checked out some of Garris' work and the two hit it off immediately.

When interviewed by writer Yohana Desta in 2014, Garris recalled:

> I loved the idea of the true story of Salem witches being brought into our world especially after visitng the location and seeing it all first hand. "Disney was quite eager for the film! I was attracted to the essence of David's idea as well as bringing the dark side of Disney to life. I mean we are talking about a little dead girl and a boy consigned to live for centuries as a cat. Setting magic in the real world has always been a theme that I'm attracted to.

> One thing I love doing over the Halloween season, and I got this from going there on a location scout for the movie was to go to Salem [Massachusetts] for this huge 11-day celebration that climaxes with a candlelight vigil to gallows hill, where the Salem witches were put to death. It's an amazing event, and I went there five or six years in a row after I went there to research the movie.

> I was the first writer when it was going to be called *Disney's Halloween House*, and there were several—almost a dozen—on the project after me. But they ended up going with most of my material, hence the way the credits were doled out. Now every woman or girl that I meet, from about five years old to 50 tells me it's their favorite movie. It definitely hit a nerve in the female psyche.

The movie's first draft was much darker. Garris told another writer:

> What I had written originally was about 12-year-olds. The kids being younger and in more jeopardy was certainly something more explicitly frightening. Later versions made two of the children older to attract a different demographic to sell more tickets and the film became more broadly comic. My version centered on the fears a younger, less mature kid would face like confronting death and being in a graveyard.

However, that first script did include having Billy the Zombie's head knocked off. Actress Karyn Malchus performed as the Headless Billy because she was short enough so that the upper torso still was the same height as Doug Jones.

As makeup supervisor Tony Gardner remembered:

> She wore this dummy head on top of a skullcap strapped to her own head, while looking through the lace of Billy's collar. The fake head had magnets mounted in the base of the neck, and there were corresponding magnets inside the neck stump that Karyn wore on her head.

> The tree branch was metal covered in foam, and the only protection Karyn's real face had was just the fiberglass skullcap covering her face from the nose up, so there was a lot of rehearsal to make sure that Karyn's false head was at exactly the right height for the branch to take Billy's head off and not her own.

Kirschner and Garris approached Spielberg to consider being involved perhaps as the director.

Garris said:

> He loved it until he found out that Disney was already involved. At that time, Disney and Amblin were very competitive in the family-film market, so neither of them wanted to be in business with the other. [But] it was very close to being a project with Steven Spielberg.

The intent was to ask actress Cloris Leachman to play the main witch. Singer Bette Midler had already made several films for Disney's Touchstone Pictures including *Down and Out in Beverly Hills*, *Ruthless People*, and *Outrageous Fortune* as well as voicing Georgette the poodle in the Disney animated feature *Oliver & Company* (1988).

When she expressed interest in the script Disney executive Jeffrey Katzenberg saw it as an opportunity to upgrade the project to a theatrical release. Midler stated in 2008 that this was her favorite of all of her films with *Oliver & Company* being another favorite. The title was changed to *Hocus Pocus* when it became a theatrical project.

Midler told television host Katie Couric:

> I'd be happy playing (Winnifred) for the rest of my life. She is completely demented. She is quite evil but she can be funny but she doesn't know how funny she is.
>
> It was the first time I had been part of an acting trio and I thought it was just so much fun. We laughed the whole time. We flew. And we got to wear crazy noses and fake teeth. I kept my fake teeth. And we just had the best time.

Since at least 1620 A.D., the phrase "hocus pocus" has been used as an incantation by magicians when performing tricks in a similar manner to using the phrase "abracadabra". Initially, magicians hoped that such exotic sounding phrases might suggest to the audience that mysterious forces were at work while at the same time offering a moment of brief distraction from what they were actually doing.

Actress Rosie O'Donnell was originally offered the role of Mary Sanderson but turned it down because she did not want to be a scary witch that killed children.

The role was offered to actress Kathy Najimy who had just appeared in Touchstone's *Sister Act* (1992). At first, she was hesitant to accept because she did not want to offend real witches by playing a negative stereotype. She urged the writers to include some mention of white witches who do protection.

However, since she was a longtime, huge Bette Midler fan, almost a borderline stalker, the opportunity to be able to work with the singer was more than enough to convince her and during the filming she revealed her fifteen year long obsession to Midler.

Najimy stated:

> It seems scarier on paper. But when you get me and Sarah and Bette in our characters and in our costumes, with the jokes everywhere and running around and bumping into each other, the sucking the lives out of kids becomes so secondary that it's not scary anymore.

You usually don't rehearse much for a film. You just rehearse that day. But we rehearsed for a month because there was flying and dancing and singing.

Hocus Pocus's choreographer Peggy Holmes didn't just work with the three actresses on the famous *I Put A Spell On You* dance number, she also instructed the witches on how to fly. Najimy explained:

[Peggy went]) driving with Bette and Sarah and I indvidually around the Disney back lot, and from our driving she developed how we flew. So Sarah was like very front forward so she would hold it. [She demonstrates miming a broom held closely to her chest] I was like very 10-and-2 while I was driving, so she was like, "That's how you'll fly."

Stunt coordinator Terry Frazee instructed the stars on how to handle the wire rigs that had them hanging thirty feet off the ground as well as the teeter rig (for close-ups) that would allow the Sanderson Sisters to swoop down on the children. Elaborate rod puppets were also used for long shots.

Sarah Jessica Parker, who played Sarah Sanderson, said:

I liked making the movie and I loved flying. It was old fashion wires and harnesses. It's joyful. It's also a dance, and there's a lot of trying to be graceful while not being sure you weren't going to be turned upside down.

I realized I could fit an entire *New York Times* newspaper up the back of the corset, and I found that the harness was comfortable, so I would just sit up there and read the *Times* while people took their breaks or changed the camera or sometimes went to lunch.

Mary's signature crooked smile was something Najimy discovered for herself during rehearsals. It was during one day in rehearsal that it was decided that Mary should be like a bloodhood to sniff out children. Early make-up concepts had her prosthetic nose longer and more snout-like to resemble a dog.

Make-up supervisor Tony Gardner said that Kevin Haney designed Mary Sanderson so that her head was like a pumpkin with her hair acting as the twisted stem.

Najimy revealed that the movie was "cut and edited completely differently than it was filmed. There are as many as five huge scenes with the witches that never made the movie

because Disney wanted the film more family friendly and so emphasized the kids more than the witches.

She said:

> One scene I love that was cut is Mary is set loose in a grocery store and begins snacking. She goes crazy when she sees toilet paper with a baby's face on it and Winifred has to drag her out.
>
> My dog Al Finney was in both *Sister Act* and *Hocus Pocus*. He is the winged dog who chases the witches out of 'Satan's' supposed suburban home.

Other missing scenes include kids attempting to push the witches into a pool and the witches being surrounded by trick-or-treaters holding out their hands.

Sarah Jessica Parker while researching her family history for the show *Who Do You Think You Are?* (2004) discovered that her 10th great-grandmother, Esther Elwell, was arrested in Salem, MA in the late 1600s for committing "sundry acts of witchcraft" and choking a neighbor to death.

Parker felt that her character was "the most fundamentally evil of all of them."

She continued:

> She is so not bright, not calculating, that it is her inate nature to be evil. For her older sisters it is a learned thing. Yet, she is still somewhat seductive. She's just awful but I love her.
>
> There was very little about our characters beyond the script itself so it gave me my first chance to really create a character like finding the voice and physical stuff. They wanted me to do a Marilyn (Monroe) voice but I found that boring so I came up with something like a small, four year old boy on helium.

Ortega recalled his first day on the set:

> What I really, really remember [is] observing Bette and Kathy and Sarah really finding their characters, in the mirror with makeup, hair, prosthetics, and I just burst out laughing. Looking at one another, you saw this chemistry come into play, and I knew we were going to have a lot of fun.

Principal photography began on October 12, 1992. The film is set in Salem, Massachusetts, but most of it was shot on sound stages in Burbank, California including the big Soundstage 2 at the Disney Studio.

Some of the daytime scenes were filmed in Salem and Marblehead, Massachusetts during two weeks of filming with principal cast including the boy Thackery going through the woods.

The elementary school is a Salem school, and the Town Hall where the big party is thrown is also local to Salem too. Allison's home is the Ropes Mansion which is now a museum and a well-known haunted tourist stop.

Of course, not everything outside was shot in Salem. The famous fountain from the opening of the television series *Friends* can be seen behind and to the right of Dani and Allison while they're celebrating the deaths of the witches.

Production was completed on February 10, 1993.

Billy the Zombie:
Hocus Pocus

In 1693, William "Billy" Butcherson was the boyfriend of the witch Winifred Sanderson. Unfortunately, Winifred's younger sister Sarah was quite a seductress and loved "playing" with men so tempted Billy to stray.

When Winifred discovered that Billy was being unfaithful with Sarah, she poisoned him on May 1, 1893 and sewed his mouth shut with a dull needle (which is why the stitches are so large) so he could not tell her secrets even in death.

Three hundred years later she awakened him with this spell:

> Unfaithful lover long since dead. Deep asleep in thy wormy bed. Wiggle thy toes, open thine eyes, twist thy fingers toward the sky. Life is sweet, be not shy, on thy feet, so sayeth I!

She resurrected him to help her retrieve her book of magic from the three children who had taken it. Billy was not completely under Winifred's enchantment because in the cemetary he tried to protect little Dani and aided the children in trying to defeat the Sanderson Sisters. When the witches were destroyed, he gleefully went back to his grave and plopped down for an eternal rest.

Certainly, when people think of witches, it is natural to also think of a black cat but it is a little odd to include a zombie, especially in the years before zombie-mania became insanely popular in comics, films, television and more.

Writer Mick Garris had zombies on his mind because he had just performed as one in Michael Jackson's music video *Thriller* (1983) as he started to write the first draft of the script for the film and felt it could be a relatively inexpensive supernatural element to add to the mix. No elaborate special effects, just some make-up.

Special effects make-up artist Tony Gardner remembered:

The intention was to create a character who would walk a fine line between grotesque—because he has been dead for quite some time—and handsome. I envisioned him as a ghoulish version of Ichabod Crane (the lanky music teacher from *The Legend of Sleepy Hollow*). He is regal, an aristocrat but very dead.

Director Kenny Ortega said he wanted Billy to be an "attractive zombie", not a drooling, dumb monster. Actor Doug Jones who played the role said that fans still tell him how Billy was their first movie crush. "It's really kind of sweet and charming to hear that," stated Jones.

Today Jones is well known for the many, many characters in prosthetic make-up that he has portrayed over the years including the fish-like Abe Sapien in the supernatural film *Hellboy* (2004) and its sequel (2008), the Pale Man (with his eyes in his palms) in *Pan's Labyrinth* (2006), the Silver Surfer in *Fantastic Four: Rise of the Silver Surfer* 2007) and most prominently as the Amphibian Man in *The Shape of Water* (2017).

His credits also include the Lead Gentlemen in television's *Buffy the Vampire Slayer* scary episode *Hush* and Commander Saru in *Star Trek: Discovery*.

However, when he auditioned for the role of Billy he was still a struggling actor with only a small handful of credits. One of his first professional jobs was portraying McDonald's marketing character Mac Tonight (a pianist crooner with the head of a crescent moon) in over twenty-seven commercials over three years.

Jones said:

> I started as a mime, many years ago, in college. That woke up my body to realizing that movement, gesturing, postures and body language are every bit as communicative as verbal dialogue is. That background is what I brought into my acting career with me.
>
> When I came out to Hollywood in 1985, I thought that I would be a sitcom star. I'm a tall, skinny, goofy guy. I thought that I would make a great funny neighbor or wacky office mate in a sitcom. When I started doing TV commercials, my agent at the time knew that I had a mime background and could put my legs behind my head, which qualified me as a contortionist.
>
> So, I was sent out for anything physical. If there was costume work, mimes or clowns, they'd send me out. What started the

ball rolling was that the first commercial I booked was for Southwest Airlines, and I was a dancing mummy.

The only studio film I had been in before (*Hocus Pocus*) was *Batman Returns* (1992) as a supporting character (listed in the credits as "Thin Clown"). I was one of Danny DeVito's henchmen in that. So (*Hocus Pocus*) was my first sort of real supporting role in a major film.

The audition was held at a dance studio. The character of Billy only had one line in the original script, which meant there wasn't really anything for Jones to read.

As Jones recalled:

> For the role of Billy, (Ortega) really wanted to see a physicality and what choreography he could throw into that character to make it a more visual piece. So he gave me a scene to act out of waking up from 300 years of being dead. "Stand up, give us what his walk would be, get from point A to point B. When you get to point B, crumple down and look up at Winifred and tell her off."
>
> I remember, as I wasn't even halfway across the floor yet, from point A to point B through this choreography, [Ortega] and the assistant casting director were laughing, tilted heads back, laughing, grabbing their sides laughing. I had no idea what I was doing, but I thought, this was going pretty good. As it turned out, before I even got home, the call came to my manager that they really wanted me in the movie, so I was tickled pink.

Gardner remembered that not only was Jones extremely talented physically but that he never complained about the make-up which took up to two and a half hours each day to apply. His Alterian company spent an entire day doing a complete headcast and bodycast of Jones and also cast his teeth as well.

Gardner said:

> His weathered skin and gaunt look was created by using one single foam latex appliance to cover his entire face and neck. I thought it was the easiest way to keep the prosthetics as thin as possible, and be able to have the wrinkles and folds line up and move well over the entire surface of his head.
>
> Because it was so thin and delicate, it took two makeup artists to apply it every day: myself and Margaret Prentice.

We exaggerated Doug's physical features. He has a small nose and a very narrow face onto which we could place the latex, reshaping his face, with hollowed cheeks and deep-set eyes.

Kenny wanted him to look innocent, a Bambi-look, with doe eyes. Doug's eyes are very expressive and stand out with the make-up so it was decided not to use colored contact lenses that we had originally considered. After the first makeup test, it was agreed upon that Doug's big brown eyes were the soul to the character, and as a result, no contact lenses would be used.

The stitches were glued into his facial appliance every day, and between shots I would disconnect them on the bottom lip so that Doug could talk and eat. It wasn't a flattering look though. He looked like a cross between a walrus and a skinny teenager trying to grow a mustache.

In addition, he wears a full body suit, long gloves with acrylic extensions on the ends of his fingers to add length, a ratty wig and big shoes with fake toes coming through them. Underneath his costume he wears the body suit with all the textural details of a zombie, exaggerated bone structure at the knees and elbows.

Doug wore foam latex gloves instead of hand appliances to save time during the prosthetic makeup application process, and also allow us to add some additional length to his finger-tips. The gloves had acrylic finger cups inside them so that the extra length of the fingers was solid instead of floppy, and the finger cups were sculpted with long nails on them that were cast in a translucent grey dental acrylic. The foam latex gloves and were not worn until just before the camera was rolling.

Given how physical Doug was as Billy, it was also nice to be able to change out his zombie gloves if they were torn up on set, as opposed to having to stop and spend valuable time repairing prosthetic hands.

Jones recalled:

They formed a dead guy mask on me, a foam latex prosthetic makeup that gave me pronounced cheek bones and a pro-nounced jawline and sunken cheeks, so they could take flesh away from places that might be decayed.

As he told writer Jessica Dwyer:

First of all, my makeup was created and applied by the amazing Tony Gardner, assisted on-set by Margaret Prentice with prosthetics sculpted by Chet Zar.

When you have the best artists in the world putting a mkeup on you, it is invigorating. Watching myself transform into Billy helped me find his voice and physical presence every day. It was also a remakrable design that was all one piece, so the entire face and neck went on quickly. Add the wig, the gloved zombie hands, the zombie leg sleeves and a torn period costume by Mary Vogt and I was ready to go.

Many filmed scenes were cut from the final version of the released film including several with the witches. Interestingly, on Jones' first night of filming he shot a scene that eventually got cut because it slowed down the pacing of the rest of the story.

As Jones once told an audience at an event:

> [I was] so terrified to see [Bette Midler] face-to-face that I didn't want to make a fool of myself. And the first time I did see her, she's wearing this bright red wig and no eyebrows and buck teeth with those dinky little lips drawn on. I got the giggles and I couldn't stop. I couldn't take her seriously because she looked so incredibly goofy.

The scene was Winifred giving directions to Billy but Billy being distracted by Sarah.

Jones continued:

> Bette wants to give me some instruction on what I should be doing next, and all the while, I'm just kind of mooning over Sarah Jessica Parker. I grabbed a piece of her blonde wig and I was stroking it. I had it caught in my fingers.
>
> And when they walked away, I kind of followed them, and I got hooked onto a lamppost in the park and just kind of had this sad moment of longing as they walked away. I *loved* that scene. It was my very first night of work and it was just kind of a magical moment for me. And unfortunately it's not in the film.

Another Billy scene that was cut took place after the *I Put a Spell on You* musical number where all the townspeople are bewitched into dancing.

Jones revealed:

> When the witches are gone, I hopped up on the stage and I boogied down myself. I got to have free run of the stage and dance however I wanted to. Kenny Ortega just wanted to let me go, take the reins off and let me have at it. I had so much

fun doing that. At some point, I kind of shook it off and exited off the stage, and that's what kind of carried me to the next scene where I'm outside of the party.

As Jones told writer Jessica Dwyer:

> I had been a slobbering fan of Bette Midler's for many years before this movie so that first night on set with her playing a scene only a foot away from her made me get the giggles like a silly fanboy.

> Later in the production when we were doing the costume party scene, she took a minute during camera set-up to tell me how funny I was and how much she loved what I was doing with my part. I thought if a spotlight were to fall from the ceiling and kill me at that very moment, it would be a glorious time to die happy.

The favorite story that Jones tells at events is that he actually had real moths in his mouth for the brief scene where he cuts his mouth open. Winifred had sealed his mouth and in the cemetary using a cross he grabbed from Max, Billy is finally able to cut through the stitches.

Ortega thought it would be funny that if when Billy finally opened his mouth for the first time in 300 years all the accumulated dust and a live moth would come flying out. However, this was in the years before CGI so it would have to be accomplished physically.

Alterian's Vance Hartwell created a latex rig much like a dental dam for Jones' mouth to stop the moths from going anywhere but out of the mouth. It was essentially a latex pocket attached between upper and lower dentures which completely blocked Jones' throat.

There was a small hole in the very back of the pocket so that Jones could cough some air through it and force the Fuller's Earth (a traditional movie effects safer alternative to real dirt) and the moths up and out of his mouth.

The rig had Fuller's Earth added to the bottom and then animal handlers came in with tweezers and gently added moths atop the dust inside the reservoir and all of this was supervised by an ASCPA representative.

During the scene, Jones would cut the stitches and blow both the moths and the dust out of his mouth. The scene had

to be filmed several times. In one instance it took so long to set up the shot and the dirt and moths remained in his mouth longer than usual that the saliva started to build up.

When Ortega yelled "action" and Jones cut the stitches and went to blow out the dust and moths a puddle of sludge just poured out of his mouth onto the ground.

Each time, Gardner glued Jones' pre-cut mouth stitches back together with a prosthetic adhesive so that it would be easy to cut.

Jones disclosed:

> When I cut my mouth open I was supposed to just say 'Bitch!' to Bette Midler. At the time, I was like, "It's a kids' Disney movie." That was a conversation that I wanted to have with Kenny Ortega on the night that we shot that scene.
>
> And I told him, "I'm not comfortable just throwing the B-word out when our audience is going to be kids expecting a Disney happy movie. There's gotta be a more creative way that's actually going to sell this movie better than that." So the line that I ended up saying was one that I came up with by myself.
>
> Kenny approved it, loved it, and that's what stayed in the movie. And that's when I cut my mouth open, coughed out the moths and the dust and said, "Wench! Trollop! You buck-toothed, mop-riding, firefly from hell!" That became a favorite quote from the film.

As a Halloween film released in July, it did not do as well as was hoped although it did make a modest profit.

Jones recalled his initial disappointment:

> When we were making this, this was one of my first feature films ever, so I was thinking, 'OK, this is the one; this is gonna be the hit that takes me to the moon.' It did not do the box-office figures at all that we had hoped for, and kind of went into obscurity in the theatrical box-office world. Not knowing what would happen in the future, I thought, 'There was my big chance. It's over.' Of course, it wasn't.
>
> Every parent now shares the movie they grew up with with their kids. I had no idea this would happen, because I didn't know what technology was going to turn into. I didn't know that *Hocus Pocus* would be one click away on every computer and TV screen in the world, and it would become like *The*

Wizard of Oz of Halloween. I had no idea it was going to do that. None of us did. It was just a happy surprise.

When I do speaking engagements and my credits are announced, *Hocus Pocus* always gets the biggest cheers. There's been talk of doing a twenty year later sequel that I would have been a part of. I loved that idea and I would just love to reprise Billy Butcherson again. I was actually approached and asked about that.

I love that character so much. He's beloved to me. So, the recent announcement of a reboot took all of us by surprise especially when none of us was asked. A cheap reboot is so unnecessary when the movie is incredibly relevant to this day and it's timeless. It doesn't need a facelift, it doesn't need it. It's timeless. You can't even tell what year it was made when you watch.

As Gardner has shared, for the initial resurrection scene of Billy:

The ground in the area where his grave was located was built off of the stage floor high enough to allow for the pneumatic rig that Terry Frazee's physical effects crew had built that would make the earth rise and fall, and also push Billy's coffin up and out of the ground.

Doug was fine will doing this stunt himself—which was good, because his makeup would have looked pretty humorous on anyone else. Once Doug was settled into the coffin, it was lowered down into the ground, a breakaway coffin lid was laid down over Doug, and then loose dirt, moss and leaves were piled on top of that. Once we got the 'all clear' and the machinery started up, Doug was on his own. I think they had their shot on the first take.

For Billy's final appearance, another grave was dug separately from the grave that Billy originally rose out of, so that there was enough depth to hide a stunt mat in the bottom of it so that Jones could fall back into the grave and completely out of shot.

Jones recalled twenty-five years after the film:

Stepping onto that set was like stepping onto an attraction at Disneyland. The Sanderson house and the cemetery were my personal favorites. Especially when I was buried alive in my grave with dirt and all, so I could push my way out of that casket to wake up when summoned.

The *Halloweentown* Saga (1998–2006)

The Disney Channel launched April 18, 1983 and despite the backlog of Disney cartoons, television shows and films the new cable channel still needed more content to fill its proposed sixteen hours a day schedule. In December 1986, it would extend to twenty-four hours a day like other cable channels.

The plan was to balance the programming with one-third existing Disney material, one-third original programming and one-third material that had been acquired from outside sources but was in "keeping with the Disney identity and values".

At first the original programming consisted of half hour television series both animated and live action as well as specials. However, in keeping with the tradition started by the original Disney weekly television show on network television, new movies made especially for the channel were created.

The first new film that premiered in October 1984 was the sports-themed *Tiger Town*. It earned the channel a Cable Ace award.

Originally these were called Disney Channel Premiere Films but starting in 1997, they were re-branded as Disney Channel Original Movies (DCOM). They were often released on home media formats like VHS and DVD within a year of their airing on the channel.

Some films were so popular that they spawned sequels to create a franchise including *High School Musical, Camp Rock, Teen Beach, The Descendents* and more including *Halloweentown*.

For many people, the mention of "Halloweentown" immediately conjures the image of Halloween Town where Jack Skellington lives in *The Nightmare Before Christmas* (1993). However, for many young people the word meant a community populated by all the creatures of that spooky holiday who

often owed their safety to a family of witches in a series of four Disney Channel Original Movies.

The premise of the series was that fantasy beings associated with Halloween like witches, warlocks, vampires, werewolves, mummies, ghosts, zombies, cat people, living skeletons, goblins and other similar creatures all live together in this town to avoid persecution from "The Mortal World". Humans have vague memories of the creatures that used to live among them and so mimic them by dressing up in costumes on Halloween.

The residents of Halloweentown can only visit the world of humans on Halloween and only with magical aid. The later films expand on when they can visit. In Halloweentown, witches and warlocks appear human and are the only ones in the town who can do magic which is hereditary in their families.

The films revolve around the Cromwell-Piper family. Agatha (nicknamed Aggie and played by Debbie Reynolds) Cromwell lives in Halloweentown but her daughter Gwen Piper (Judith Hoag) married a human mortal she met on Halloween and forsook the fantastic world and her magic. She is widowed and raising her three children Marnie (Kimberly J. Brown), Dylan (Joey Zimmerman) and Sophie (Emily Roeske) as completely human with no awareness of their magic heritage.

Halloweentown (1998)

Marnie Piper (Kimberly J. Brown) is a thirteen year old girl who can't understand why her mother will not allow her or her two younger siblings to participate in any Halloween activities. Her grandmother Aggie (Debbie Reynolds) shows up for her annual Halloween visit and reads the children a bedtime story about a place called "Halloweentown".

Later that night, Marnie overhears an argument between her grandmother and mother and discovers they are all witches. Aggie needs to train Marnie in using her powers or she will lose them. In addition, Aggie needs help with uncovering why citizens of Halloweentown are disappearing.

When Aggie leaves to return home, Marnie and her siblings follow her onto a magical bus and arrive in Halloweentown. Aggie agrees to train Marnie but needs to first take care of a mysterious hooded demon she has seen in her cauldron who

threatens the town. Marnie's mother arrives but she and Aggie are frozen in time by the demon just like the missing citizens.

In order to defeat the demon, a talisman must be placed in a large jack-o-lantern in the center of the town. The demon turns out to be the mayor, Kalabar, who is bitter that Marnie's mother married a human mortal instead of him. He intends to take over the mortal world.

Marnie drops the talisman inside the jack-o-lantern which weakens Kalabar and unfreezes all his captives. The entire Cromwell-Piper family use their combined powers to defeat him. Aggie decides to stay in the mortal world and train her grandchildren.

Halloweentown II: Kalabar's Revenge (2001)

Marnie has spent two years being trained by her grandmother Aggie. During a Halloween party, Marnie tries to impress a cute new boy by showing him her grandmother's secret room. Shortly afterwards, Aggie senses something wrong in Halloweentown.

Accompanied by Marnie, they discover that the town and its residents have all been turned into a dreary, dull mirror-image of The Mortal World with all the creatures now human.

The boy Marnie was trying to impress named Kal was the son of Kalabar and has stolen Aggie's spell book from the secret room to prevent Aggie from helping against the effects of his Grey Spell.

Aggie tries to find her spare spell book in Halloweentown but it has been sold by a junk dealer to Kalabar. Aggie becomes another victim of the Grey Spell while Kalabar's son attempts to turn The Mortal World into a monster movie. A handsome golem is sent to distract Marnie's mother at a party from helping out. At the party, all the guests are transformed into various monsters based on the costumes that they were wearing.

Marnie is able to free Aggie but they are trapped in Halloweentown. Contacting her siblings in The Mortal World, the Piper children are able to develop a new spell that opens the portal between the two worlds permanently.

Marnie confronts Kal and takes both spell books from him and breaks his spells. Kal is sent away never to return.

Halloween High (Halloweentown III) (2004)

Originally intended as the final film in a trilogy, it is the last Halloweentown film to feature Kimberly J. Brown as Marnie and Emily Roeske who retired from acting after making this movie as Sophie.

As Marnie starts a new school year, she proposes to the Halloweentown High Council to allow her to bring a group of Halloweentown students to her own high school in The Mortal World to create better understanding between the two worlds.

The Council worries about the Knights of the Iron Dagger who have sworn to destroy all things magical in the human world but permit Marnie to take the students when she bets all the Cromwell magic that her plan will work. If not, her entire family will lose their magical abilites on midnight of Halloween.

The Halloweentown students are magically given human appearances so they can blend in as exchange students from Canada. Aggie becomes a substitue teacher at the school to keep an eye on things. At first fearful, the students at Marnie's urging gradually join sports teams and other school activities, making new friends in the process.

Unfortunately, odd things begin happening including the students briefly reverting to their real appearances at a mall and a disappearance of one of the students. Aggie starts to develop a romance with the school principal who turns out to be the last Knight of the Iron Dagger. However, he only knew about the students real identities because of Dalloway the head of the Halloweentown High Council who wants to keep Halloweentown isolated.

The students use the Hallowen carnival to show what their lives in Halloweentown are really like and the mundane tableaus in the haunted house end up boring the humans. Dalloway brings the prop monsters to life and Flannigan incites a mob to corner the new students who eventually reveal who they really are.

The crowd accepts them and Flannigan renounces his knighthood and accepts Aggie. Dalloway claims the Cromwell magic but when Marnie's mother shows the Council the events of the evening, they return the Cromwell magic and imprison

Dalloway. A portal opens in the carnival haunted house and crowds of children from Halloweentown cross over to enjoy the festivities with the children of the human world.

Return to Halloweentown (2006)

Marnie (now portrayed by Sara Paxton) is eighteen-years old and decides to change her college plans and attend Witch University in Halloweentown on a full scholarship because of her previous good deeds.

However, at the school, students are forbidden to use magic and instead study more mundane historical subjects. While she makes new friends, she also makes three new enemies called the Sinister Sisters, a group of spoiled, manipulative mean girls. Marnie finds a box with the name "S. Cromwell" on it and learns it contains a magical amulet only a Cromwell can use to control anyone which is why it is locked away.

She journeys to the past and discovers that the "S" stands for "Splendora" which was her grandmother's original first name and meets with the young witch who gives her the key to the box.

Marnie's principal and Professor Grogg are members of a mysterious group called Dominion and they steal the gift. The Sinister Sisters turn Marnie's brother into a dog to force her to use the amulet so they can control Halloweentown. The brother will stay a dog once Halloween passes if he is not turned back.

Marnie tricks them and destroys the amulet. The agents of Dominion and the Sinister Sisters are captured by an under-cover detective of the Anti-Dominion League and they are all stripped of their magic and arrested.

It turns out that the amulet was not really destroyed and Marnie's brother finds that she left it for him in a book and it now belongs to him. Supposedly, this event could spawn another sequel.

The reason for Kimberly J. Brown not appearing in this final film is shrouded in controversy with mulitple conflicting explanations.

The official Disney explanation was that Brown was filming another film *Big Bad Wolf* (2006) about college students

encountering a werewolf at the time and there were scheduling conflicts between the two productions.

However, according to Brown those conflicts had been resolved:

> Well, let me just say that I wanted to do the fourth one and was fully available for the shoot. Nothing makes me happier than playing Marnie. Disney decided not to use me for the fourth one, I'm don't know why. I was definitely disappointed not to do it. Ultimately … it's a decision that came down to Disney and I don't know specifically.

Paxton who replaced her in the role was clueless as to why Brown was not cast. She said:

> [Disney] asked me if I was interested in playing Marnie and I said I was. It sounded like a lot of fun. I don't know [what happened to Kimberly J. Brown]! I just know they called me and said, "Do you want to play Marnie?" and I said, "Yeah!"

Paxton had just finished filming *Aquamarine (2006)* for 20th Century Fox. She sang in the film and had signed a record deal with Epic Records. It had been rumored that *Return to Halloweentown* might be done as a musical like *High School Musical* that was released that same year which may be a reason the actress was cast.

Executive producer Sheri Singer stated about the re-casting:

> That was not something we wanted to do. We could not come to terms that we felt were fair. We just weren't able to. We couldn't make the deal work.

Return to Halloweentown director David Jackson said:

> The character she played was younger than the actress actually was by enough years that we felt like as a collective group that it was better to recast someone who was younger. It kind of came down to that.

He added that it was also felt that the original audience who knew Brown in the role had grown up and was no longer the demographic for the series and that the story was not reliant on the first three installments. However, Joey Zimmerman, Judith Hoag and Debbie Reynolds were retained from the first three films.

In fact, Millicent Martin had been cast to take over the role of Aggie Cromwell because Reynolds had an existing conflict

but when it got resolved Reynolds was hired and a new part was written for Martin.

The *Return to Halloweentown* premiere was the most-watched Disney Channel Original Movie ever among adults 18 to 34 (1 million viewers) and adults 18 to 49 (1.9 million).

Disney Channel Worldwide president of entertainment Gary Marsh said:

> This fourth movie in the *Halloweentown* franchise continues our incredible streak of stellar ratings, not just for the premiere, but across the weekend, and across all demos, including adults.
>
> For kids and families, the unique 'spooky-funny' sensibility coupled with extraordinary casting, music and special effects, helped build this into one of the premiere movie franchises on television.

The movie's debut finished second only to ESPN's October 16 *Monday Night Football* coverage of the Chicago Bears come-from-behind win against the Arizona Cardinals, which tackled an 11.7 rating and some 14.2 million viewers. However, that same week reruns of *Halloween High* (ranked #8) and the original *Halloweentown* (ranked #11) also scored high with viewers.

However, the film did receive and continues to receive criticism for not casting Brown in the role of Marnie with many Disney fans disliking Paxton's interpretation of the character.

The *Halloweentown* franchise captured the spirit of Halloween in a way that other films have not and is still much beloved even today.

The story of *Halloweentown* was created by Sheri Singer and her husband Steve White who were executive producers on the film. The idea came from Singer's step-daughter who asked her "Where do all the creatures from Halloween go the rest of the year when it's not October 31?"

The pair pitched the idea as a made-for-television movie to NBC. After *The Wonderful World of Disney* programming ended in 1991, Disney transitioned into a six-movie deal with NBC.

NBC was initially interested in the concept but then after Paul Bernbaum was brought in to write the actual screenplay, the network decided it was "too young" despite Bernbaum's adding some genuine spookiness. Bernbaum said, "It got really scary sometimes."

Since it was considered as being for a young audience, they took the idea to Disney and the studio also passed on it. However after the success of *Under Wraps* (1997), the first officially branded DCOM, about three twelve-year olds who discover a mummy, the Disney Channel re-considered the proposal.

However, now that the idea was at Disney, it was readjusted with additional writing by Jon Cooksey and Ali Matheson to appeal to an even younger audience by making it lighter in tone. Bernbaum would be a writer on all four of the films.

Writer Paul Bernbaum had named Marnie, Dylan and Sophie after his own children. Aggie was the nickname of actress Debbie Reynolds' late friend, actress Agnes Moorehead who had played a grandmother witch on the television series *Bewitched*.

Singer said:

> We were able to be very whimsical. We needed to create these really interesting characters. They were fun and slightly scary, but not too scary.

Rather than build a city set on some studio back lot, the production chose St. Helens, a small town outside of Portland, Oregon to stand-in for Halloweentown. Because of a volcano that had erupted in 1980, it had become mostly a "ghost town" so the locals were welcoming to the crew because it generated much needed income.

Singer recalled:

> They were so grateful to have us there and so easy to work with. We had a good crew up there and it fit the demands of the movie. We made all these storefronts. It was really fun and became very iconic.

Director DuWayne Dunham remembered:

> The Disney Channel was just starting to make these kinds of family movies. I had come in and met with them and they gave me this project called *Halloweentown*. It was very well-written, it just was big, because it was written as a feature.
>
> We spent some time trying to keep the integrity of the story but get it down, where we could afford to make the movie. We tried to populate this story with some real funny characters: Benny, the taxi driver was pretty funny. And we had the two-headed coffee-drinker. One of my favorites was the big fat guy

who went in the steam room and shrunk up, and came out real skinny. We just did funny things like that that kept it light and entertaining, and really kept the story moving.

It was a fun, fun shoot because we were in this little town, up north of Portland, Oregon. The town was kind of deserted. We took over the whole town square, everything. It was ideal—like shooting on the back lot.

Dunham fell in love with the color scheme of St. Helens, and admitted they got lucky, seeing as how the film budget was so small. The filming was done in five weeks during the hot summer of 1998.

Robin Thomas, who played the movie's villain Kalabar, had to be taken to a local doctor after blowing out his vocal cords during the confrontation scene at the end of the film and it took a week to recover.

With no body microphone, Thomas said:

I was having to project my voice down. There were fans blowing. [I was] 150 feet or so from the camera. That was challenging. I blew my pipes out.

Reynolds used to write all her lines for each day on large yellow legal pads because the print was too small on the script copies.

Originally budgeted at twenty to thirty million dollars, now that the project was at the Disney Channel, the budget was trimmed to roughly four million dollars. The most expensive special effect remaining in the script was Benny, the taxi-driving skeleton, who was an elaborate animatronics figure, with the actor dubbing in the lines after filming.

A core group of actors wore multiple different costumes and make-up to create the illusion of a crowded town. Director Dunham remembered:

We had just enough [extras], and we would double up and change costumes and make it look like there were more and different people and that sort of thing.

Joey Zimmerman, who plays Marnie's brother Dylan, said that these extras struggled through the one of the hottest summers in the city on record. Zimmerman said, "People were just passing out...the fish guy mask, and the crazy alien mask."

Despite the budget restrictions, the original film was an unexpectedly huge hit and spawned three sequels and a local Halloween celebration.

The *Halloweentown* movie franchise actually has many similarities to the *Harry Potter* films.

A young teen who always assumed they were just a normal human discovers they have magical powers and learns of a fantasy world inhabited with strange creatures where they must defeat the evil plans of a frightening and powerful wizard. The teen is part of a magical family and needs to be trained in how to properly use their power by an older mentor who has magical abilities as well.

As witch Aggie Cromwell says in the original *Halloweentown* film, "Being normal is vastly overrated."

The first Harry Potter book had appeared in limited release roughly a year before the first *Halloweentown* movie was shown so it is just an amazing coincidence in the core similarities between the two franchises. Of course, the Disney Channel film lacked the spectacular special effects, make-up and epic storytelling of the Potter films but it captured the spirit of All Hallows Eve for a generation of eager young viewers.

As Marnie Piper says in the first film, "Halloween is cool. It's ancient. It's strange."

Actress Debbie Reynolds was the first person to be cast for the original film.

Director DuWayne Dunham stated:

> I'm not quite sure the genesis of how Debbie got involved. We wanted something of a name [to get involved], and Debbie Reynolds is terrific. We all jumped at the opportunity to work with her. And she was; she was great! [Laughs] You know, comes from the school of one take. "What's the matter, I didn't do it right? I have to do it again?" [she'd ask]. It was great.
>
> Debbie came from a time where you came prepared, and you knew your stuff, and you delivered. It should be one take, and move on. I think she was an education and an inspiration to all of the other actors, especially the young kids.

As executive producer Sheri Singer recalled:

> Debbie had decided she wanted to open herself up to doing some television. When we saw the list, we took one look at

her name and said, 'omigod, would she really do it?' This is absolutely unbelievably blessed and terrific idea for casting. And she did. We never went to anyone else.

Reynolds once said that she took the role as so her granddaughter, actress Billie Lourd, would watch something Debbie was in and actually enjoy it. In addition, Reynolds was having some financial trouble with some property in Las Vegas and needed some money.

During her short breaks during the filming, Reynolds would stroll over to an appreciative crowd of fans and introduce herself by saying, "Hello, I'm Princess Leia's mom." Her daughter was actress Carrie Fisher who played that role in the *Star Wars* films.

Kimberly J. Brown who played her granddaughter in the film enthused:

> She made it a point to tell us as kids, 'Always make time for fans and say 'hello'. That has stuck with me over the years. She appreciated the ability to entertain and make people happy, so she taught me what a gift that was to be able to do that for people.
>
> When you hear you're going to work with a legend of that magnitude, you never know how this person's going to be. But she was warm and gracious and it was such a good example to work with somebody like that and have her impact me so much not only professionally, but personally over the years.
>
> She was so talented and wise, which easily could have gone to her head, but instead she went out of her way to help others shine as brightly as they could. She'd try to move huge ladders on set just to help the crew, and looked out for every actor no matter the size their role.
>
> Debbie is an amazing human being, so giving and full of grace and humility, and she has the best sense of humor, ever. She just couldn't share enough of her wisdom with me when we were on the set—she had so much experience and she just wanted people to have fun and enjoy themselves. Getting to work with her has been one of the best experiences of my acting career.

Originally, they wanted a blonde to play the role of Marnie but brown-haired Kimberly Jean Brown's audition blew everyone away.

Brown first got into acting at age five, appearing on stage in Broadway productions of *Four Baboons Adoring the Sun, Les*

Miserables (in which she sang solo as Young Cosette), and the Tony-winning revival of *Showboat*.

She was just coming off the soap opera *Guiding Light* where she had received an Emmy nomination for playing the part of Marah Lewis from 1993 to 1998 when she was cast in the *Halloweentown* role. She also had a career as a voice actress and supplied a voice for Pixar's *A Bug's Life* (1998) as well as in a commercial telling the Trix Rabbit that the cereal was for kids.

As Brown told an interviewer:

> Being a young teen, it was so exciting to be part of it all. I love Marnie and everything that she stood for, so I'm really happy when people tell me how much she meant to them. Marnie always knew there was something different about her, and when she did find out about her magic, she wanted to know everything she could and really fully live in that and be herself.
>
> She was just always really cool in that way. I admired her determination and her sense of humor and her willingness to take on her family legacy. Who wouldn't want fly a broom and make things magically appear?
>
> The broom flying scene in the first movie was probably one of my favorites to shoot. That was actually our last day. We did it in front of a big blue scene in the studio, and I just remember that just feeling like a special day because it was Debbie and I up on a broom for hours. I loved that we got to see (Marnie) figure out how to be a teenager but also how to be a witch at the same time.

When actress Judith Hoag played the role of Gwen she was only seventeen years older than Brown who was playing her oldest daughter which meant that Gwen must have been a child bride.

Hoag had played the key role of April O'Neill in the first live action *Teenage Mutant Ninja Turtles* (1990) movie. She went on to appear in many movies and television shows including most recently recurring roles in *Nashville* and *The Magicians*.

Hoag recalled:

> I had an agent; it was just another audition. Michael Healey, who was a head of Disney Channel, had a son who was a big *Ninja Turtles* fan. When I walked in, Michael said "I'm so excited that you're here, we're huge *Ninja Turtles* fans in our house." At some point I did a little autograph for his son, and

posed for photos. I thought that it was a sweet script. And hearing that Debbie Reynolds was attached to it, I was like "I'm in!"

Zimmerman, who played her son was a big fan of the TMNT movie, said:

I wanted to be a professional, so I waited until after filming the entire first movie before exploding about *TMNT*.

Hoag told an interviewer:

Gwen was described to me as a Martha Stewart kind of character, back during her pre-prison days. She was the quint-essential perfect person. Her house was perfect and her hair was perfect. Everything she cooked was perfect.

I thought Gwen is pretending to be something that she's not, and she wasn't doing it well. She didn't want (her children) to celebrate Halloween even though she was from Halloweentown. Gwen's not comfortable in her skin.

Sara Paxton who played the part of Marnie Piper in the final film *Return to Halloweentown* said:

It was so much fun! Lucas [Grabeel] was great. We filmed us kissing but it was cut from the film. The whole cast was great. We got to do stunts and special effects. Probably the most challenging stunt was when I had to be hanging from a broom and flying without a harness.

I was flying through the air on this broom with Lucas and me on the back of it. I was so scared I started crying. Lucas tried to cheer me up and make me feel better. Also, I would have to wave my arms in the air and pretend to make a spell, and then I would have to pretend that something had happened. They added the special effects later. It was pretty hard pretending that I was making things float and stuff like that.

I had watched all of the (*Halloweentown*) movies when I was little. That's why I was so excited to get the part. I love those movies! My film was shot in Salt Lake City, Utah. We couldn't really find a lot to do there, because it's more like a snow-boarding and ski town and it was summertime. So we'd just hang around together and watch TV and order pizza.

The first one was shot in Oregon, but I believe the other two were shot in Salt Lake City. Actually, most Disney Channel Original Movies are shot with the same production company

in Utah. I went there when I was twelve to film my first Disney movie [2001's *Hounded*].

It's six years later so the people there didn't really recognize me. But they have a picture of every single movie on the wall in the production office so I pointed to [*Hounded*] and said, "That's me!" Happy memories came flooding back!

Director of *Return to Halloweentown* Jackson said:

[Paxton] was great and wonderful to work with and I felt like she had a young spirit that the story needed. I have no regrets about recasting the role with her.

While *Halloweentown* may have been the second DCOM to ever go into production after *Brink !* (1998) about inline skating, by the time it actually came out it was the fourth ever DCOM to be released.

In that first film, the Piper children are introduced to Halloweentown through a book read to them by their grandmother. Brown has revealed that several copies of the book were specially made for the movie, and are, in fact, entirely finished books. Brown was able to take one of the books as a souvenir.

Brown recalled:

They had an artist draw that picture of me too so it would look a little like me. It really is a beautiful book! But there are only a few copies made for the shoot.

There was a different ending planned for the film. Marnie was to place the talisman in the middle of a magical forest. As Marnie walked through the forest to accomplish the task, she grew older and older with each step so there was the danger that she would die of old age before doing the deed.

That idea got so far along that the production company made a mold of Brown's head in order to achieve the necessary make-up effects. Since the ending was changed, Brown ended up keeping the headpiece for herself as well as the broom she rode.

The sequel to the original film *Halloweentown II: Kalabar's Revenge* was filmed in Vancouver during the winter of that year. The day actress Brown who was then sixteen years old flew up to Canada was when she first met Daniel Kountz.

Kountz played the sequel's new villain, Kal, and would, years later, become Brown's boyfriend in real life.

The pair reconnected in May 2016 to work on a project and have been a couple ever since.

Brown said:

> It didn't even cross my mind (when we did the movie). He was in a serious relationship. We got along great, had a lot of fun and he was sweet and everything, but it just, we never went there. Things kind of slowly turned romantic, which was completely unexpected for both of us because neither of us were looking.
>
> All of a sudden it was just everywhere … and I was like, 'What!?' … It was amazing to us that it became prominent in the news for a minute.

During filming, Kountz got quite the surprise when it came time to conjure the portal to Halloweentown. The script reads "Kal says spell and walks through the portal." He assumed that he would be given a spell to say, but that didn't happen.

When it came time for the scene, he was asked if he had prepared a spell and the young actor not wanting to seem unprofessional answered "yes".

He got inspiration from a choir song he learned in school. "I just pulled that out of nowhere, and they ended up using it," Kountz recalls, "and I think it actually worked out pretty well."

Halloweentown High was shot in Salt Lake City, Utah. Both the interior and exterior (for carnival scenes) of Juan Diego High School, a Catholic High School was used in the filming. Posters were carefully placed and appropriate filming angles were necessary to obscure Catholic-related artwork and statues.

The scenes at the mall were filmed in Cottonwood Mall in Holladay, Utah, about 30 minutes from Salt Lake City.

The high school was the same one used in the DCOM *The Luck of the Irish* (2001) that had basketball competitions as a key element. The gym was used for both films with Aggie actually teaching basketball during gym class. Many shots reveal the same lockers and classrooms.

Brown was asked for her input into the script. After she left the franchise, she continued to act and worked on various

projects, including studying improv, writing sketch comedy, developing some scripts and running her own YouTube channel. She also co-authored the thirty-two page Halloween children's book "Poppins Pumpkin Patch Parade."

Scenes from the first Halloweentown movie were filmed in the Riverfront District in St. Helens, Oregon. Every Halloween season since the movie premiered, the town gets into the spirt of the movie by installing its own Jack O' Lantern in Courthouse Plaza (that was used for Halloweentown's town square), along with other scary touches like pumpkin-themed flags flanking the official building.

The town's businesses, merchants, and local government stage an annual "Spirit of Halloweentown" festival for locals and tourists that lasts the entire month of October. The town always decorates the streets to replicate scenes from the franchise.

The event became even more widely popular in 2015, when actress Brown attended. Attendance increased dramatically and Brown also attended the following year.

Brown said:

> The city recreates the town square from Halloweentown as it was featured prominently in the movies. The townspeople will dress the town square and much of the downtown to look like it did in Halloweentown and for the past two years, I went out to kick things off, light the pumpkin and get the month-long activities started. It's so much fun—people come out in costume, fans of the movie, it's a great experience—very fun.

In 2017, the entire "Piper family" Kimberly J. Brown, Judith Hoag, Joey Zimmerman and Emily Roeske, from the movie franchise showed up to dedicate a special monument to Reynolds during the October 14th lighting of the Jack O' Lantern at Courthouse Plaza and the casting of a "spell" from the movie. Between 40,000 to 50,000 people visited the event in 2017.

Reynolds died on December 28, 2016, at age 84, one day after her daughter Carrie Fisher died. For many years on Halloween, Reynolds would wear her Aggie costume and surprise young trick-or-treaters who happened to knock on her door.

Brown said:

> We wanted to do a special tribute to her and her role as
> Grandma Aggie and have a small monument set up there
> for her. It was nice to go back and honor Debbie. It's such an
> honor that people want to come and hang out and see where it
> was filmed. Never in my wildest dreams could I have imagined
> this is what we would be doing two decades later.

Why has the Halloweentown franchise remained so popular
even to new audiences?

Brown said:

> If I may be so bold to pontificate, I think the movies have
> remained so popular for several reasons. For one thing,
> several people like the idea of a town where it's Halloween all
> the time—there's the whole element of a place where magic
> exists and being able to do things with magic powers—people
> really enjoy that fantasy element of the series.
>
> There's also the aspect of there being a family as the main
> characters—they kind of have the best of both worlds, being
> able to live both in the 'normal' world and in the more magical,
> fantastical Halloweentown world.
>
> My character, Marnie, was thirteen years old when she dis-
> covered she had these magical powers, which she learned to
> embrace. I think that's something that people can relate to,
> especially teenagers or people who are just becoming teenag-
> ers—there are so many changes going on in a person's life at
> that age. I think seeing a character who was undergoing these
> radical, magical changes in her life that she was having to get
> used to was something they could relate to.

Disney has no official plans to continue or reboot the franchise but creator Singer said she is eager to do a fifth movie:

> I'd have to get Disney Channel to get on-board, but I would
> like to. I have ideas of how I would do it. There was some talk
> about a year and a half ago but then it didn't happen. I have
> pitched the idea of doing it as a musical. There's also ways to
> do a prequel. It's not something I haven't brought up several
> times before.

DISNEY PARKS

While the coronavirus outbreak made all Disney theme parks worldwide into ghost towns, once they are up and running again to full capacity, it might still be possible to encounter a ghost or two in those areas and not just the audio-animatronics kind in the Haunted Mansion.

Places like hotels where many people have come and gone over the decades and where emotions were often at their peak are often cited as good locations for a ghost sighting. Disney theme parks have a similar profile and regrettably, there have actually been people who have died while at the parks. In addition, some people have scattered the ashes of loved ones in the parks although Disney does its best to prevent it.

Ghosts are sometimes just be a spirit who didn't want to pass over for whatever reason including not even realizing that they are dead. More than a few people might like spending their afterlife in a Disney theme park for all eternity.

Undeniably, some sightings described as being paranormal are nothing more than a misidentification or an optical illusion that is a trick of the light. After all, the Haunted Mansion ballroom scene is based on the same premise of being in a lighted room at night and looking out a window and seeing images on the outside lawn that are merely a reflection from the lighted room.

Articles have been written and unofficial tours given of the haunts of supposedly ghostly entities at the Disney theme parks. None have ever been verified despite the stories of cast members and guests who reportedly encountered these spirits more than once.

In the 1980s, a woman named Dolly Young who was riding the famous Disneyland Matterhorn roller coaster

was thrown from her bobsled and killed by an oncoming bobsled. Cast Members who work on the ride claim her ghost still lingers in a section where she died that they call Dolly's Dip and can hear strange sounds at night.

Bogden Delaurot who died in the Rivers of America still seems to splash in the waters while Thomas Cleveland who died on the Monorail track has been seen running along the beam. The young woman named Debbie Stone who was crushed to death in the America Sings attraction reportedly roams the area and while the attraction was still in operation sometimes gently warned fellow cast members who got too close to the rotating walls.

Mr. One Way on Disneyland's Space Mountain will appear in an empty seat on a ride vehicle but disappears before the final tunnel at the end of the ride.

At Disneyland, the ghost of a young boy cries near the exit of the Haunted Mansion looking for his mother while at Walt Disney World, a young boy rides in a doombuggy and leans out to smile at riders behind him.

WDW's Pirates of the Caribbean is supposedly home to a construction worker named George who died in the attraction. Cast members say "good morning" and "good night" to him over the PA system each day to prevent him from causing mischief.

Roy O. Disney has been seen walking down WDW's Main Street but also at other locations like Walt's apartment at Disneyland. Of course, Walt has been seen at different locations in Disneyland and always seems to be enjoying himself.

These are just a few of the many ghost stories that have been reported and we all know that at a Disney theme park anything is possible.

Mickey's Not So Scary Halloween Party

Mickey's Not So Scary Halloween Party did not exist when the Magic Kingdom opened but two highly popular events inspired its creation.

At Walt Disney World, the very first Mickey's Very Merry Christmas Party was held on December 16, 1983 for one night only but then expanded to two nights in 1989, then three nights in 1990 and its popularity continued to increase so that today, it runs for multiple weeks.

This separate hard ticketed event offered to a limited number of guests after the Magic Kingdom closed for the night was a great guest satisfier with new things added to it each year.

The second inspiration was an event at a competing theme park.

Halloween Horror Nights began at Universal Studios Florida in 1991 for three nights and was instantly popular so that today, it also runs for multiple weeks. Designed as the ultimate in an interactive scary experience, it sparked the creation of similar events at amusement venues not only in Central Florida but also in Southern California.

The Disney Company decided that perhaps a family friendly alternative celebration to the Universal event along the same lines as Mickey's Very Merry Christmas Party might appeal especially to families with young children. Those holiday offerings were generating tens of thousands of additional sales from theme park guests and local residents so another similar party seemed a great idea.

WDW has previously experimented with some small Halloween themed promotions as early as 1972 but most often in the individual resorts.

In 1975 to help attract locals and guests to the new Lake Buena Vista Shopping Village, the Village Halloween Party

was introduced where children (encouraged to attend in costume) could go with their parents trick-or-treating at the various stores and restaurants. Another experiment was the one night separate ticketed Halloween Hysteria event at the Magic Kingdom held after operating hours in 1979.

It wasn't until October 31, 1995 that the first Mickey's Not So Scary Halloween Party debuted. Like the first year of MVMCP, it was held for only one night to determine if there was any interest. The cost was $16.95.

By October 1997, it increased to two nights and in 1999 increased again to three nights. Two years later in 2001, it grew to five nights and two years after that in 2003 to ten nights. By 2005, it was boosted to fifteen nights and in 2016 there were twenty-nine nights. Just like MVMCP, new offerings were introduced each year. The event now takes place on selected nights in late August, September, October and sometimes November first.

Depending upon which night an adult attends, today, it can cost a hefty fee up to a premium price per person for Halloween night.

There are many reasons for the popularity of the event. First, it provides a safer and more magical environment for young children to go trick-or-treating for quality candy than visiting their local neighborhoods. Second, the limited number of people in the park provides easier access to favorite attractions.

Finally, during the event, the Magic Kingdom provides some unique experiences that don't exist normally from a special "Mickey's Boo To You" parade to eerie projections on the castle and unique stage shows in addition to Disney character dance parties.

Since 2005, the event included an exclusive fireworks show titled *Happy HalloWishes: A Grim Grinning Ghosts' Spooktacular in the Sky* with Halloween themed music. This fireworks show was replaced with a new one in 2019 designed to run several years.

The new fireworks show hosted by Jack Skellington and his dog Zero entitled *Disney's Not So Spooky Spectacular* features Mickey, Minnie, Donald and Goofy on a trick-or-treating

adventure, as they are drawn to a mysterious haunted house. The show also included dancing skeletons and ghosts, lasers, new lighting, projections on Sleeping Beauty Castle along with some troublemaking Disney villains.

In addition, several limited edition items of merchandise from pins to ornaments to balloons to apparel are sold only during the event. A special limited edition Sorcerers of the Magic Kingdom card is handed out at the event.

Of course, one of the key components is the opportunity to get free candy at a variety of locations on a special trick-or-treat trail. In 2016, roughly 285 tons of candy was handed out during all the parties including 40 different kinds of brand-name candies like Snickers, Milky Way, Butterfingers, M&Ms and Kit Kats as well as other offerings including Cheez-Its, Goldfish Crackers, and Apple Slices. Allergen free candy and other treats are also available so that children with allergies could still participate.

There are special character meet-and-greet opportunities and photo opportunities not available during the regular operating hours. The Disney characters like Mickey, Minnie, Donald, Daisy and Winnie the Pooh and his friends are in their Halloween costumes, something that can only be seen at the event.

The PhotoPass photographers have thirty different images that can be digitally added to a guest photo like holding a poison apple over a cauldron, holding a frightful flaming pumpkin, hitching a ride with the ghosts near the Haunted Mansion or meeting the Headless Horseman in person at the entrance to Magic Kingdom.

Special food offerings are available from a spider cupcake to candy corn flavored popcorn. Some of these special treats include at the Main Street Bakery the Not-So-Poison Apple Cupcake (spiced apple cupcake with pecan crunch and buttercream), the Halloween Cinnamon Roll (cinnamon roll topped with icing and a chocolate spider web), and the Pumpkin Cheesecake topped with a chocolate Mickey Pumpkin.

At Casey's Corner the Minnie Witch Brownie is topped with a white chocolate piece featuring the Minnie Mouse dressed in her Halloween best.

At Aloha Isle the Hitchhiking Ghost Dessert is a cream puff filled with cookies and cream mousse and topped with a chocolate piece featuring the Hitchhiking Ghosts.

At Pecos Bills Tall Tale Inn the Worms and Dirt is chocolate pudding topped with gluten-friendly cake crumbs, gummy worms, and a chocolate gravestone.

In the Liberty Square Market, the Madame Leota Dessert is a vanilla tart shell filled with toasted marshmallow pastry crème and topped with crispy pearls, chocolate, and a hard candy garnish.

Storybook Treats offers the Maleficent Dessert which is a lime soft-serve in a black waffle cone and topped with purple sugar and chocolate horns.

Gaston's Tavern serves the Oogie Boogie Meringue which is a pomegranate-cherry gelée with gummy worms and topped with glow-in-the-dark meringue.

With the increased popularity of the event, Disney had to set some guidelines not only for safety concerns but because of the situation where some adults were attired so accurately that other guests mistook them for official Disney character performers. At one time the Disney Store sold adult costumes that were very authentic but no longer does so.

For legal and entertainment reasons, Disney does not want non-Disney employees pretending to be Disney characters, taking pictures with guests and giving autographs.

The latest guidelines include the following:

- Disney may deny admission to anyone or remove anyone who is wearing attire that is considered inappropriate or could detract from other guests' experiences.

- Guests may dress as their favorite characters, but cannot pose for pictures or sign autographs.

- Costumes must be family-friendly and not obstructive, offensive, violent or objectionable.

- Costumes must not contain weapons that resemble or could be mistaken for real weapons.

- Costumes may not contain sharp or pointed objects, or materials that might accidentally strike another guest.

- Guests who do not abide by the guidelines may be refused entry or removed unless their costumes can be modified to acceptable standards.

For guests ages 14 and up:

- Layered costumes or costume props that surround the entire body are strongly discouraged and subject to additional security screening.
- Costumes may not reach or drag the ground.
- Capes should not go below the waist.
- Themed T-shirts, shirts, sweatshirts and hats are acceptable.
- Transparent wings, plastic light sabers, toy swords and tutus are OK. Headwear must not cover the face.
- Masks are not allowed.

For guests ages 13 and under:

- Costumes and some masks may be worn. Masks cannot cover the entire face, and eyes must be visible.

In recent years, the party has officially started at 7 p.m. inside Magic Kingdom. Disney Halloween party guests with special wristbands are allowed to enter the park starting as early as 4 p.m. with the following special events scheduled during the evening:

- Mickey's "Boo-To-You" Halloween Parade—9:15 p.m. and 11:15 p.m. About 15 minutes before the parade begins, the Headless Horseman trots through Liberty Square on his black horse and continues down Main Street. The parade features Disney characters in Halloween regalia and the ghostly inhabitants of The Haunted Mansion like the gravediggers who scrape their shovels on the ground creating sparks.
- Disney's Not So Spooky Spectacular fireworks—10:15 p.m.
- *Hocus Pocus Villain Spelltacular*—8:30 p.m., 10:45 p.m. and 12 a.m. at the Castle Forecourt Stage. The show is held exclusively during the party and features the Sanderson Sisters, Winifred, Mary and Sarah, along with other Disney villains such as Dr. Facilier, Ooogie Boogie

and Maleficent. *Hocus Pocus Villain Spelltacular* replaced the *Villains Mix 'n' Mingle*.

- Dance parties—all night long!

To enhance the experience, some attractions receive temporary "spooktacular" overlays including Pirates of the Caribbean, Mad Tea Party, Space Mountain and Monsters Inc. Laugh Floor.

A crew of live pirate performers appears throughout Pirates of the Caribbean. A pirate prisoner hassles guests to help him escape and some pirates sprinkled throughout the attraction try to recruit guests for their crew.

Mad Tea Party gets special lighting, fog and music, while Space Mountain goes completely dark. Over at the Laugh Floor in the Monster World, the comedic monsters learn more about the Human World holiday called Halloween with seasonal jokes.

The dance parties include *Monstrous Scream-O-Ween Ball* with Mike Wazowski and Sulley from *Monsters Inc.* in Tomorrowland. At Cosmic Ray's Starlight Café, the Villain Kids from the *Descendants* franchise appear in dance videos for the *Disney DescenDANCE Party*.

A Dapper Dans-style ghostly group called Cadaver Dans pops up throughout the night for performances in front of The Frontier Trading Post in Frontierland. They crack jokes and sing songs like "Happy Trails To You" and "Boo to You."

Cruella's Halloween Hide-a-Way is a special dining experience at Tony's Town Square Restaurant starting around 9:30pm that allows guests to mingle with the villainess and enjoy hors d'oeuvres and sweets along with access to a reserved viewing section for the 11:15 parade. This is a seperately ticketed experience above the regular admission to the event.

Because of the pandemic restrictions, the entire event was cancelled for October 2020, the first time in twenty-five years.

"While assessing ... Mickey's Not-So-Scary Halloween Party, we determined that many of its hallmarks—stage shows, parades and fireworks—are unable to take place in this new, unprecedented environment," Disney said in an announcement on its blog. "With that in mind, we have made

the difficult decision to cancel this year's Mickey's Not-So-Scary Halloween Party."

Disneyland's Mickey's Halloween Party in September and October was replaced in 2019 and supposedly for the future with a separate ticketed Oogie Boogie Bash: A Disney Halloween Party at Disney's California Adventure.

Disneyland still has the Main Street Pumpkin Festival that includes the giant Mickey Mouse Pumpkin and lots of unique Disney-themed hand carved pumpkins in Town Square. The Ray Bradbury Halloween Tree in Frontierland is appropriately decorated and lit.

Space Mountain is refitted as Ghost Galaxy. In this version of the ride, guests travel to the far reaches of space where ghostly occurrences have been detected. The outside of the attraction sets the tone with loud, scary shrieks emanating from the mountain and creepy lighting effects.

Of course, the Haunted Mansion is refitted as a *Nightmare Before Christmas* experience called the Haunted Mansion Holiday.

During Halloween Time at Disneyland, a specific "Happiest Haunts Tour" for an extra price is held that focuses around the specific Halloween attractions and story of certain Halloween elements in the park.

At Disney California Adventure for the special Halloween party, Oogie Boogie (the villain from *A Nightmare Before Christmas*) has taken over the park and his oversized silhouette welcomes guests into the park.

There is a ten foot tall Headless Horseman statue that has smoke coming out of the horse's nostrils.

The World of Color has a show overlay entitled *Villanious!* telling the story of a little girl named Shelley Marie created by Disney animator Eric Goldberg as a tribute to Frankenstein author Mary Shelley. Shelley Marie has to decide whether to be a princess or a villain for her Halloween costume, and goes on a journey that teaches her that there's a little villain in all of us.

Hollywood Land hosts the *DescenDance Party* and the *Mickey's Trick and Treat* show.

The Frightfully Fun Parade starts over by Paradise Gardens Park and winds its way through DCA. Following the Headless

Horseman, the parade is lead by Minnie and Mickey Mouse, in Halloween outfits, and features a number of villains including the Evil Queen, Dr. Facilier, Cruella de Vil, Hades and Ursula, among others as well as Jack Skellington and Sally, the Hitchhiking Ghosts from the Haunted Mansion and the Cheshire Cat.

Guardians of the Galaxy: Monsters After Dark attraction overlay centers around the guest serving as bait to distract the monsters that have been released from their cages from eating Baby Groot.

Radiator Screams has costumed *Cars* characters, and ride overlays including Mater's Graveyard JamBOOree, Luigi's Honkin' Haul-O-Ween, Fillmore's Jack-Oil-Lanterns, Flo's Spider-Car and Witchy Miss Lizzie's shop.

In Cars Land, Mater is attired as a vampire with Lightning McQueen dressed as a superhero with a flying cape. Others include Cruz Ramirez (pirate), Red the Fire Truck (clown) and DJ (punk rocker). Again for reasons related to pandemic restrictions, this event was cancelled for 2020.

Tales of the Twilight Zone Tower of Terror

It was Halloween night, October 31, 1939, when a freakish thunder and lightning storm descended on the Hollywood Hills while the elite of the film community found sanctuary in the prestigious and popular Hollywood Tower Hotel's elegant lobby.

Among those checking in that night were young singer Carolyn Crosson and her actor boyfriend Gilbert London as well as child actress Sally Shine in blond curls and frilly dress (reminiscent of actress Shirley Temple) with her stern governess Emeline Partridge.

Sally clutched a Charlotte Clark Mickey Mouse doll. Overworked bellman Dewey Todd assisted them all into the elevator to take them to the top floor where a special party that had started roughly forty minutes earlier is still going on at the Tip Top Club.

They stepped in, the doors closed, and seconds later as the elevator made its way to the top of the hotel, its passengers, and an entire guest wing of the hotel simply vanished when lightning struck the building, leaving a burnt scar and a gaping hole on the outside. Supposedly, the elevator then plummeted out of control to the basement but it mysteriously disappeared before it reached the bottom.

The hotel is frozen in a twilight zone of time and space, and while the exterior has fallen into disrepair over the years with overgrown vegetation, the interior remains frighteningly untouched from the way it was that fateful 1939 Halloween night with hotel personnel eerily acting as if it is still 1939 and everything is fine.

Rumors abound that the missing five people from the elevator still roam the upper floors beckoning new visitors to join them in the Fifth Dimension.

That roughly minute and a half pre-show video that guests see depicting that horrific evening was directed by award winning director Joe Dante known for his horror films like *The Howling* and *Gremlins* as well as directing a segment of the 1983 *The Twilight Zone—The Movie*.

The set that he used to film those scenes for the attraction was built on a soundstage in a studio in Culver City for the shooting by Theme Park Productions. It was then dismantled and reassembled in the lobby of the actual attraction in Florida so it would look exactly as it was in the video.

Show producer Leanne Nakayama remembered:

> The most exciting part was being able to get a sneak preview of what the lobby looked like. We were able to see the set full size and to see it in reality with all the paint and the color and people walking through it. Then to be able to see this set with all the lighting and the characters walking through it in black-and-white brought it to life and gave it its own history.
>
> It was like it really was there in 1939 and it was great. I believed it. I was there for it being filmed but when I saw the video I believed these guys were there and checking in and they got in the elevator.

Writer Rod Serling who created *The Twilight Zone* television series died in June 1975 but thanks to clever mixing of video compositing as well as the voice work of Mark Silverman, who was personally selected by Serling's widow Carol after hearing hundreds of audition tapes, Serling is able to host this "lost" episode of *The Twilight Zone*.

Walt Disney Imagineers screened each of the original 156 episodes of the series twice to capture the mood of the series. Some of the episodes were screened three or four times to get ideas for storylines, props and set designs.

They observed Rod Serling's opening and closing comments separately at least ten times each to determine the most representative quotes and characteristic phrases used by Serling.

The uncanny vocal imitation of Serling by Silverman states:

> Hollywood. 1939. Amid the glitz and the glitter of a bustling young movie town at the height of its golden age, The Hollywood Tower Hotel was a star in its own right, a beacon for the show business elite.

Now something is about to happen that will change all that. The time is now, on an evening very much like the one we have just witnessed. Tonight's story on *The Twilight Zone* is somewhat unique and calls for a different kind of introduction.

This, as you may recognize, is a maintenance service elevator, still in operation, waiting for you. We invite you, if you dare, to step aboard because in tonight's episode, you are the star. And this elevator travels directly to...The Twilight Zone!

The image and narration "Tonight's story on *The Twilight Zone* is somewhat unique and calls for a different kind of introduction," comes from Serling's intro at the beginning of a 1961 TZ episode, "It's a Good Life," where he is standing in front of a map where a town has disappeared, not in front of an elevator.

That episode told the story of little Anthony Fremont who wishes people into the cornfield and among other things hates people singing. So it is interesting that the poster in the lobby indicates that Anthony Fremont's Orchestra is playing Big Band music in the Tip Top Club starting at 7:30pm on the unmarked thirteenth floor. Oddly enough, Joe Dante directed the segment "It's a Good Life" in *Twilight Zone—The Movie.*

Child actress Lindsay Ridgeway at the age of seven portrayed Sally Shine in the video. She later appeared on the ABC-TV show *Boy Meets World* as the little sister Morgan (seasons 3-7). At the age of eleven, she recreated the Sally role for the 1997 Disney ABC television movie *Tower of Terror.*

The original elaborate back story for the Disney MGM Tower of Terror is in actuality a Halloween story appropriate for an episode of the popular cult television program hosted by Rod Serling that began in 1959 and lasted until 1964.

While today, variations of the iconic and popular attraction have been at four different Disney theme parks worldwide, it was not the first choice when Disney decided in 1989 to expand Disney MGM Studios to meet the unexpected demand by a surge of attendance.

The first idea that was suggested was an elaborate Roger Rabbit Toontown with several attractions, shops and food and beverage locations.

Then, with hopes that the *Dick Tracy* Touchstone film would spark a successful and financially lucrative franchise

like Tim Burton's *Batman* had a year earlier, the idea was discussed to build a 1930s era Chicago street where Sunset Boulevard is today.

Among other things, it would have included a warehouse that held the Dick Tracy Crimestoppers attraction where guests in vehicles in a high speed chase using the same vehicle later used in Indiana Jones and the Temple of Mara attraction would be shooting with tommy guns at gangsters using the same technology later incorporated into Buzz Lightyear's Space Ranger Spin.

In late 1989, CEO Michael Eisner pitched the idea to filmmaker Mel Brooks to colloborate on a new Disney theme park attraction in hopes it would also lead to Brooks producing films for Disney. After several trips to Imagineering, Mel wanted to combine scary and funny into a Castle Young Frankenstein that would have had a Bavarian village leading to a drawbridge and the castle.

The idea evolved into Mel Brooks' Hollywood Horror Hotel. The Imagineers jokingly referred to the project as Hotel Mel. Guests would have seen this huge abandoned hotel that may be haunted and through television monitors be informed that Mel Brooks was directing a new comedy horror movie inside.

Guests would be given a chance to visit the "Hot Set" and maybe even get to be an extra in the film. They would have boarded golf carts (guided by a magnetic wire embedded in the floor) and would experience a coven of witches cooking in their cauldron in the hotel kitchen, encounter Quasimodo the hotel "bellboy", and even visit the men's room where Dracula is trying to shave himself in a mirror where he can't see his reflection and the wolfman is combing himself while Frankenstein is in a stall trying to grab the Mummy's wrappings to use as toilet paper.

It was Brooks' intention that it be a comedic version of the Haunted Mansion. However, despite many outrageous gags, nobody could come up with a coherent story to tie it all together and the price for creating these elaborate audio-animatronics figures was cost prohibitive.

Other ideas were pitched including an attraction featuring the various characters that appeared in author Stephen

King's novels as well as a partially walking tour narrated by Vincent Price (who had recorded the original Disneyland Paris Phantom Manor narration) about a group of movie stars who had been staying at the hotel but mysteriously disappeared.

Throughout the tour, guests would discover clues and when they finally entered the elevator what had happened to those missing people became very clear but it was too late to get out.

Eisner suggested making the hotel an actual in-park Disney resort themed to a "film noir" murder mystery revolving around the hotel manager who had gone crazy that would have included costumed staff interacting with guests and a haunted elevator experience. It was even suggested having resort guests brought directly from the airport in a 1939 vehicle with the shades drawn to immerse them in the time period.

While building Disneyland Paris, there were plans for Frontierland to have an attraction called Geyser Mountain located near Phantom Manor that would have combined a roller coaster with a free fall experience, basically the geyser shooting a vehicle vertically high up in the air. It was never built although the freefall element was considered for another never built attraction centered on the story of *Journey to the Center of the Earth.*

Imagineers realized they might be able to incorporate this freefall idea into the haunted elevator. Since Disney MGM Studios was themed to the Hollywood of the 1930s and 1940s, it seemed logical to have a classic Hollywood hotel from that era.

The Hollywood Tower Hotel was a "star among the stars" that hosted the celebrity elite of 1930s Hollywood. On the hotel is a plaque indicating that the hotel was built in 1917 and in two decades it became as popular a place for Hollywood's rich and famous as the real Hollywood Hotels that inspired its architecture and lore: the Hollywood Roosevelt, the Biltmore, the Mission Inn and the Chateau Marmont.

However, Imagineers also wanted to connect the attraction with some film reference like other attractions at the park. After calling around to see what appropriate movies might be available to license and the cost, they eventually settled on using *The Twilight Zone* as the storyline "hook" since the series

was still well-known and beloved and dealt with the "paranormal" and ordinary people being taken to a new dimension.

In so doing, the tone of the attraction shifted into being spookier and much more of the thrill ride that Eisner wanted to attract an older audience.

At the time work began on the attraction, United Technologies was the sponsor of the Living Seas pavilion at Epcot. UT owned a subsidiary, Otis Elevator that had pioneered the development of the safety elevator in 1852 that would lock it in place if the ropes failed.

Originally, because of their reputation, they balked at the idea of being involved with an "unsafe" elevator but were persuaded it would be good publicity.

The self-guided vehicle was assigned to Eaton-Kenway, a manufacturer of computerized palette drivers for automated warehouse inventory transport. There were challenges getting both systems to work in tandem.

The horizontal movement into the Fifth Dimension is an element that is unique to the original Disney MGM Studios version. Every week the *TZ* television show began with Serling telling viewers that, with the key of imagination, one unlocks the door to another dimension.

The idea of a Fifth Dimension was shown in the *Little Girl Lost* episode (March 1962) where a little girl named Tina falls into another dimension through the wall behind her bed. The premise for the Tower of Terror attraction is that the ill-fated elevator passengers have fallen into a dimension and have been trapped there never aging for decades. They are not ghosts but frozen in time and space.

In the Disney MGM Studios attraction, the guests' elevator leave the lift shaft and passes through the Fifth Dimension where guests get a glimpse of the 1939 passengers motioning them to go deeper and join them. The elevator then goes into another lift shaft for the drop.

The Tower of Terror actually employs more than one type of vehicle in order to enable riders to leave the elevator shaft and pass through the Fifth Dimension. Guests sit in Autonomous Guided Vehicles (AGVs), which rise up to the corridor scene in a Vertical Vehicle Conveyance (VVC).

When they reach the Fifth Dimension corridor, the AGVs exit not on a track like a traditional dark ride vehicle but are guided by a magnetic wire under the floor. This technology was originally developed for the ride vehicles in Epcot's Universe of Energy attraction and The Great Movie Ride.

When they reach the far end of the corridor, they lock into another vertical motion cab, which handles the actual drop sequence.

The AGVs are powered by onboard batteries, which are charged while riders are unloading. At any one time, up to eight of these vehicles could be circulating around the Tower of Terror's ride system. Ten were originally built so two would be available for backup.

While there really are two drop shafts on the original Tower of Terror, there are actually four elevators that lift the AGVs up to the Fifth Dimension scene—two of these merge into a single corridor scene. This enables the ride to have an increased capacity.

Unlike other amusement park drop rides like Magic Mountain's Freefall, guests are not in fact being pulled down by gravity. In fact, they are moving faster than the speed of gravity to a top speed of 39 miles per hour.

Once the AGV vehicles are locked into the Vertical Vehicle Conveyance (the elevator housing), they are pulled by cables connected to two enormous motors which are 12 feet tall, 35 feet long and weigh a massive 132,000 pounds. So the VVC is both pulled up and pulled down.

When the attraction was going through the test and adjust phase, it was found that the VVC was being pulled down so rapidly that it was compressing the air at the bottom of the shaft and blowing out the walls so adjustments had to be made.

The attraction is only 199 feet tall because Federal regulations would have required a flashing red beacon at the top to warn aircraft if it was 200 or more feet tall and that would have conflicted with the theming of the story the Imagineers were trying to tell. For years, the tower was the tallest WDW attraction. Today, it is Expedition Everest at 199.5 feet.

Due to its height, the rear façade of the building can be seen from the Morocco Pavilion in Epcot's World Showcase. So the

architectural elements and color palette for that part of the building were chosen to blend in from the distance as part of the skyline of the Morocco Pavilion.

The color would not have been common on a 1930s Hollywood hotel although most guests would never realize that oddity but if they do, it is just one more disturbing element to make them feel uneasy.

Because of its height, lightning did indeed strike the structure while it was being built and also afterwards so there are lightning rods installed at the top. The building is composed of 1,500 tons of steel, 145,800 cubic feet of concrete, and 27,000 individual roof tiles.

Construction began in 1992 on the area that had formerly been a cast member parking lot. As concrete was getting ready to be poured, a sinkhole opened up under the site. The sinkhole was filled and pounded down and the placement of the building was shifted before concrete and steelwork was begun.

Disney marketing jumped the gun and came out with promotional tie-ins, commercials and opening date teasers but because the ride system was utilizing new technology, the test-and-adjust phase to assure safety took longer than expected.

The computer code had to be written and revised. The Imagineers tested thirty-three different drop sequences before settling on the final one. Although marketing announced the attraction would be open July 4, 1994, it did not open until July 22 where it was so popular that wait times could be as much as three and a half hours. The cost for building it has been estimated as a hundred and fifty million dollars.

Through the years, the Tower of Terror has received updates to the drop sequences and additional visuals in show scenes.

In 1996, it was modified for two "twice the fright" drops. In 1999, a triple drop was included with faster accelaration and more rumbling. In celebration of the attraction's tenth anniversary in 2004, randomized patterns of drops and lifts were added, where the ride vehicle would drop or rise various distances at different intervals for up to five to eight drops per ride. The Florida slogan was now: "Never the Same Fear Twice!"

However despite the changes, the overall ride experience is very much the same as when it debuted. With the removal

of the Sorcerer Mickey hat from the park, the tower is now marketed as the new icon for Disney Hollywood Studios.

Disney California Adventure opened a version in 2004 that was based on one for Disneyland Paris that did not open until 2007. However, because of different construction requirements in France, there are differences.

Without the horizontal movement into the Fifth Dimension (to save Disney money and maintenance), both these attractions feature three elevator shafts with each shaft having its own separate ride and its own separate operating system.

Rod Serling's voice declares: "You are the passengers on a most uncommon elevator... about to take the strangest journey of your lives. Your destination? Unknown; but this much is clear: a reservation has been made in your name for an extended stay."

The California version closed on January 2, 2017 to be converted into Guardians of the Galaxy: Mission Breakout! that opened May 2017.

A similar attraction that opened at Tokyo DisneySea in Japan in 2006 dropped the Twilight Zone reference since it was determined that Japanese guests had no familiarity or emotional connection to a 1960s American television show.

The new storyline revolved around the fictional Hotel Hightower and its owner Harrison Hightower III and his collection of stolen, mysterious artifacts with the elevator incident happening New Year's Eve 1899 when Harrison disappeared.

Just as in the television show, host Serling has a final commentary at the end of the original attraction:

> A warm welcome back to those of you who made it, and a friendly word of warning, something you won't find in any guide book.
>
> The next time you check into a deserted hotel on the dark side of Hollywood, make sure you know just what kind of vacancy you're filling. Or you may find yourself a permanent resident... of the Twilight Zone.

Walt Disney World's Tower of Terror

The free Walt Disney World park guide map brochure from when the attraction opened in July 1994 stated: "Your next stop...a mysterious Hollywood hotel where the elevator takes a sudden detour into the fifth dimension and plummets straight down...from the thirteenth floor!"

At WDW, when it came to immersive theming, the Imagineers outdid themselves with things to make guests feel uneasy before they experienced the elevator.

Of course what makes an elevator frightening is the combined fears of claustrophobia and agoraphobia (a fear of being trapped with no escape that leads to panic attacks) not to mention being out of control.

When guests are walking down Sunset Boulevard toward the attraction, in the background they hear upbeat Swing music of the time period by artists like Benny Goodman and Tommy Dorsey including *Don't Sit Under the Apple Tree, Song of India, Juke Box Saturday Night, Three Foolish Things, Sing, Sing, Sing,* and more.

However, as guests enter the queue line, they hear more melancholy music. The music has an eerie, ghostly haunting sound that was achieved with a Lexicon 480L box for an "echo return". That means that on channels one and two is the source audio and on channels three and four is the return from the reverb so the reverb can be controlled throughout the piece. In addition a "Room" filter was used on the reverb so there is less of a stereotypical reverb sound.

Here the playlist loop of those songs in the queue:

- *Alabamy Home*—Gotham Stompers
- *Another World*—Johnny Hodges
- *Can't Get Started*—Benny Berigan

- *Dear Old Southland*—Noble Sissle
- *Deep Purple*—Turner Layton
- *Delta Mood*—Cootie Williams
- *Inside*—Fats Waller
- *Jeep's Blues*—Johnny Hodges
- *Jitterbug's Lullaby*—Johnny Hodges
- *Jungle Drums*—Sidney Bechet
- *Mood Indigo*—Duke Ellington
- *Pyramid*—Johnny Hodges
- *Remember*—Red Norvo
- *Sleepy Time Gal*—Glenn Miller
- *There's A House in Harlem*—Henry Allen
- *There's No Two Ways About It*—Frankie Newton
- *Uptown Blues*—Jimmy Lunceford
- *We'll Meet Again*—Vera Lynn
- *When the Sun Sets Down South*—Nobles Singers
- *Wishing (Will Make it So)*—Vera Lynn

Outside in the courtyard of the Legends of Hollywood store at the beginning of Sunset Boulevard, partially hidden by a tree, is a billboard depicting the Hollywood Hotel in its heyday. This is an example of story foreshadowing so that later when guests see the decrepit hotel at the far end of the street, they get a sense of foreboding of how much it has fallen into decline after the incident.

Another example of foreshadowing is by the Route 66 sign further down on Sunset where actor Gilbert London's abandoned suitcase is still waiting to be picked up. London was one of the ill-fated guests in the elevator on that fateful Halloween night in 1939 when lightning struck the hotel.

The stone monument gates at the entrance (that also serves as a concealed bathroom facility) to the attraction were inspired by the Hollywoodland Gates in California. The original structure was built in 1923. It is located on Beachwood Drive at Westshire Drive. The Hollywoodland Gates were built to let everyone know that they were entering a very prestigious part of Hollywood.

It never seems to occur to guests that once they pass the entrance gates, they don't enter the hotel at its main entrance. That entrance with the covered porte-cochère for cars to drop off or pick up guests is now the exit of the attraction. Guests are directed to take a side garden entrance to get to the lobby.

The grounds of the Hollywood Tower Hotel were inspired by the chaparral-covered hills of California's Griffith Park and Elysian Park. Since the hotel has supposedly been "deserted", there are the signs of neglect everywhere.

The queue takes guests pass broken stoneware, an old fountain with dead vines, and a cracked, empty pool. Once extravagant landscaping is now overgrown and crumbling overseen by silent statuary. The latticed walkways are very similar to ones at the Mission Inn hotel gardens in Riverside.

Besides the haunting background music, guests can hear screaming. The Imagineers enhanced the sounds of screams because it was discovered that when some people were really scared that they were sometimes too scared to scream. The screams also serve as an early warning of what to expect as well as to increase the excitement of the foolishly brave about what is to come.

The interior of the Lobby was inspired by the Los Angeles Biltmore Hotel (the ceiling is practically identical as are the adjacent archways) that was built in 1923 and is filled with wonderful details to make the fantasy real that are too often missed.

Luggage is still on the rolling carts, dead flowers in vases are on some of the tables, a coat and hat are strewn carelessly on the counter and unpicked up mail is in the room slots. It is as if people would return at any second to resume their activities.

The Mahjongg game (a popular pastime in the 1930s) in the lobby was set up by professional players of the game to be in progress so that guests who knew how to play the game could see that it was authentic.

What makes it spooky is that if the players left the table during the game, they would have pushed their chairs away from the table to get up. Their chairs are still in the position as if people were sitting there playing the game and then suddenly vanished.

On the wall in the lobby by the concierge's desk is a silver framed "13 Diamond" award from AAA. In actuality the award would only go up to the number five. Thirteen is an unlucky number.

The clock in the lobby has stopped at 8:05, when lightning struck the hotel at this time. Eight plus five equals thirteen.

The directory in the lobby for amenities, located between the inoperable elevators has some missing letters that have fallen off and are at the bottom of the glass case that originally warned "evil Tower UR (you are) doomed" but after the fall of the New York Trade Center Twin Towers during 9/11, the letters that spell "evil tower" were removed.

Some of the bronze sculptures featured in the lobby are the actual work of 19th century French sculptor Auguste Moreau.

It is often pointed out that on the lobby's concierge desk is an issue of a *Photoplay* magazine that has "Four Pages of Hilarious Star Caricatures by Walt Disney". That fun fact has been cut and pasted in just about every listing for the attraction. However, there is more to that amusing bit of trivia. It is the January 1939 issue of *Photoplay* with a cover of actress Hedy Lamarr.

It's an infamous issue because it contained an article (anonymously written by gossip columnist Sheilah Graham) that revealed several unwed Hollywood couples like Carol Lombard and Clark Gable who were living together. It prompted some quick marriages by studios to avoid bad publicity.

The four pages by Walt Disney were actually to promote the latest Silly Symphony short cartoon *Mother Goose Goes Hollywood* that had been released late in December 1938 and was still appearing in theaters.

The celebrity caricatures portraying famous Mother Goose characters like Simple Simon and Little Boy Blue were not done by Walt Disney himself as he had long stop doing drawing. They were based on the work of Disney storyman and caricaturist Thornton ("T.") Hee. Hee had been hired specifically to work on this cartoon because of his skill in doing caricatures.

To make things spookier, because of his skill in caricatures, T. Hee was loaned out and did the design for the Cliff Robertson version of the infamous Caesar ventriloquist dummy from the Twilight Zone episode *Caesar and Me*.

In the magazine, two pages are in black, white and red and the last two pages in black, white and blue. The caricatures from the film include movie stars who would have been very familiar to audiences at the time like the Marx Brothers, W.C. Fields, Charlie McCarthy, Greta Garbo, Edward G. Robinson. Laurel and Hardy, Fred Astaire, Clark Gable, Katherine Hepburn and more.

It is natural that a hotel catering to Hollywood celebrities would have a copy of the magazine, but it is ten months old... another indication that something is not quite right here.

Everything in the lobby is covered by dust and cobwebs. There's a set of leather chairs that are genuine Renaissance antiques. Similar sets of these 17th century Portuguese renaissance chairs are in New York's Metropolitan Museum and London's Victoria and Albert Museum. Other chairs were from the exclusive Jonathan Club, a well-known Los Angeles landmark built in the 1920s.

In order to find the appropriate style of furniture that was needed to fit the themed time period for this attraction, Imagineers went to garage sales, auctions, antique stores, and flea markets. In some cases Imagineers, were unable to find the type of furniture that they were looking for so items had to be re-created. The sofas in front of the fireplace were built from scratch using a 1920s furniture catalog as a pattern.

In the libraries are some lamps with HTH (Hollywood Tower Hotel) on them. These were built for the attraction using flapper dresses from the 1920's for the material. The libraries have a plethora of references to characters from *The Twilight Zone* television series as well as replicas of iconic props from the episodes.

Some of these are only found at the version in Disney's Hollywood Studios while other versions have some examples missing from the Florida version. For instance, Disney's California Adventure had the broken stopwatch from *A Kind of Stopwatch*, the red toy telephone from *Long Distance Call,* the box camera from *A Most Unusual Camera*, and the electric razor and typewriter from *A Thing About Machines.*

Among the items in the DHS libraries are the Mystic Seer devil-headed machine from *Nick of Time,* the book *To Serve*

Man from the episode of the same name ("It's a cookbook!"), Henry Bemis' glasses from *Time Enough at Last*, and the miniature gold-suited spaceman figure from *The Invaders*. The row of thin, tightly packed books on a shelf each contain a script for an episode of the television series.

The right library has an envelope with Rod Serling's name on it behind a cage and the left library has an envelope with Victoria West's name on it both referencing *A World of His Own*. The trumpet from *A Passage for Trumpet* is sitting on top of some sheet music. In one of the libraries the sheet music is entitled *What! No Mickey Mouse?* (1932) by Irving Caesar. In the other library the sheet music is *The Wedding Party of Mickey Mouse* (1931).

The boilers look like faces, often with fiery eyes or mouths. On the left side of the service elevator is an inspection certificate dated October 31, 1939 (the night of the incident) and signed by "Cadwallader". Cadwallader was a character on an episode of the *Twilight Zone* entitled *Escape Clause* where it was revealed he was the Devil. The certificate number is 10259. *The Twilight Zone* series premiered October 2, 1959.

In the unload areas are the slot machine from *The Fever*, the infamous Caesar ventriloquist dummy from *Caesar and Me*, and the flying saucer spaceship from *The Invaders*.

While it has been cited that the design of the architecture of the attraction was inspired by the Biltmore Hotel, Mission Inn and even elements from the Chateau Marmont, there is another inspiration that is often missed.

The Hollywood Tower is a large apartment building on 6200 Franklin Avenue in Los Angeles that was built in 1929. It became "sophisticated living for film luminaries" during the Golden Age of Hollywood and was placed on the Register of Historic Places by the U.S. Department of Interior in 1988.

Its large neon "Hollywood Tower" sign from the side of the building can be seen clearly from the northbound lane of the Hollywood 101 Freeway. It has been cited with its sign and the ascending design of the central building (only seven stories high) as one of the inspirations for the exterior of Florida's Twilight Zone Tower of Terror attraction. The building gets ample screen time in the Disney comedy *Midnight Madness* (1980) and was a well known Hollywood landmark.

Speaking of screen time, *Tower of Terror* shown on October 26, 1997, on ABC's *The Wonderful World of Disney* weekly television program was the first film based on a Disney theme park attraction. While it was primarily filmed in Hollywood, some of it was filmed at the attraction in Orlando, Florida.

Music was by Louis Febre. He met his mentor, John Debney, who had done extensive musical work for Disney, in 1996 and worked with him on *Doctor Who The Movie* (1996). Febre is perhaps best known for his work on the *Smallville* TV series.

The roughly ninety-minute movie was written and directed by D.J. McHale who had previously worked as a writer for the *Encyclopedia Brown* television series as well as several *After School Specials* and was the co-creator (with Ned Kandel), writer and director on the Nickoleoden tv series *Are You Afraid of the Dark?* So he was well-versed in shows for young people as well as horror when he was given the opportunity to direct this movie. Today, he is probably best known as the author of the young adult science-fiction/fantasy *Pendragon* book series of novels.

McHale said:

> I was never a horror fan but I loved scary stories like the compilations of short stories supposedly written by Alfred Hitchcock. I felt *Tower of Terror* was really normal people you might know and that you feel like you could relate to, who are caught up in a bigger-than-life adventure. That's what comes out of my head, I don't know why, but that's what comes out.

The story has only the slightest connection to the storyline of the actual attraction and no reference to the *Twilight Zone*.

Disgraced reporter Buzzy Crocker (Steve Guttenberg who that same year appeared in the straight-to-video *Casper: A Spirited Beginning)* was fired from the *Los Angeles Banner* newspaper for submitting a story that turned out to be false. He now works for a sleazy supermarket tabloid called *The National Inquisitor* assisted by his young niece Anna (Kirsten Dunst who that same year appeared in an episode of *The Outer Limits*).

An elderly woman named Abigail Gregory comes to Buzzy with a story about an incident she witnessed at a now abandoned luxury hotel back in 1939 where five hotel guests mysteriously disappeared. Gregory claims that the nanny of child film star Sally Shine was a witch who cast a curse that backfired.

Thinking the mystery might give him a great story and get him a job on a legitmate newspaper, Buzzy investigates the closed hotel. He does find a book of spells and Abigail insists that if items belonging to each the passengers are found and the events of that night are repeated the curse will be broken. Buzzy and his niece enlist the assistance of the hotel caretaker who happens to be the grandson of the bellhop who was in the elevator.

Buzzy tries to set up some fake photos of the ghosts for his story for the tabloid but some of the real ghosts appear to try and frighten him off. Anna accuses the nanny of cursing the guests but the ghosts come to her defense.

Buzzy's girlfriend Jill (Nia Peeples) while also researching the story discovers that Abigail is the sister of Sally Shine and was jealous of her younger sister's success. In fact, no one remembered Abigail's birthday on October 31st so she is the one who cursed Sally.

Buzzy has located a lock of Sally's hair, the nanny's handkerchief, the bellboy's spare hat, the actor's Oxford spectacles and the female singer's locket. In addition the elevator has been repaired but all of this is not to free the spirits but for Abigail to complete the curse.

Anna gets trapped in the elevator with the ghosts but the ghost of Sally makes it out and the elevator gets stuck on the 11th floor. Sally appears to Abigail and reveals that the party on the top floor was to have been a surprise birthday party for Abigail. Sally gives her the present she had for Abigail on that night. Abigail doesn't know how to stop the spell.

Buzzy, his girlfriend, Abigail and Sally board a service elevator and catch up with the others on the 11th floor. Anna manages to get out from an emergency escape hatch just as lightning once again strikes the hotel and both elevators plummet toward the basement. Sally and her older sister reconcile and that breaks the curse as they dissolve into golden sparkles that safely stops both elevators before they crash.

The other ghosts ascend to the Tip Top Club in all its former glory and then go on to Heaven along with the other party attendees who had also been trapped. With the curse broken, the Hollywood Tower Hotel is restored and re-opened.

The Early Development of the Haunted Mansion

When Walt Disney conceived of building an amusement venue, the concept of a haunted house was always part of the dream. It would have been an attraction where it was always Halloween 24 hours a day, seven days a week where spirits would gather in the perpetual darkness.

Haunted Mansion authority Jeff Baham has suggested that one of Walt's earliest experiences with a haunted house was the Sauer house in Kansas City, Missouri built by Anton Sauer in 1871. Walt was friends with Gus Eyssell who lived with his grandmother Marie Sauer, the widow of Anton's son.

The house is surrounded by many myths including a hidden treasure and secret tunnels. Several deaths had taken place on the property including Anton's widow who supposed hanged herself in one of the rooms.

Over twenty-four pages list the various known haunted houses in Missouri and even in Marceline, Missouri where Walt grew up was the story of a misty-white female apparition that would appear by the railroad bridge. As young boys, Walt and Roy loved playing in an old house that was rumored to be haunted. After some unknown incident, they never returned.

The Haunted House (1929) was a black-and-white Mickey Mouse theatrical short cartoon that was animated by Ub Iwerks with music by Carl Stalling. State censors were not upset by the skeletons or Mickey being threatened but were concerned because there were gags involving a chamber pot and an outhouse.

On a dark and stormy night, Mickey Mouse hesitates to take shelter in deserted house but the branches of a tree blown in the wind prods him into the refuge where he finds himself in total darkness. He is startled by a large spider and several bats. A cloaked figure confronts him and compels him to play

the organ in the room so several skeletons could dance. When the music ends, Mickey runs away but even outside he finds a skeleton in the outhouse.

Variety reviewed the film February 12, 1930: "Mickey Mouse in a haunted villa is fast with laughs throughout. Culminates in Mickey being compelled to play an eerie organ while a ballet of skeletons dance weird capers. Delightfully mad, this short can be added to any bill and improve it thereby."

Certainly, "haunted" dark rides were popular in trolley parks and later amusement parks. The iconic Haunted Preztel (because the ride track twisted back and forth like the shape of a pretzel) was built in 1927 for Bushkill Park in Pennsylvania. It featured scary heads popping up from the floor, a hallway of doors hiding who-knows-what, a body trying to get out of a coffin and more very similar experiences to what was in the original Haunted Mansion.

Walt definitely saw the small haunted house at the Beverly Park Amusement Center located on the corner of Beverly and LaCienega Boulevards in Beverly Hills where he took his young daughters to play.

He was also familiar with the Haunted Shack at Knott's Berry Farm advertised as "The Ghostliest Place in Ghost Town" with its illusions where water seemed to run uphill, small children at one end of the room would seem taller than their older siblings on the other end and chairs that seemed to balance on just two legs among other illusions.

Walt often had many different people tackle a project, sometimes without letting them know that others were working on the same thing. Artist Herb Ryman had originally drawn a haunted house for the first aerial view of Disneyland.

Later, Walt had Imagineer Harper Goff do a sketch of a dilapidated old house on the top of a small hill overlooking a church and a graveyard on a side street near the end of Main Street U.S.A. Guests would have looked through the large windows to see the ghostly activity inside.

By 1957, when Walt gave an interview to the BBC about his plans for a retirement home for ghosts, he envisioned it being located in an area of Frontierland that had a New Orleans theme. Ken Anderson had just moved over to WED

Imagineering from the studio, and Walt turned to his "jack of all trades" to develop some possibilities.

As historian Paul Anderson told me:

> We always hear about 'the group of Imagineers' that went out to research the Haunted Mansion. Actually, 'the group' was just Ken in the beginning.

Anderson (1909–1993) had a bachelor's degree in architecture and intended to pursue a career as an architect, but kept getting sidetracked. He was employed at MGM Studios as a sketch artist working on films like *The Painted Veil* and *What Every Woman Knows*.

One day, as he was driving by the Disney's Hyperion studio in early 1934, he went in and applied on a whim, even though he told his wife, Polly, that he didn't know how to draw cartoons. Impressed with his portfolio, Disney hired him, and Anderson began his career at the studio in 1934, contributing to many animated classics as art director beginning with *Snow White and the Seven Dwarfs* (1937).

Since he had an architectural background, he was able to come up with innovative perspectives on such Silly Symphony cartoons as *Goddess of Spring* and *Three Orphan Kittens* that had never before been used in animation.

Ken Anderson's official credits list such titles at Disney as art direction, art supervision, story, color, styling, layout, production, and character development. He worked on the classic scene of the dwarfs dancing with *Snow White*, but it became apparent that his talents lay not in animation, but in such areas as production design on such films as *Sleeping Beauty* and *101 Dalmatians*.

Specializing in character design in his later years, Anderson designed such characters as Shere Khan in *The Jungle Book* and Elliott in *Pete's Dragon*.

Anderson also helped design many parts of Fantasyland, like the early dark rides of Snow White's Scary Adventures, Mr. Toad's Wild Ride, Storybook Land Canal Boat experience and others.

He retired on March 31, 1978, but continued to consult at WED Enterprises (now Walt Disney Imagineering). He was honored with the Disney Legends award in 1991. Anderson

was 84 years old when he died. Forty-four of those years had been spent in the service of the Disney Company.

Knowing of his background in architecture as well as his understanding of animation storytelling, Walt assigned Anderson to come up with concepts for what he called the "ghost house".

Anderson discovered in the Disney Studio library a book entitled *Decorative Art of Victoria's Era* (1950) where he found a photograph of the Shipley-Lydecker House in Baltimore, Maryland taken in 1937. He used that picture as the basis for his 1958 sketch of the exterior of the haunted mansion. Artist Sam McKim later used it as the basis for his concept painting.

At first, the attraction was going to be a "walk-through" experience.

Anderson was greatly influenced by his experiences taking walking tours at the Winchester Mystery House in San Jose, California.

Sometimes called the "ghost mansion", this popular tourist attraction has doors and staircases that lead nowhere and a maze of rooms that were constantly being redone by the widow of the maker of the Winchester rifle.

She believed that the ghostly victims of the Winchester rifle had cursed her family and were haunting her to keep building more and more rooms for their earthbound spirits. It was even rumored that through "automatic writing" she received building directions which she passed along to the carpenters

Ken Anderson had two pages of notes on the Winchester House, from the size of the tour group (maximum of 20), the mix of adults and children (roughly four times the number of adults to children), the maximum/minimum entrance and exit time in each area (25–60 seconds), the maximum/minimum time the guide spoke in each area (32 seconds to three-and-a-half minutes), as well as a variety of notes like "average group well behaved" and "rooms are all empty—nothing to touch".

Anderson strongly believed that a cohesive story was necessary to guide Disney guests through the Haunted Mansion. Not only was storytelling an important element of the Disney Brand and had positioned Disney's "dark rides" as different from carnival amusement park dark rides, but storytelling would be

necessary to move guests through the experience rather than have them dawdle in one area and clog the flow of traffic.

In 1957, Anderson developed four story concepts, all of which feature elements reflected in the final version of the attraction that was eventually opened at Disneyland on August 9, 1969.

According to Anderson's best known storyline, a well-known and feared pirate captain quietly retired to private life in a seaside community, like the famed Captain Henry Morgan. He changed his name and used some of his ill-gotten booty to establish himself as a respected and prosperous man. To make his life even more complete, he chose a lucky eighteen-year-old to be his bride and bear him many children.

The only restriction he gave her was to stay out of the attic of their magnificent mansion. Of course, the curious girl couldn't resist and, on their wedding day before the ceremony, but dressed in her wedding gown, she snuck up into the cluttered attic and found a locked trunk that she forced open.

Inside the trunk were souvenirs and documents from the man's previous life. The pirate captain caught her in the attic and, enraged that his secret might be revealed to the community by this foolish girl, he tossed her out the window to her death.

In the Haunted Mansion attraction that was finally built, guests actually relive this experience of being tossed out the window. Next time, look to your right as you leave the attic through the window and you will see that the shingles on the roof of the mansion do not match the ones on the outside of the mansions at Disneyland or Walt Disney World. Like a medium, you have become the girl and see what she saw, including the house from which she fell to her death.

That's also the reason you are falling backward as you drop down just as she did. The caretaker at the bottom is not scared by the graveyard but by you since you are now the final ghost to enter it so that there will be a 1,000 happy haunts. He is looking at you and shaking not the graveyard filled with ghosts.

The girl's ghost haunted her fiancé so mercilessly that the only way he could find peace was by hanging himself. However,

their passions were so intense that their spirits were bound to the mansion for all eternity. Their continuing struggle, even after death, attracted other ghosts, including some who came to celebrate a wedding that will never be held.

This story would have been shared with guests by a butler or maid who worked in the mansion as they guided guests through the walk-through attraction.

Another Anderson version was about Bloodmere Manor, which was the lakeside estate of "the unfortunate Blood family". It was built around 1800 in the swampy bayous near New Orleans and was moved to Disneyland intact because it was an example of early architecture from that region for guests to enjoy. The concept was similar to Henry Ford relocating famous buildings for his Greenfield Village.

The mansion had not been occupied for some time and was badly in need of repair, so the Disney Company started the work of restoration as soon as it arrived at Disneyland, but "strangely enough...the work of each day was destroyed during the night...and the night watchman reported that when he had passed the house he'd heard eerie screams and seen weird lights... In fact, we are sorry to report that the latest tragedy of all occurred here in Disneyland...when one of our carpenters engaged in restoration work on the house disappeared completely from sight...and he has not been seen or heard from since. The house is now too dangerous to live in, but we have succeeded in making it safe enough for a visit...when accompanied by our trained and competent guide, a former butler of the household."

A third version had Walt himself as the narrator on tape as the guests wandered through the house to go to a ghostly wedding celebration.

Another version focused on the Headless Horseman from the Disney animated film *The Legend of Sleepy Hollow* (1949) about Ichabod Crane on Halloween night. This version also featured a wedding, this time between Monsieur Bogeyman and Mlle. Vampire. The bride jilts the groom at the altar, sparking chaos and the need to quickly exit the mansion.

Here is a closer look at Ken Anderson's second revision of the Bloodmere Manor version of the Haunted Mansion, dated

September 17, 1957. It is one of the most detailed (24 pages, double-spaced) and atmospheric of the versions that Anderson submitted. Here is the first page:

> Guests will be admitted to the grounds through a large wrought-iron pedestrian-and-vehicle gate typical of New Orleans, circa 1800. The ticket booth will be located in the brick and plaster gatehouse which terminates the wrought-iron fence. Posted conspicuously on the gatehouse are copies of the *Times Picayune* and *Leslie's* magazine, with headlines about atrocities connected with the ghost house in the past.
>
> The approach to the house will be along paths lined with azaleas and moss-festooned magnolias and southern oak trees. The garden shows evidence of a once well-planned symmetry and beauty, but is now overgrown and obviously out of control.
>
> Vines and moss combined in the tall trees shut out much of the sunlight and lend mystery to the shadowy exterior of the house. Being set well back from the street behind the grove of trees, the house will be scarcely visible until close upon it. It appears to be in a state of dilapidation common to all ghost houses. First at one upstairs window and then another, a girl's face appears momentarily, screams, and is throttled by a large hairy hand which draws her back into the darkness.

Notations on this revision also indicate that Anderson had used his experience at the Winchester House to plan audience flow. He estimated that a group of no more than 40 guests would gather on the front porch to enter the house. At regularly spaced intervals of one-and-a-half minutes, around 8 groups of 40 guests each (320 guests total) could be in the house simultaneously, or a possible 16,000 visitors in a 10-hour schedule.

Anderson wrote:

> If the show in each room lasts a minute, it would leave 15 seconds to enter the room and 15 seconds to clear the room. We are conducting tests with groups of 40 people, using the *Zorro* sets [on the backlot of the Disney Studio in Burbank], to determine the practicality of this timing.
>
> In room clearance tests so far, times ranged from 15 seconds to 25 seconds, for an average of 20 seconds. As soon as construction of the test mock-ups for optical illusions are completed, we will utilize them for further crowd capacity tests; which will

include a one-minute show of the illusions. A tour of the house should take an average of about 12 minutes to complete.

The first episode of Disney's popular weekly television program *Zorro* appeared on ABC in October 1957, but workers had started building the sets in June 1955 and they were the Disney Studio's first permanent sets, costing more than $100,000. In 1957, the partial mock-up for the attraction was built on these sets and test audiences went through the different rooms.

For the front porch of the mansion, Anderson had written a one-and-a-half minute speech to be recorded by Walt Disney, which would have explained the strange history of the house and ended with Walt explaining:

> The guide is made necessary by another strange characteristic of the house. It has rotted so long in the dank vastness of its lost hiding place in the swamps that not even southern California sunshine or the best efforts of electricians and illumination engineers can dispel the dimness of the bayous... it mysteriously remains always night within the house...the night in which all ghosts are condemned to live.
>
> Now we cannot promise you that anything at all will occur during your visit...since it is usually in the wee small hours that the departed ones live it up... However, be prepared to see and hear something or other, and take whatever precautions you please. We recommend that you stay close together during your visit and please...above all...obey the guide's instructions. Thank you.

Using Anderson's own notes, as well as excerpts from interviews I did with him, we will go on a step-by-step walking tour of Bloodmere Manor, one of the earliest prototypes for the final Haunted Mansion. This information is from Anderson's September 17, 1957, final draft.

In the proposal, the Disney Company has relocated an authentic 1800s mansion from the swampy bayous around New Orleans to Disneyland, and strange occurrences have happened, including noises and people disappearing, but it will be safe enough as long as guests stay close to their butler guide.

Once inside the house, the guests would immediately experience some sound effects and even an invisible ghost writing

on the wall: "Foolish mortals... go home!" However, a butler appears and assures the guests they don't need to worry, "He's only a ghost writer!"

This is the first use of the term "foolish mortals" in connection with the mansion.

The butler explains that the last group he took through had the good fortune to see a good deal of ghostly activity. As the butler talks, a panel in the wall behind him opens and a "huge, hairy arm gropes menacingly", but the butler easily avoids it and warns the guests not to get too close to the walls and to stay with the group at all times during their visit "because Hairy the Arm, who was the insane brute of a man-servant for the old Blood family, delights in picking off stray visitors".

The group then passes through a gallery of portraits leading into the Library. The butler instructs the guests to come to the dead center so he can describe the portraits of the infamous ghosts because:

> The unfortunate Blood Family, which inhabited the house in life, had a tremendous circle of acquaintances and an international reputation as hosts.
>
> The supreme tragedy of the house occurred while the Blood Family was hosting numerous friends on the eve of the real-life wedding of their beautiful daughter. An event too horrible to mention prevented the wedding and it has been rumored that, on every anniversary for the last 150 years, the ghosts have been attempting to complete the ceremony which would lift the curse on the house.

An amazing thing about these portraits is that at first glance they appear quite normal, "but on second glance, the eyes of each portrait appear to stare back directly at the viewer and follow him relentlessly wherever he moves".

The guests are then led into a huge, dimly lit library. As the butler points out some of the items in the room, the group is joined by the "Lonesome Ghost" who is shunned by other ghosts because he likes people better than his ghostly peers.

At first, the group only hears the ghost, but then the butler directs them to look at the huge mirror hanging over the fireplace and the guests see not only their own reflection, but the image of the Lonesome Ghost apparently moving through

the group as he speaks. (This would have been a version of the Pepper's Ghost illusion.)

The Lonesome Ghost is excited because "two of our ghosts from prominent old ghost families are getting married" today. The ghost directs the guests' attention to more portraits in the Library. As he talks about each portrait, an eerie light illuminates it and the portrait changes.

Here are some of Ken Anderson's suggestions from 1957:

> As a typical example of the type of reaction, a portrait of the blue-blooded relative will seem to fill up with blue blood like a bottle filling with liquid, sound effects and all. Also, a maiden aunt with an austere face will coyly wink and the portrait of a gay blade will disintegrate ala Dorian Gray, etc.

Hairy the Arm makes another grab for the butler, who tells the group they will need to wait in the room for a bit, but the Lonesome Ghost suggests another alternative and suddenly the group hears his voice from an adjoining room beyond the walls. "Oh dear me," moans Lonesome, "I forgot you mortals can't walk through the walls... You'll have to use the bookcase..."

A bookcase creaks open allowing the guests to enter a room called the Gallery where they get to experience a screaming female ghost whose head separates from her body. It is the ghost of Anne Boleyn who was beheaded by her husband. "Of course, she'll have to pull herself together in time for the wedding," remarks Lonesome who will now disappear from the group for a while when the guests start to leave.

As the butler tries to lead the group out a large double door, the shadowy figure of Hairy the Arm is seen as it throws a knife which sticks in the wall across the room, forcing the guide to take the group through a secret wall panel.

In this new room, the butler is on the bedroom level when the group arrives at one end on a raised platform separated by a railing from the main floor. Originally, this platform was only a foot or two above the rest of the room, but now it has three separate levels so all the guests can see equally well into the bedroom.

There are a series of ghostly gags that take place here, including "five hideous little Charles Addams-type children

monsters who sit up in bed and glower at the visitors as they chorus: 'EEK! PEOPLE!'. A door opens revealing an invisible bather taking a bath using a visible sponge, brush, and wash cloth, and singing 'I'll Be Glad WhenYou're Dead You Rascal You'..." (It's our old friend, Lonesome, getting prepared for the wedding.)

During these displays, Hairy the Arm pulls the butler into the wall and the room goes pitch black with only the sounds of fighting and then silence. The lights come back on with a disheveled butler appearing to usher the guests into a large oval room called the Salon.

The room slants toward a large bay window that displays a windy moonlit scene of distant bayous. As the guests watch, clouds obscure the moon, there are flashes of thunder and lightning, and ghostly skeletons seem to rise from marble tombs and float toward them. There is a distant sound of pounding hoofs that signal the approach of the Headless Horseman, who is eventually seen galloping through the tops of the small trees and overgrown shrubs.

A fireplace near the guests mysteriously rises and Lonesome reappears to invite them to follow him to the wedding. The guests enter an octagonal-shaped room with rough unfinished walls and ceiling and windows on three sides with broken panes.

Suddenly, the storm breaks outside in full intensity with rain drenching the windows and more arriving ghosts (some with skeleton umbrellas). A series of brilliant lightning flashes reveal the transparency of the ceiling. As it becomes transparent, guests can see at the highest point in the peaked ceiling the ghost of a figure in full dress clothes...hanging by the neck.

Since the room seems to be filling up, the guests are ushered into another short mirrored hallway and as they look in the mirrors they see not only their own reflections, but the transparent reflections of ghostly visitors heading in the same direction.

Anderson wanted some of those ghosts to be famous, like Dracula, Frankenstein, the Hunchback of Notre Dame, the Phantom of the Opera, Scrooge and Marley, Little Eva and Simon Legree, Jack the Ripper, the Canterville Ghost, Captain

Hook, King Tut, and so forth. According to his notes, black-light would be used in this effect, as well.

Eventually, the guests would arrive in a large octagonal-shaped room with mirrors on all sides. Even the doors are mirrored, so that guests can clearly see all the ghosts in the mirrors who are attending the wedding and chattering away about the wedding gifts of a matched set of poisoned darts, guillotine book ends, etc. The Lonesome Ghost mingles through the group of ghosts.

The sound of wedding bells causes all the ghosts to disappear, leaving only the reflection of the guests who move into the great hall, where the wedding is to take place. On the lower floor is a long table with a wedding cake, candles, and flowers, all covered in cobwebs. An invisible ghost plays an old pump organ.

The groom appears, as does the bride on the opposite side who floats toward him. He tenderly reaches out and takes her head off and kisses it. She retaliates with a resounding slap. This action is repeated several times. This causes lights to flash, thunder claps, rattling shutters. The groom kisses her again and is slapped again.

Suddenly, the music gets faster and faster to crazy rhythm. Footprints run all around the floor and walls below, while furniture is upset and the organ is now joined by various floating jazz instruments. The storm builds to a climax. The ceiling collapses and lets the rain in.

As things intensify, the butler leads the guest into the Trophy Room, where the skulls of ghostly animals on the wall stare back at the group as the portraits did in the Portrait Hall. The group is rushed through a fireplace, still hearing the pounding rain and the loud chaos behind them. As they are led outside, they are surprised to see that it is not raining at all. (This is many years before the Enchanted Tiki Room, which used a similar effect at the end of the show.)

The butler attempts to discuss the Blood Family crypt and graves which the guests still have to visit, but Hairy the Arm grabs the butler and pulls him back into the house with a bloodcurdling yell. The tour is finished and apparently so is the poor tour guide.

Anderson even thought that an attraction should end in an area where guests could purchase merchandise related to their experiences. This concept later became commonplace at Disney theme parks, but here is the first time it is introduced. In the garden crypt:

> Visitors will be given the opportunity to buy pieces of ghost wedding cake neatly wrapped in shroud material, and tied with a bow of ribbon...suitable for placing under the pillow for inducing dreams; Lonesome Ghost lapel buttons, which plug a visit to the Ghost House; or Lonesome Ghost balloons, complete with floating China silk shrouds.

> In the high-walled and fenced garden, the visitors may take many paths all leading to the exit. There will be knee bones, foot bones, and skulls protruding occasionally from the silent paths. A statue in a secluded spot in the unkempt, overgrown garden animates mysteriously at timed intervals. In one corner of the garden is a typical graveyard with epitaphs to be inspected while closer to the exit gate is a wishing well with an echo effect.

Anderson moved back from WED to the studio in the late 1950s for a variety of reasons (including that, with the mounting costs on *Sleeping Beauty*, the animation department needed to be brought back under control, which is why Anderson proposed using xerography to save costs on hand inking cels) and spent much of the next several years working on the Disney animated feature films.

In 1964, Walt assigned the task of the Haunted Mansion to Marc Davis, Claude Coats, and X. Atencio. Imagineers Rolly Crump and Yale Gracey had been developing some illusions for a "Museum of the Weird" which would have been a "spill area" near the mansion where guests could enter and exit at their leisure before going through the main attraction, or after they had experienced it.

When Walt died, there was a struggle over creative direction between Marc Davis and Claude Coats. Davis wanted to emphasize characters and humor while Coats wanted to emphasize a terrifying atmosphere. Much of Coats' influence is seen in the first part of the attraction and much of Davis' contribution is in the second part.

This disjointed approach resulted in cast members and guests creating their own cohesive storyline for the attraction using bits and pieces of the various storylines from the original proposals.

Looking over Anderson's concepts from the late 1950s, it becomes apparent that he should receive greater recognition for his contribution to the attraction.

Just the short summary of one of his proposals reveals many elements, from the transparent ceiling revealing a hanged gentleman, to portraits which transformed humorously before your eyes, to looking in a glass reflection to see both a guest and a ghost, which are some of the most memorable experiences in the current Haunted Mansion.

With the introduction of the "doombuggies" to transport guests through the attraction, some of the things that Anderson had suggested were now no longer necessary or even effective since the pace of moving through the attraction was now controlled mechanically.

Today, the Haunted Mansion like Pirates of the Caribbean are considered iconic milestones in theme park attractions and still delight guests of all ages. Even though changes have been made to both attractions over the decades, their original core spirit still exists.

Master Gracey:
Haunted Mansion Illusioner

Yale Gracey was called an "Illusioner" in the days before the term "Imagineer" was officially coined. For those who worked with him, his boyish love of magic and the creation of unusual effects made him a modern Merlin the magician.

The prominent special effects in the Haunted Mansion were the work of Gracey. Today, if his name is known at all, it is because it is mistakenly believed that "Master Gracey" was the master of the haunted house—thanks to a tombstone in the outside graveyard written by Imagineeer X. Atencio, show writer for the attraction, that declares: "Master Gracey, laid to rest, no mourning please, at his request."

The belief that Gracey is the master of the mansion is so beguiling that it has retroactively been taken as fact so that even the horrible 2003 live-action film starring Eddie Murphy, and based on the Disney attraction, tried to make it officially part of the story.

As X. Atencio has said, at the turn of the century, the term "master" meant a boy too young to be called "mister." There are many examples in literature including "Master Lord Fauntleroy."

Atencio was trying to offer a tribute to his friend, the boyish Gracey, not make him the owner and master of the house. He was also trying to honor Gracey's many contributions to the project, especially the fact that his boyhood fondness for magic resulted in some of the illusions in the attraction.

Some misguided Disney cast members have even gone so far as to indicate that the aging "Dorian Grey" style portrait is a representation of "Master Gracey" or that the hanging man in the stretching gallery is the "master." None of those assumptions were intended by the original Imagineers.

Gracey was born in Shanghai, China in September 3, 1910. He was the son of the American consul and attended an

English boarding school. Among other training, he attended the Art Institute of Chicago, Art Center School of Design in Los Angeles, and the Chouinard Art Institute.

He joined the Disney Studios in 1939 as a layout artist working on *Pinocchio* and then later animated features including *Fantasia*. He continued to work on Disney animated films, including doing layouts and backgrounds on most of the Donald Duck shorts directed by Jack Hannah.

With the Disney Studios curtailing its productions of animated short cartoons, Hannah and most of his unit was shut down and left the Studios around 1959 to work for Walter Lantz and produce animated cartoons with Woody Woodpecker, Gabby Gator, and others.

One of the few who didn't go with Hannah was Gracey, who by then had found a home at WED. Walt Disney had noticed Gracey spending time during his lunch hours with making little gadgets and illusions.

One Saturday afternoon, on one of Walt's fabled tours of his artists' offices to poke around to see what they were doing, he found a mock-up Gracey had made of falling snow.

Walt was so impressed that Gracey was given a pair of rooms to develop new effects. His first assignment was to refresh some of the Fantasyland attractions, like coming up with the endless steam of tea pouring from the Mad Hatter's pot.

At first, Gracey was not assigned to specific projects, but just given unprecedented freedom to do research and development on things that Walt might make use of in some future project. It is important to remember that Gracey had no formal training at all in any of this, but just his own hands-on experimentation and reading.

Gracey was teamed up with Rolly Crump around 1959 and the two worked on several projects together, from updating the Fantasyland attractions (including volcano effects in Peter Pan's Flight) to early concept work for the Haunted Mansion.

Yale later admitted he had never seen a firefly in his life after he recreated the firefly effect for the Blue Bayou area of Pirates of the Caribbean.

Imagineer Rock Hall told me in an interview in 2010:

Delicate effects such as Blue Bayou fireflies were a specialty of his. He constantly complained that the replacements were never done according to the original design and every time someone tried to improve on them they fouled their performance in one way or another. Yale could show you the right way to build a firefly like no one else could.

Gracey grew up as a shy young boy, fascinated by issues of *Popular Mechanics* magazine and he had a complete set of the *The Boy Mechanic* series of books published by *Popular Mechanics* in the early teens of the 20th century.

The Boy Mechanic series featured hundreds of projects for boys from magic tricks to building kites and tie racks to making boomerangs. Some of the other projects may see a little outdated today—including chemical photography and coal furnaces.

In addition, some of these projects include the use of gunpowder, mercury, sulfuric acid, nitric acid, hydrogen, and other things that would be highly inappropriate for young boys to handle in these more enlightened times to build devices.

The Boy Mechanic series sparked in Gracey an interest in gadgetry and magic that eventually led to him creating many amazing effects at Disney theme parks, like a pixie dust projector used in Space Mountain to block out the surrounding structure.

The famous ghosts in the ballroom scene of the Haunted Mansion owe their magic not to holographic projections or, as Imagineer Tony Baxter loves to quip "real ghosts," but to the "Pepper's Ghost" illusion that was refined by magician Henry Pepper in 1862 for his stage act.

Gracey first encountered this amazing yet simple illusion in *The Boy Mechanic*, Volume 1 page 52 from 1913. There were multiple volumes of *The Boy Mechanic* published over the years. His original collection contained just four volumes. Crump, who also does magic as a hobby, has a 1916 reprint of Volume 1 in his personal collection.

There have been many reprints over the years, including an excellent facsimile edition in 1988. Supposedly, girls would not be interested in these adventurous projects, but there is one picture of a girl in the book making a lampshade.

Here is the explanation from Gracey's copy of Volume 1, page 52 from 1913.

The title page declares:

THE BOY MECHANIC: 700 THINGS FOR BOYS TO DO

HOW TO CONSTRUCT WIRELESS OUTFITS, BOATS, CAMP EQUIPMENT, AERIAL GLIDERS, KITES, SELF-PROPELLED VEHICLES ENGINES, MOTORS, ELECTRICAL APPARATUS, CAMERAS AND HUNDREDS OF OTHER THINGS WHICH DELIGHT EVERY BOY

WITH 800 ILLUSTRATIONS

COPYRIGHTED, 1913, BY H. H. WINDSOR CHICAGO POPULAR MECHANICS CO. PUBLISHERS

A Miniature "Pepper's Ghost" Illusion

Probably many readers have seen a "Pepper's Ghost" illusion at some amusement place. As there shown, the audience is generally seated in a dark room at the end of which there is a stage with black hangings. One of the audience is invited onto the stage, where he is placed in an upright open coffin.

A white shroud is thrown over his body, and his clothes and flesh gradually fade away till nothing but his skeleton remains, which immediately begins to dance a horrible rattling jig. The skeleton then fades away and the man is restored again.

A simple explanation is given in the model engineer. Between the audience and the coffin is a sheet of transparent glass, inclined at an angle so as to reflect objects located behind the scenes, but so clear as to be invisible to the audience and the man in the coffin.

At the beginning the stage is lighted only from behind the glass. Hence the coffin and its occupant are seen through the glass very plainly. The lights in front of the glass (behind the scenes) are now raised very gradually as those behind the glass are turned down, until it is dark there.

The perfectly black surface behind the glass now acts like the silver backing for a mirror, and the object upon which the light is now turned -- in this case the skeleton -- is reflected in the glass, appearing to the audience as if really occupying the stage.

The model, which requires no special skill except that of carpentry, is constructed as shown in the drawings.

The box containing the stage should be 14 inches by 7 inches by 7-1/2 inches, inside dimensions. The box need not be made of particularly good wood, as the entire interior, with the exception of the glass, figures and lights, should be colored a dull black. This can well be done by painting with a solution of lampblack in turpentine. If everything is not black, especially the joints and background near A, the illusion will be spoiled.

The glass should be the clearest possible, and must be thoroughly cleansed. Its edges should nowhere be visible, and it should be free from scratches and imperfections. The figure A should be a doll about 4 inches high, dressed in brilliant, light-colored garments.

The skeleton is made of papier maché, and can be bought at Japanese stores. It should preferably be one with arms suspended by small spiral springs, giving a limp, loose-jointed effect. The method of causing the skeleton to dance is shown in the front view.

The figure is hung from the neck by a blackened stiff wire attached to the hammer wire of an electric bell, from which the gong has been removed. When the bell works he will kick against the rear wall, and wave his arms up and down, thus giving as realistic a dance as anyone, could expect from a skeleton.

The lights, L and M, should be miniature electric lamps, which can be run by three dry cells. They need to give a fairly strong light, especially L, which should have a conical tin reflector to increase its brilliancy and prevent its being reflected in the glass.

Since the stage should be some distance from the audience, to aid the illusion, the angle of the glass and the inclination of the doll, A, has been so designed that if the stage is placed on a mantle or other high shelf, the image of A will appear upright to an observer sitting in a chair some distance away, within the limits of an ordinary room. If it is desired to place the box lower down, other angles for the image and glass may be found necessary, but the proper tilt can be found readily by experiment.

The electric connections are so simple that they are not shown in the drawings. All that is necessary is a two-point switch by which either L or M can be placed in circuit with the battery and a press button in circuit with the bell and its cell.

If a gradual transformation is desired, a double-pointed rheostat could be used, so that as one light dims the other increases in brilliancy, by the insertion and removal of resistance coils.

With a clear glass and a dark room this model has proved to be fully as bewildering as its prototype.

To demonstrate the effect and how it worked for Walt Disney, Gracey built a working miniature model. It was a box about three feet square. There was a slot at the top of the front side where a viewer could look. Pushing a button the lights come on and the ghosts sweep through the scale model. It is now housed at the Magic Castle in Southern California.

Gracey built another model of a skeleton ghost playing a pipe organ using the Pepper's Ghost illusion that was showcased on the *Disneyland 10th Anniversary* January 3,1965 episode of the *Walt Disney's Wonderful World of Color*.

One afternoon Walt came to see what Gracey and Crump were working on and decided that all three of them should go catch an afternoon matinee of the new William Castle movie *13 Ghosts* (1960).

The film featured the gimmick "Illusion—O" which were cardboard glasses with colored filters given to each member of the audience. If they looked through the red lens they could see the ghosts but if they looked through the blue lens, the ghosts disappeared. Periodically a caption flashes on the screen to alert the audience to put on their glasses because a ghost was going to appear.

The plot was that reclusive Dr. Zorba died and left his eerie mansion to his family. Zorba was an occultist and had collected twelve ghosts who could only be seen through special goggles. Hidden somewhere in the house is a fortune so the family stays and deals with the ghosts to try and find it.

"It was an absolutely horrible movie," Crump recalled. "We didn't learn anything except maybe what not to try to do."

One afternoon, Crump casually asked Gracey if he had ever seen a ghost and was surprised by Gracey's response.

When he was ten years old, young Master Gracey went to visit his aunt back East and stayed with his cousins in one big bedroom. They had a great deal of fun together.

Near the end of the trip that summer, his mother asked him what he enjoyed most about the visit. Without hesitation, he responded that he enjoyed "the little old woman who lives in the closet who comes out each night to read stories to us."

The other children became upset and tried to silence Gracey from sharing the secret, but were unsuccessful. Gracey's mother did some research at the local library and discovered that there was a woman who looked just like the one Gracey described who once owned the house but had died some time earlier.

As the children feared, once Gracey blurted out the story, the old woman never appeared again to read stories to the children.

"Yale would never make anything up. He was about as straight as they came," Crump said at a presentation. "As far as I'm concerned it's true. It can't be any truer than that."

In the February 1971 issue of the magazine *Famous Monsters of Filmland* #82, shortly after the Haunted Mansion opened at Disneyland, Gracey shared his thoughts about the mansion in these previously forgotten quotes:

> Often I simply don't know that something couldn't be done. I would develop a concept and gather various gadgets and materials and keep trying until it worked. When we built the illusions we were surprised to find how effective they actually were.

> People enjoy being frightened but we couldn't make the attraction too scary because of the droves of children that would be coming. We decided to add the element of comedy. It's like adding a wink of an eye to the end of a ghost story. Someday I would like to design a real scare house. Some of the illusions that weren't used in the Haunted Mansion would send chills through anyone I know.

One paragraph in the story included the following statement: "Using refracted images, half-silvered mirrors, Audio-Animatronics and projectimation, Gracey and his ghostly helpers designed and built enough illusions to fill the new attraction twice over."

The term "projectimation" was never used anywhere else and referred to the effect of Madame Leota's head in the crystal ball and the four singing busts.

It was a new effect discovered by Gracey when he experimented with using film of Hans Conried's talking head from the Magic Mirror on the 1956 Disney television show episode *Our Unsung Villains* and projecting it on a bust of Beethoven. While it didn't sync exactly, it appeared as if the bust came to life and began talking and encouraged Gracey to develop it even further.

Unfortunately, many of the most fantastic (and never re-created) effects that Gracey and Crump developed were never used in the attraction when it was changed from a walk-through event (with more time for guests to see an effect evolve) to a moving vehicle, which meant the animation had to be short cycled because it could not be determined whether a guest would see the beginning, middle or end of the cycle of action.

Guests pass a room where they see the coffin lid before it is being lifted, in the process of being lifted, as it shakes in the air or has dropped back into place. That is the voice of X. Atencio plaintively crying "Let me out!"

As Crump once lamented about one of those never-used effects:

> There was one gag that Yale and I came up with. We developed the whole story for that room. It was a Sea Captain's room. That's where he lived. He had killed his wife, and bricked her up in the fireplace. He drowned out at sea. As the story goes, he would periodically come back to his room. We actually had a full scale mock-up of this on the soundstage to show Walt.
>
> You'd see the curtains blowing. You could see the ocean off in the distance, the waves breaking. You could hear the cry of a coyote or wolf. We had a lot of special effects that we'd put into that.
>
> Then all of a sudden, this skeleton with a rain slicker and hat holding a lantern appears slowly but surely in the middle of the room. We actually had a shower of water that was coming off of him onto the floor. It looked like water was running all over the floor.
>
> It was one hell of an illusion! As he kind of turns and looks around the room, you see her ghost skeleton appear behind the bricks—and all of a sudden she comes flying out! She has

a white silk outfit on, she raises her arms, and with her mouth wide open, screaming, coming right at him and you—they both just disappear.

I think that would have done the job. That was the best piece of Pepper's Ghost that'd been done. Of course, that went down the tubes, because everything in there was now quick-cycle animation.

Yale and I worked for a year developing illusions. Because I wasn't involved in the final Haunted Mansion at all, I would say that out of all of the illusions that Yale and I did, 25 percent were used. That was based on the change of the storyline, because when we worked on it, it was a walkthrough.

When they made it into a ride that eliminated a lot of the illusions that we had presented, because they wouldn't work in a ride. They would only work if you had the audience standing still for a bit. I really think that would have made the Mansion, a far better attraction than what it is.

In 2010, Imagineer Rock Hall who began working at Disney in 1982 on the New Fantasyland told me:

For most of my time there (at WED) I was located at the Tujunga building. My office was there and for much of the time I shared that office with Yale Gracey.

Yale was a sweet mild-mannered guy, polite and respectful at all times. He worked at a very meticulous pace, setting up his illusions with everything done to a precise level. He got a real kick out of illusions that were done with the unique use of optics. Parabolic mirrors, Pepper's Ghost type effects, sculpture and lighting tricks, you name it.

He always said that the best effects were simple effects like finding out that a sculpted face when vacuum formed and viewed from the back seems to follow you. This was an accidental development that Yale discovered and ended up using in the hallway at the Haunted Mansion.

He talked a lot about Walt and the way it used to be. Walt gave the people he trusted *carte blanche* to create and design using their own unique ideas to help his visions come true. It was great back in those days he said. Every day became fun and rewarding. He also talked a lot about a book that Walt gave him in which many of his co-workers had signed and decorated.

As you might imagine every animator left his mark in Yale's book. He showed everyone this book and was so proud of it. I believe this was one of his favorite things. Unfortunately I seem to remember that this was stolen from him and never recovered. This would be a very valuable book and its loss absolutely crushed him.

Now mind you Yale told me all this after lunch. Yale had two martinis at lunch. Yale always had his martini lunches; it was his tradition. The last thing I remember him working on was a parabolic reflection of a hummingbird sipping from a flower.

This created a virtual image out in space. He was great with these types of effects. The sinking ship in a bottle effect was very similar with video projections replacing drum projectors and more mechanical animation.

After thirty-six years with the company, Gracey retired October 4, 1975. He continued to consult on special effects and lighting for attractions at Walt Disney World and EPCOT Center in Florida.

He was quiet and not much has been written about him since he was not a self-promoter. Perhaps the most mysterious thing about him was his death.

On September 5, 1983, 73-year-old Yale and his wife Beverly were in a cabana at the Bel Air Bay Club on the beach at Pacific Palisades when a transient broke in at 2:30 a.m. and tragically shot to death the sleeping Imagineer and wounded his wife.

The motivation behind this senseless murder is still not known to this day. The assailant fled on to the beach and was never caught. There were no suspects.

Writer Rick West interviewed Yale's friend Imagineer Marc Davis about this incident for *Theme Park Adventure* magazine:

Yale Gracey was a very fascinating, interesting guy, whose life was very, very unique.

He had a cabana down at the beach, Santa Monica, with his wife. This was a club kind of thing. They went down there one night and spent the night in their little cabana. Somehow or another, somebody came along. We don't know what happened for sure. There are thoughts but nobody really knows for sure.

Somebody shot Yale to death and wounded his wife in this cabana. Here was this guy who created all of these magic

things. If you wanted fireflies, this was the guy who would figure out how to do them. He was the guy who created the fire effects for Pirates, and the magic effects for the Haunted Mansion. All of that was Yale Gracey.

He was a great guy. I never drink a Manhattan without saying...[my wife] Alice and I agree on this..."Here's to Yale!'"Because that's all he drank. He made an enormous contribution to the Disney attractions. It was a great loss.

Yale married Beverly in 1946 and they raised two sons named Wayne and Lucky.

The Gracey brothers clearly loved their father, who would often do homemade magic tricks around the kitchen table at dinner for them. One of the things he left them was a huge box of homemade magic tricks, but without any instructions on how to work them.

Wayne told me: "We also inherited his collection of his smoking pipes. He loved his pipes and you will see him with one in just about every photo. Dad was always a 'tinkerer'. He figured that if he just kept working at something he would figure it out. He was a professional photographer and his work was on the cover of several magazines. Sometimes the cover featured artwork he did."

On September 30, 2017 I was a speaker at the Disneyana Fan Club Happy Haunts evening event at the Disneyland Hotel Magic Kingdom ballroom where the Haunted Mansion was being honored. I had the opportunity to talk with Gracey's two sons who also attended the event. Unfortunately, only a month later their mother passed away on November first.

Both of Gracey's sons spent had a little time working in Imagineering themselves, primarily in "traffic" which meant delivering mail and doing errands.

Wayne told me:

> Mom didn't work at Disney. He met her somewhere else and it was not love at first sight for her. Dad really had to be persistent. He was ten years older than she was but once they got married, nobody could have loved each other more.
>
> Dad took me into the ballroom of the Haunted Mansion and pointed at these mannequins hanging on the other side of this glass to try to explain to me what he was trying to do

and I didn't get it at all. Then, when I rode the attraction, it all made sense to me.

Lucky told me:

> We still have Dad's copy of the *Boy Mechanic* books where he got the idea. In fact, we have a handwritten journal he did listing all the illusions he built and how they worked. He always tried to do it the simple way because at Disneyland these things had to run 16 hours every day of the week for years.

In preparation for the event, the men had looked around to see if they could bring anything interesting to show. They found the original skull for the Hatbox Ghost in the back of a closet before their trip down to the event. It had been rejected because it was too scary and stark so a different head was sculpted for the short-lived figure in the original attraction.

Yale Gracey was the master of creating things that had never been created before and making them seem natural and realistic whether it was the city in flames in the Pirates of the Caribbean attraction (that was so realistic that the Anaheim fire department insisted on an emergency switch to shut it off so they could tell what was the real fire and to diminish some of the other related effects, like a smoky smell) or the Hatbox Ghost in the Haunted Mansion where its head would disappear from its shoulders and then reappear in the hatbox it was holding.

Imagineer John Hench recalled:

> Whenever we needed a special effect, we went to Yale. Sometimes it took a while to get what we were asking for, however, because along the way he'd develop other marvelous effects we could use.

Imagineer Bob Gurr said:

> He'd literally sit in his room and fiddle with stuff, and occasionally invent something. Walt was totally happy with that... Yale was good at figuring out physical gags. Then somebody working on a project would find a way to weave Yale's gag into their show story. He would often have things on the shelf that we could use later.

DISNEY WITCHES

Witches have had a long history with Halloween. Legends tell of witches gathering twice a year when the seasons changed on April 30 (the eve of May Day) and on October 31 (All Hallow's Eve).

The witches would gather on these nights, called the Witches' Sabbath, to celebrate with the devil. It was widely assumed that the gatherings included promiscuous sex, naked dancing, and gluttonous feasting on the flesh of human infants with the devil himself actively participating.

These traditional superstitions and more were brought over to America from Europe. Just as with any group, Wiccans, witches, neopagans and others who include the practice of some form of witchcraft in their beliefs and life-styles are all different with different agendas. Witchcraft remains a deeply personal practice.

It wasn't until the early Renaissance that our modern perception of what a witch looks like was probably formed by the work of German painter and printmaker Albrecht Dürer.

In *Witch Riding Backwards on a Goat* (circa 1500) a naked crone sits on top of a horned goat (a symbol of the devil). She has withered, drooping breasts and her mouth is open as she shrieks spells. She is even clutching a broomstick which was considered an icon of womanhood (men witches rode demon horses when they flew).

Generally images of witches in artwork depicted an under-lying misogyny. Since it was generally older women who were often accused, it is not unusual that the image of a woman bent over with warts or a hooked nose became standard. Of course, in the 20th century, witches were often scantily clad enchantresses that were less Salem and more sexy.

In modern culture, the witch has been portrayed as a benevolent, nose-twitching suburban housewife; an awkward teenager learning to control her powers and a trio of charmed sisters battling the forces of evil.

Since the many worlds of Disney feature various forms of magic, it is not unusual to find that the Disney universe includes a wide variety of witch characters from Eglantine Price (*Bedknobs and Broomsticks*) to Ursula the sea witch (*The Little Mermaid*) to the broom-flying, pointy-hatted witch in the Silly Symphony *Babes in the Woods*.

Miss Eglantine Price is a patriotic woman living in World War II England. She is also a witch in training taking a mail-order Witchcraft Correspondence Course with Professor Emelius Browne. She hopes to learn as her final lesson the spell for Substitutiary Locomotion, the power to give life to inanimate objects. When the lessons unexpectedly stop, she goes in search of the Professor and the spell.

When Nazis invade her hometown, she is able to enchant all of the armor in the castle and lead a magical army on her broomstick to drive the invaders out of England. However, they have left a bomb that blows up her workshop with all her witchcraft notes, equipment, and supplies like the Poisoned Dragon's Liver, so when it's destroyed it deactivates all of her spells and she must be content to live the rest of her life as a normal woman.

The witch in the Silly Symphony *Babes in the Woods* (1932) is unnamed in this very loose adaptation of the Hansel and Gretel story. While several animators worked on the character, Norm Ferguson who would later animate the witch in *Snow White* handles the scenes of her inside the cottage. Lucille La Verne provides the voice for the witch as she would in *Snow White*. At the end, the witch falls into a cauldron of her own potion and petrifies into stone so the area is now called Witch Rock.

The Evil Queen and Wicked Witch

The Evil Queen and Wicked Witch in Disney's first animated feature film *Snow White and the Seven Dwarfs* (1937) is one of the most iconic villains of all time and can still generate a feeling of dread for modern audiences.

Actress Mariette Hartley (who starred in the 1973 Disney movie *The Mystery of Dracula's Castle*) mentioned how the Disney witch terrified her as a young girl in the October 27, 1979 issue of *Family Weekly*:

> The thought of witches terrified me. That's because the first film I saw, when I was four years old, was *Snow White and the Seven Dwarfs*. I was so frightened of the witch that, for years afterward, especially on Halloween, I had nightmares about witches. The one in *Snow White* was so graphic, so close to reality. I'll never forget those long, red fingernails.

The character of the Evil Queen/Wicked Witch is completely evil with no redeeming qualities at all. She doesn't kill Snow White with a poisoned apple but puts her into a coma-like sleeping death that she hopes the dwarfs will mistake for actual death and bury the little princess alive. This act is not in retaliation for anything Snow White has done or said but purely as an act of vanity.

The impact of the character and the film as a whole was thanks to Walt Disney's ruthless editing of superficial scenes that disrupted the emotional continuity of the story.

The well-known animated film is a sanitized version of the original tale recorded by brothers Jacob and Wilhelm Grimm and published in 1812. The Grimms were German scholars, researchers and authors who collected folktales but almost immediately started making changes in the stories in subsquent editions to match their own philosophies.

In the first version of the story, the Queen was Snow White's mother (not her stepmother), the young girl was rescued by her father (no prince in the story), the queen painted her face to disguise herself, and Snow White was almost killed twice by the disguised Queen before finally biting into a poisoned apple.

As late as a March 1937 story conference, Walt suggested alluding to the first two attempts. Walt said:

> Downstairs she could be building up to the disguise—choosing something so no one would recognize her. 'Ah, the old pedlar woman!' like she remembers it...'The pedlar woman—what could she sell?—Combs soaked in poison—the hair will stiffen like a board. A corset—lace it tight!' So many people remember those old things from the fairy tale.

Walt chose the fairy tale for his first film for several reasons including that it was a good, solid story with lots of interesting character possibilities. However, an emotional reason was that when he was a fifteen year old boy, he saw a film version at Kansas City's huge Convention Hall in January 1917. It was a reward for his work as a *Kansas City Star* newspaper boy.

Four prints of the film were projected on a giant four-sided screen suspended in the middle of the hall. Walt was in a loft gallery seat so he could see two different screens at once.

Walt wrote in 1938:

> My impression of the picture stayed with me through the years. From the spot where I viewed the picture I was able to watch two screens at the same time. I could look at one screen and tell what was going to happen on the next. I remember the show very well, and I am sure it will remain a vivid reality with me the rest of my life.

The 1916 Paramount silent film had elements that Walt later incorporated into his final film including giving the dwarfs individual names (and some of the bits of business done by the dwarfs), an animal warning the dwarfs that Snow White was in trouble and the apple rolling out of the hand of the collapsed Snow White among other things.

One element that he did not borrow was that in the black-and-white film the queen (Queen Brangomar) and the witch (Witch Hex) were two separate characters in order for

the witch to have some comedic moments while the queen remained a true threat.

Of course, the original proposal for Disney's witch was also to make her an exaggerated comic looking crone similar to the version that had appeared in the Silly Symphony short *Babes in the Wood* (1932), a brief re-telling of the famous Hansel and Gretel story but incorporating little male gnomes to save the children.

An early story conference suggested that when the Queen transformed "warts pop out of her face –Ping! Ping! Ping! Also hairs out of the warts." However, as the Disney film kept developing, it was obvious that a more serious approach needed to be taken for the characters of the Queen and Witch in the feature film to create a genuine sense of danger.

An October 22, 1934 story outline stated:

> The Queen: A mixture of Lady Macbeth and the Big Bad Wolf—her beauty is sinister, mature, plenty of curves—she becomes ugly and menacing when scheming and mixing her poitons—Magic fluids transform her into an old witch-like hag—Her dialogue and action are over-dramatic, verging on the ridiculous...

The scenes for the Queen and the Witch were co-written by Joe Grant who designed the characters, Bill Cottrell who would direct the Queen and Witch scenes and Dorothy Ann Blank, a former East Coast newspaper woman in her late 30s at the time who struggled over the dialog often writing and rewriting. She is the one credited specifically with the "Mirror, mirror on the wall" and the magic spell speeches.

Walt and his brother Roy had been working closely with Hal Horne, publicity director for United Artists that had been distributing the Disney shorts and who employed Blank. When Horne left United Artists, Blank became am member of the Disney Studio in 1936 and brought a unique female perspective to the two characters.

Fellow storyman and character designer Joe Grant was laudatory about her contributions and frequently sketched her surreptitiously. She eventually confronted him, demanding to know why he was drawing her.

"I'm modeling your face for one of our characters in *Snow White*." replied Grant. "The Evil Queen."

He was fascinated by her arched eyebrows, her almond-shaped eyes, and her long, straight nose. However, the final version of the character was a combination of other inspirations as well including some current movie actresses Joan Crawford, Katherine Hepburn and Helen Gahagan as well as masks by W.T. Benda.

Grant would base his model sheet for the Witch on the face of actress Lucille La Verne who was providing the voice for the character. She had a small build, long-hair, very intense eyes, and a husky voice and had no hesitation sacrificing her looks for her craft.

At voice recording sessions, he would sketch her furiously. He noticed La Verne's changing attitude and posture when voicing the Queen and Witch, and sketched those poses down for reference.

Grant had been given an interpretation of the character done early in production by artist Gustaf Tenggren but he would greatly refine it making the character very much his own design.

Grant said:

> The Witch was conceived before Lucille (Laverne, the voice for the character) was cast but I would say that she inspired the final model sheet. We picked up her expressions, which were very broad and caricatured. What inspired me about the character was John Barrymore in *Dr. Jekyll and Mr. Hyde* (1931) like the bug eyes for the Witch.

Layout artist Ken O'Connor shared with Steve Hulett the following memory from the Carthay Circle premiere of the film:

> I was sitting near John Barrymore when the shot of the Queen's castle above the mist came on with the Queen poling across the marsh in a little boat. He was bouncing up and down in his seat he was so excited. Barrymore was an artist as well as an actor, and he knew the kind of work that went into something like that.

The staff had a clear idea of how evil and crafty the Witch needed to be portrayed. On the evening of October 30, 1934 (the day before Halloween) to convince his staff that they could and should make an animated feature, Walt gave them

all money to go and have dinner. When they returned, he had them sit in an empty soundstage at the Hyperion Studio while he acted out the entire story and all the characters.

As artist Ken Anderson remembered:

> [Walt] proceeded to intrigue us from eight o'clock until early midnight acting and telling the story. He became all these characters. He became the dwarfs. He became the witch. He so thrilled us with the complete recitation of all the characters that he had created that we were just carried away. We wanted to do this!

Art Babbitt was assigned as the lead animator on the Queen and rejected using much of the rotoscope footage. Although up to that time, he was primarily known for his outstanding animation on Goofy, Babbitt had a passion for movement analysis and did study the live action footage but refused to be confined by it.

It was difficult for the animators to capture her regal beauty and graceful movements since she did not do the usual broad gestures and facial expressions common in animation. Both Snow White and the Queen have two lip colors, with the upper lip being darker to help give greater dimension to the character's mouth.

For the transformation scene, Bob Stokes did much of the animation of the queen questioning the mirror, descending the steps to the laboratory, and the business with the book. Sam Dawson also assisted on that scene. It was Babbitt who had her turn the pages, recite the spell, mix the chemicals and the business with the glass.

Norm Ferguson was assigned as the lead animator on the witch with John Lounsberry as his main assistant. Tony Rivera also assisted. Ferguson was known for his animation on Pluto and the Big Bad Wolf.

Fergy, as he was called, had a loose drawing style that allowed for a lot of expressiveness in his characters. Lounsberry was a fine draftsman and was able to compensate for any of Fergy's technical flaws in this style of drawing.

Grant said:

> It wasn't good drawing but (Ferguson) put such character into the animation. Everything was extreme, you know and it just felt right.

Many believe that the real magic of the Queen and the Witch was because of their distinctive voices both done by the same actress.

Lucille La Verne was born November 7, 1872 and died March 4, 1945 at the age of 72 from cancer. She had just turned 65 years old when the film premiered.

After doing the roles of the Queen and the Witch, she retired from acting and became a co-owner of a successful nightclub. She was first diagnosed with cancer in 1933, forcing her to have two surgeries. The cancer resurfaced in 1937, after which she then retired from acting and had more surgery. The cancer came back for a third time in January 1945, and claimed her life four months later.

She was an accomplished stage and film actress with a lengthy and celebrated career in both venues when she was hired to do the voice. Her most famous onscreen performance prior to *Snow White* was probably the toothless, cackling insurrectionist in *A Tale of Two Cities* (1935).

She began acting on stage as a child and later had her own traveling theatrical company that toured the U.S. and Europe as well as briefly having a New York theater named after her.

She had received acclaim for her portrayal of Lady Macbeth when she was only fourteen years old and years later she played the role of Shylock in *The Merchant of Venice*. Although she played many lead roles, she specialized in character parts especially unlikeable old hags, slum mothers and rough frontierswomen including a hillbilly matriarch.

She had many silent film credits including *Orphans of the Storm* (1921) where as an old harridan she harrassed poor little Dorothy Gish. Her debut in sound films included *Little Caesar* (1930) with Edward G. Robinson where she was a slatternly underworld fence and *Sinner's Holiday* (1930) where she played petty crook Jimmy Cagney's mother.

Bill Cottrell remembered in an interview with historian David Johnson:

> [Lucille] was mostly a stage actress. When the voices were brought in, there were radio shows that had witches in them, old crones. They all had a pattern that was a cliché, almost as if crones all talk this same way and so on.

After seeing a bunch of these, they all seemed rather uninteresting because you'd heard the same thing on radio for so many years. Lucille Laverne was brought in late one afternoon. She was almost brusque. This was a no-nonsense character. She took the script from me and read it without looking at the storyboard. You could have made a take of that voice that she read as the Queen.

She was a professional actress, and I think when she was told the Queen is a vain, imperialistic personality she visualized something. She read the lines beautifully and then when she went into the Witch with the maniacal laugh; it rang over the soundstage. It was blood curdling.

We weren't thinking of having one actress do both parts. With the Queen's voice, no one read with any great authority or with anything outstanding. We made a test of her voice and ran it for Walt. He said, "That's it!"

She was rather serious and she lived in Pasadena, I believe. I enjoyed her performance very much and I appreciated it and I enjoyed being with her on the set. She was not that outgoing. I think for her it was just a business thing. Come in and shoot it and go home.

At first Cottrell and Grant didn't feel she quite captured the sense of menace as the Witch. Overhearing this conversation, Lucille excused herself for a moment and left the room. When she returned, she did the lines again and amazed Cottrell and Grant.

Since they had no experience dealing with live performers, they asked what she had done in preparation outside the room in order to get into just the right sound for the character.

Lucille smiled, "I just took out my teeth."

Grant remembered:

Lucille was already a very famous stage and film actress. She was very willing and very obliging. When she first did the voice we didn't think it was 'witchy' enough and then she came up with the idea of taking her teeth out.

As a result of it, it gave that wet sort of sound. Her jaws collapsed and she was the witch. She was a pro. We did not have to do too many takes with her, only to try a different interpretation. She was dressed with a cape on.

Some at the studio though Lucille sounded too old for the queen but as director Dave Hand said:

> The main point of argument is really that La Verne knows how to deliver lines. We are willing to sacrifice a little to get that correct delivery, that punch we need.

When one of the writers of the scenes suggested a change in the Witch's dialogue, Walt responded:

> All the dialogue sounded bad to me until she [Lucille] read it.

By having Lucille voice both roles helped unify the two characters despite the differences in their voices and performances. It was now clear that the two characters were just different facets of the same person. The crippled evil inside the Queen manifested itself physically when she transformed into the Witch.

Over the decades, official materials from the Walt Disney Company have sometimes depicted them as being different entities. The Queen's name has sometimes been given as "Queen Grimhilde" in some old publicity material and comics, but the Walt Disney Company does not acknowledge that name as canon.

Lucille La Verne reprised her role as the Evil Queen/Wicked Witch in two radio performances. The Chase & Sandborn radio show starring Edgar Bergen and Charlie McCarthy on December 19, 1937 just two days before the premiere of the film featured the film's cast including Lucille playing both the Queen and the Witch. McCarthy tricks the witch and locks her and her apples in a closet to protect Snow White.

Bergen said at one point:

> Doc is trying to tell you the Queen is here. You won't like her. She turns into a witch and kills people. She's jealous of Snow White and she's trying to kill her. She's even gone so far as to put poison in apples.

"That sounds like a lot of applesauce, Bergen," replied Charlie.

On the *Mickey Mouse Theater of the Air* episode entitled *Snow White Day* on January 9, 1938, the witch approaches Walt with a basket of apples and says, "Hello, Disney! Have a bite?"

After Lucille's death many other actresses took over the role in animation, on stage and in live action.

Today, voice actress Susanne Blakeslee often does the roles in animation and video games. She has also voiced Malificent, Lady Tremaine, Cruella de Ville and others.

Louise Chamis was the voice of the Queen and the Witch in the original version of the theme park show *Fantasmic!* and also voiced the characters in *Disney on Ice* shows from 1986—2001 as well as some video games.

Actress Lana Parrilla played the Evil Queen in the *Once Upon A Time* television series and said, said that whenever she watched the animated feature film as a young girl she rooted for and "loved the evil queen—every time the evil queen came on, I was like 'OK!' She was just so fascinating to me."

Co-creator of the series Adam Horowitz said that his earliest Disney memory was seeing a re-release of Disney's *Snow White* when he was "terrified by the Evil Queen while also being unable to look away and that stuck with me through the years."

Jane Fowler who was working at the studio and later married Jack Boyd did live action reference modeling for the Queen but they also brought in a woman whose name no one seems to remember who had acted in feature films.

It was not unusual for Disney to film several different performers for a particular character. For instance, both Hans Conreid and actor Henry Brandon donned the costume of Captain Hook for live action footage reference.

Bill Cottrell who directed the scenes of the Queen and the Witch told historian Dave Johnson:

> We wanted to shoot live action of the character in costume to establish her, particularly with the queen and the witch, to establish certain actions and motions rather than let the animator have to figure it all out. We were doing it to playback and (Lucille La Verne) was not able to do it very well to playback.
>
> She just heard it and it's synced so that her action is synced with the voice so as she moves. Even though it was her own voice, somehow or other I think the timing confused her or something wasn't right. She was not used to that type of thing, so she would act the way she was thinking at the time, regardless of the voice.
>
> She was not in sync with the tempo. She was used to a stage play wherein she had time to make a speech, time to move across the stage and so forth. So we had to get a substitute.

Ward Kimball remembered that they brought in actor Nestor Paiva who had done the villain in the long running Los Angeles stage play *The Drunkard* to perform scenes as the Witch. Kimball said, "He knew all those old stage gestures. The Witch (animation by Ferguson) was much broader: twice, three times as broad as the rotoscope performance."

Marge Champion who did live action reference modeling for the character of Snow White remembered:

> For the Witch, they used Paul Godkin, who was also one of my father's pupils at the dance school but also studied with a woman named Carmelita Marachi. I remember filming scenes with him as the Witch. Paul and I danced together in a show called *Beggar's Holiday*. It was at the Broadway Theater. We got to be great friends.

However, Godkin was soon replaced by Don Brodie as the live action reference model for the witch. Brodie (May 29, 1904—January 8, 2001) did the voice of Devil Donald in *Donald's Better Self* (1938), The carnival barker in *Pinocchio* (1940), live action reference modeling for Gepetto and even several minor Disney live action roles including appearing as a saloon patron in *Hot Lead and Cold Feet* (1978)

Brodie was contracted to work for ten weeks from eight in the morning until six in the evening, although some days he was excused as early as noon. He remembers there was often two cameras set up to record the action and he recalls that Dave Hand directed him

Both he and Lucille were filmed for the cauldron scene using a wooden tub. He was also filmed rowing the raft with a long pole and for the climb up the mountain for the climatic scene.

Brodie told Johnson:

> I enjoyed doing her. It's a challenge for an actor. I didn't use a mask. I did makeup because they wanted my facial expressions. I made up the eyes and then I put the nose on with spirit gum. My hair was inside my cap, inside the hood. Long straggly grey hair was inside the hood.

The climatic scene of the film is when the old witch plunges supposedly to her death. The strain of the chase on the elderly witch as she desperately climbs up a rocky mountain, the rainstorm that increases in intensity (mirroring her escalating

anger and hate), the cross-cutting between the witch and the dwarfs close on her trail all builds the suspense.

Walt's description of the scene in a story conference held on May 1, 1937:

> When the Witch stops to look back and pant, we should have a moment's hesitation. Have her growl when she is trying to loosen the rock. She would be laughing to herself when she says lines 'That will crush their bones. The meddlesome fools'.
>
> Don't show the vultures coming into this scene. It is too confusing and takes your attention away from the Witch's actions. When she is ready to pry the rock loose, get a shot of the vultures looking at each other and then back at her...Here we have a shot of the dwarfs coming along. Suddenly, there is a shout of 'Look out!' We see the dwarfs scrambling to escape the oncoming boulder.
>
> Then cut above and immediately bring the lightning flash. We see her prying up the rock, letting out a laugh, then bang goes the lightning. We want to get over that she is not struck by the lightning, only blinded by it.

There is a real sense of danger because the witch is totally vulnerable. She is unrecognizable as the queen so has no royal status or protection. She is not accompanied by her Huntsman or any type of guards. She does not have access to her potions. In addition, she is now trapped in an aged body.

As live action reference actor Don Brodie told historian Dave Johnson:

> I became exhausted a couple of times because when I had to climb that mountain. I must have climbed that mountain at least...You see, they had this scaffolding built like a mountain. It went clear up the stage.
>
> Now it's a big stage probably 35-40 feet up. It took up the entire stage. And I had to climb that thing twenty times, at least twenty times. It was very exhausting. I didn't do it all in one day. But there were times when I would climb it two or three times and a couple of days later three or four times again to get the action exactly the way they wanted it.
>
> My action was crawling up this scaffolding which was boards like a ladder. There were places for me to put my feet and things that I grabbed a hold of that looked like a rock.

And I pulled myself up and then I looked back at the dwarfs, you see. Then some of the fake rocks that they had, I'd push 'em down and the dwarfs would duck and the rocks would go bouncing over their heads. Several times climbing the mountain, my cape would get stuck and I'd trip and it got in the way several times.

As animation historian John Canemaker has pointed out:

The witch's end begins with the dwarfs jumping to conclusions: seeing an old woman leave their cottage, they assume (a) she is the wicked queen (whom they have never laid eyes on) and (b) she has harmed the princess (though they never peek inside the cottage to confirm it). They are correct but it is all an assumption. Disney story logic is sometimes ignored when necessary.

It could be argued that the animals had shown them a sense of urgency about the situation and Sleepy does make the casual remark that it may be because the queen has gotten to Snow White.

Unlike the original story, Snow White is not the one responsible for the death of the queen. It is the queen's poor decisions as well as the hand of nature in the form of a lightning bolt done by special effects artist Josh Meador that collapses her rocky perch and sends her to her supposed doom.

When people complained that the Wicked Witch in *Snow White and the Seven Dwarfs* was too frightening for children, Walt would tell reporters:

I showed Snow White to my own two daughters when they were small and when they came to me later and said they wanted to play witch, I figured it was all right to let the other kids see it.

That was not completely accurate, as I found out when I asked Diane about it. She was three and a half years old at the time she first saw the film.

I was born after *Three Little Pigs* and just prior to Snow White. I remember very well I was sitting there on the sound stage [at the Disney Studio] watching [*Snow White and the Seven Dwarfs*]. When the Queen gulped down her potion and began to turn into the Witch, I became so terrified I was sitting there with my hands in front of my face peeking through my fingers... sometimes not peeking at all. And crying...just being so terribly

afraid and screaming in terror, over and over again and suddenly finding myself outside the soundstage, just outside that big door, with a strange man looking down at me...not unkindly.

Daddy was there at the screening. He was interested in my reaction and he was a little bit upset at me, you know. But, he said, and it's true, children love to be scared especially if it turns out all right in the end.

I remember one of my favorite games when I was little was 'Old Witch.' And my dad or my Uncle Bill (Cottrell) would be the Old Witch. They'd chase Sharon and I all over the house and we'd go in a little dark corner and scream 'The Old Witch is Coming!' We'd scream and hide our heads and just love it. We loved to be scared... like having somebody sneak out from behind a corner and say 'Boo!' like at Halloween. You're covering your face but you're peeking to see what's coming next.

Actually the Disney version is much less scary than the original in many aspects including the death of the queen who is forced to dance to her death at Snow White's wedding. On the original release, the United Kingdom insisted the film be advertised as unsuitable for small children and that children under the age of 16 years old had to be accompanied by an adult, a ban that was not lifted until the mid 1950s.

Famously, Walt cut several things from *Snow White* including the dwarfs eating soup and building the little princess a bed in order to keep the story focused and moving swiftly. Some things featuring the Evil queen/Wicked Witch also ended up on the cutting room floor.

It was debated that when the evil queen found out she had been deceived by the Huntsman that in a mad rage she smashed the mirror and that act transformed her into the hag. Walt decided that the transformation needed to be deliberate and not accidental.

Originally, the queen was to have had peacocks and seven black panthers. However, having a panther as a sidekick seemed too strong an image that would diminish her own power and would be distracting. The peacock motif was later incorporated into the design of her throne.

One completely animated and ink-and-painted scene lasting approximately thirty-five seconds was cut.

Sequence 9A takes place in the Queen's dungeon laboratory where the Witch stands over her cauldron. In the film, when all the Dwarfs finally doze off to sleep after their singing and dancing at the cottage, the story cuts back to this scene. In the version the audience saw, the steam clears and the witch is seen dunking the apple into her poisonous brew.

However that scene was not originally meant to start with the apple-dunking. The scene actually began with a long shot that slowly moves in on the cackling Witch. Her Raven is seen stage-right perched atop the skull upon the table.

With a poison-filled vial grasped tightly in her right hand, she stirs the boiling cauldron counter-clockwise with her left. The Witch, in a speech seemingly inspired by the witches in the Shakespeare play *Macbeth*, intones:

> Boil cauldron, boil.
> Boil cauldron, boil.
> Death within your depths I see
> For one who dares to rival me.

During this spell, vapor rises from the bubbling brew to briefly take the shape of skulls. She then tips the vial to add the last deadly ingredient and the yellow mixture turns a sickish green, and the spell concludes with:

> Brew the magical recipe.
> Boil cauldron, boil!

A huge blast of steam fills the room. When the air begins to clear, the sequence continues with the dunking of the apple.

According to historian J.B. Kaufman, this scene was directed by Bill Cottrell and voiced by Lucille LaVerne. It was fully animated, inked, painted and photographed by September 1937.

Then in November, just one month before the premiere, the scene of the Witch dunking the apple was re-shot and became the new beginning for the sequence in order to speed things up.

The Witch and Raven were animated by Norm Ferguson. Special effect animation was completed by George Rowley (cauldron bubbles and steam), Paul Satterfield (steam and liquid in vial), and Reuben Timmons (steam).

Both the Evil Queen and the Wicked Witch have appeared on a host of merchandise and in story books over the decades.

A life-sized Snow White Wicked Witch animatronic (61 inches high weighing about 25 pounds) was sold online by Spirit Halloween from 2016 through 2019. When activated, the hand with the poisoned apple moved, the head tilted forward and back and the mouth moved to lines like "All alone, my pet? Go on. Have a bite. This is no ordinary apple. It's a magic wishing apple." It sold for $200. The animatronic was the last remaining flat-squared base animatronic by Gemmy Industries

Both the Evil Queen and the Wicked Witch appeared in the Disney theme parks as well.

The Candy Cauldron shop is on the West Side of Disney Springs in Orlando, Florida. It is designed to be reminiscent of the Evil Queen's dungeon laboratory. The Wicked Witch figure is near the entrance, offering an apple to people who enter. The walls are decorated with scenes of her secret room of spell books, potion bottles, and bubbling cauldrons. The shop is known for its various candy and caramel apples.

Disney Archivist Dave Smith wrote to me to explain about the figure of the Wicked Witch at Disneyland who was in a cage that rattled while she tried to entice guests to unlock her prison and let her out.

Smith wrote:

> The Witch in the cage was originally made by the former WED Display and Design Department at Walt Disney World, under Jim McNalis, for use in 1975 Emporium windows in the Magic Kingdom park promoting *Snow White and the Seven Dwarfs.*
>
> When the Disneyana Shop opened on Main Street, U.S.A. at Disneyland in 1976, the Witch, animated and with added audio, moved west to become a major display piece in that shop. Later on it was used in the Villain's Lair shop in Fantasyland and Le Bat en Rouge in New Orleans Square.

McNails was the one who wrote the script for the new dialogue and recorded it on tape imitating the witch's voice.

Perhaps the most prominent showcasing of the Wicked Witch was in the dark ride Snow White's Adventures that opened in Fantasyland in Disneyland in July 1955 and later at Walt Disney World, Tokyo Disneyland and Disneyland Paris.

The attraction might have been called The Wicked Witch's Adventures since the character is featured several times through the second half of the attraction. For over twenty-five years Snow White herself did not appear in the ride since the intent was that the guests were supposed to take her place as they rode in the little mine car. Nobody got that concept.

In January 1961 a number of changes and improvements were made to the ride by a team of Imagineers headed by Yale Gracey. Additional scene details were added, lighting readjusted and newly built and re-mechanized Witch figures were installed in various areas in the ride.

In 1983, with the major remodeling of Fantasyland under Tony Baxter, significant changes were made to the dark ride including adding Snow White herself.

When the Witch offered guests in the ride vehicle the poisoned apple in one scene, guests frequently grabbed at the apple and some brought it home as a souvenir. During the 1983 rehab, the ever-missing poisoned apple was replaced with an image of an apple projected by means of a parabolic mirror so there was nothing physical to grab.

In another scene the Queen stands before her Magic Mirror with her back to the guests and her beautiful reflection saying, "Magic Mirror on the wall..." She then spins and faces the guests and has become the ugly witch.

"With this disguise, I'll fool them all!" she croaks. This effect is achieved by two models —one queen and one witch—rotating on different sides of the 'mirror', which is actually a sheet of transparent glass.

The original mural for Disneyland's *Snow White Adventure's* attraction was divided into four sections. These were meant to represent the seven major scenes encountered by guests inside--Diamond Mine, Quaint Forest, Dwarfs' Cottage, Queen's Vultures, Witch Stirring Her Cauldron, Haunted Forest, and Witch Boulder.

Animator/imagineer Ken Anderson who worked on the original film was one of the driving forces behind the creation of the Snow White attraction. In addition to helping design the ride itself, he was also called upon to rough sketch the initial artwork for these enormous mural images.

Anderson's sepia pencil sketches were traced onto two illustration board, re-adapted and 'Disneyfied' by artist Paul Hartley, then painted in full color at the Disney Studio. The Hartley illustration boards were then taken to the theme park. The images were projected onto four large canvas panels where several artists working together traced, painted, and re-'Disneyfied' the mural art.

Additional painting was completed as necessary then a final seal of lacquer was applied for a shiny finish and to protect against fading from sunlight. Fading did take place and so the mural was repainted frequently over the years so that the characters started to look "off model".

A section of the mural featured the Witch in her dungeon stirring her cauldron with a bone. The artwork was clearly adapted from another of Gustaf Tenggren's original publicity sketches and also from art found in the 1948 Little Golden Book. This mural was demolished during the Fantasyland overhaul.

The attraction was removed from Walt Disney World in 2012 and replaced by the Princess Fairytale Hall. The Seven Dwarfs Mine Train with some of the figures from the attraction incorporated into the scenes in the roller coaster opened in 2014. At the end of this attraction as the vehicle pulls into the station, guests see the figure of the Wicked Witch at the cottage door. She is cackling and has the poisoned apple in her basket.

Animator Ward Kimball told me:

> I was at the premiere in 1937. We were worried. It was being shown at the Carthay Circle Hollywood. Movie stars were sitting in seats. (My wife) Betty and I sat behind Clark Gable and Carol Lombard and he got upset when Snow White was poisoned.

> He started to sniffle and borrowed a handkerchief. That type of reaction is hard to get with a cartoon because after all you are exaggerating and caricaturing and the tendency is to do a put on. Not Walt! I think that was the key to his secret."

As animator Ollie Johnson said:

> The remarkable thing is that it is a story where one drawing is trying to murder another drawing but Walt made it all appear so believable that it became legendary.

The Marvelous Mad Madam Mim

One of the Disney witches who despite her popularity has never been fully documented is the marvelous Mad Madam Mim who appears on lots of merchandise, in comic book stories and much more besides her occasional cameo appearances in animation.

While Madam Mim is cited as the main villainess of Disney's animated feature film *The Sword in The Stone* (1963), her character and short scene are completely irrelevant to the story. She appears approximately an hour into the film and appears for only roughly ten minutes total and is never seen again since she is not really a credible threat.

The film is loosely based on the novel *The Once and Future King* by author T.H. White first published in 1958.

The book collects and extensively revises several shorter novels by White published from 1938 to 1940 in order to make the narrative smoother and more adult, with much new material added as well as the elimination of things from the previous books including the character of Mim who appeared in the first novel.

In Chapter 6 of the 1938 edition (pages 74 -100), when Wart and Sir Kay are hunting for a lost arrow, they are tricked by Mim to come into her cottage where she captures and imprisons them. She intends to cook and eat them for her dinner. A goat in the next cage escapes with Wart's help and brings Merlin to rescue the pair which he does when he defeats Mim in a magical duel and she dies.

Walt Disney obtained the screen rights to White's work in 1939. Like so many Disney animated feature film projects, various attempts were made to develop the story over the years. In 1944 Walt announced that the film was soon to go into production. Full story board drawings were created as early as 1949.

Disney storyman Bill Peet knew adapting the complex book would be a challenge: "Getting a more direct story line called for a lot of sifting and sorting. Walt questioned the first version of my screenplay, pointing out that it should have had more substance. So I made an all-out effort by enlarging on the more dramatic aspects of the story."

Peet decided to resurrect Mim as a character for the film and incorporate the magical duel as it would be a visual treat. In one of his proposals for an alternate opening, he intended to have Madam Mim usurp the throne of England by trying to kill young Arthur before he ever pulled the sword and her using a raven to do surveillance for her.

It was the first Disney animated feature to be directed by just one director, Wolfgang Reitherman. It was only the second Disney animated feature to be entirely written by just one storyman, Bill Peet, who had previously done the same on *101 Dalmatians* (1961).

The Sword in the Stone was the first Disney animated feature to have songs by Richard and Robert Sherman including a memorable solo tune for Mim to quickly define the vanity and power of the new character for the audience titled simply *Mad Madam Mim*:

> With only a touch
> I have the power
> Zim zabberim zim
> To wither a flower
> I find delight in the gruesome and grim
> 'Cause I'm the magnificent, marvelous
> Mad Madam Mim
>
> I can be huge, fill the whole house
> I can be tiny, small as a mouse
> Black sorcery is my dish of tea
> It comes easy to me
> 'Cause I'm the magnificent, marvelous
> Mad Madam Mim!
>
> I can be beautiful, lovely and fair
> Silvery voice, long purple hair
> La la la la, la la la la la
> La la la la la, la la la la la la

But it's only skin deep
For, zim zabberim zim
I am an ugly old creep
The magnificent, marvelous
Mad, mad, mad, mad Madam Mim!

As Peet remembered:

When I designed Madam Mim, Walt said, "Who is this frowzy old lady? Bill, why can't we have a big, tall dame with black hair?" I said, "Walt, we always do that. She has to be a counterpart to Merlin. He's an old eccentric, and so she has to be too. They have to match."

Animator Frank Thomas wrote:

The mad Madam Mim was a contrast of wild actions and restraint with unexpected outbursts accenting her overall timing. Walt had cautioned his animators, "Don't be broad when there is no reason." But this was the perfect place for startling activity. Storyman Bill Peet gave us the wizard's duel, a perfect use of animation, maintaining personalities through a surprising change in forms and exciting action.

Animator Andreas Deja said:

When Madam Mim appeared on the screen I was blown away. There is great sophistication in her design, and her acting is fresh and full of life.

Walt Disney assigned Milt Kahl and Frank Thomas to this character, knowing that if you combine their creative forces, nothing but great stuff would come out. Milt had perfected the way he drew hands in his animated scenes. The fingertips are squared off, and the fingernails are placed with realistic perspective.

To give the design contrast, her body is kept short and chubby, her arms and legs are very thin and boney. Both animators just loved working on Mim, and they agreed that there should have been more of her in the movie.

Frank had a lot of fun with her dialogue scenes. His acting is eccentric, too, but it feels very believable and grounded. Milt's animation is full of inventive moves, like funky dance steps and hops. When Mim turns into a 'beautiful' witch, her moves are almost risque.

Mim is a charmingly memorable character despite her vindictive nature and the Wizard's Duel scene demonstrates

a mastery of animation but Merlin's lesson that brains can overcome the threat of brawn had already been established in a previous scene where Wart had been transformed into a small fish in the moat.

It can be argued that Mim is meant to represent a personification of evil who only uses her skills for her own delight or to cause harm to others in order to counterbalance Merlin's goodness that is used to help others but both her verbal and visual antics evoke more laughter than genuine fear.

Madam Mim is indeed a very powerful witch although Disney often refers to her as a sorceress to avoid challenges in other countries where the portrayal of witches may be problematic.

She has many extraordinary talents including, being able to fly on her broomstick like a traditional witch, disappear, change size and appearance from ugly to beautiful as well as transform in to any animal, vegetable, mineral or monster (real or imaginary).

Animator Frank Thomas wrote:

> Mim was first seen cheating at solitaire, which for her was as moral and honorable an attitude as we ever saw her have. She could transform herself into anything, never played fair, was an out-and-out liar and was naturally a poor loser which is why she had to cheat. On four different occasions she proclaims she has won even though no one is competing with her.
>
> With the voice of Martha Wentworth, she was a cross between an aging spoiled brat and a young crotchty hag. She was a great character, being alive and vibrant and fun to animate, but the story was not constructed to use her in more than one cameo appearance.

Verna Martha Wentworth had a long radio career beginning in the early 1920s that included playing the role of The Wintergreen Witch on *The Cinnamon Bear* (1937) radio program. She provided voices for a few Warner Brothers animated shorts in the 1930s as well as Jenny Wren in Walt Disney's 1935 Silly Symphony *Who Killed Cock Robin?*

She had an extensive career as a film actress during the 1940s and 1950s as well as appearing frequently in television shows of the 1950s.

She did voice over work in Disney's *101 Dalmatians* (1961) providing the voices for the characters of Nanny, Queenie the Cow and Lucy the Goose. Two years later for *The Sword in the Stone* she provided the voice for Madam Mim and the overweight Granny squirrel. It was her last credited film appearance before her retirement and death at age 84 on March 8, 1974.

Peet drew the first sketches of Mim and several of his later children storybooks have short little witches in bloomers and scraggly hair that were very obviously inspired by his Madam Mim designs.

It was Disney Legend Milt Kahl who redesigned the character and animated her scenes in the cottage and some during the Wizard's Duel. Animator Frank Thomas did a lot of the work on her in the duel scene as well.

When director Woolie Reitherman saw Kahl's first rough drawings of Merlin and Mim, he remarked to the animator that they could be displayed in a museum. Kahl's classic response was: "Aw, you're full of it!"

In September 2017, I interviewed Disney Legend Floyd Norman who worked as an assistant to Milt Kahl on Mim:

> So with the decision made on the next animated feature, the attention shifted over to working on *The Sword in the Stone*. Naturally, most of the key animators and their assistants would be located in D-wing on the first floor of the Animation Building.
>
> Milt Kahl was not simply a presence in D-wing; he was a force. He was known as the 'Dragon of D-wing' or 'The Terror of D-wing'. It was well known Kahl did not suffer fools and woe be to those who failed to please the master animator. However, kids like me followed orders back in the 1960s even though I was initially very scared to be told I was to be his assistant.
>
> Kahl was well-known for his insistence on the best in every scene he animated. He demanded solid draftsmanship and hated those who took shortcuts. He worked with incredible efficiency and wasted not a single drawing. Even the lines on his paper were chosen carefully. At the end of the day, young scavengers would raid the animator's waste baskets for discarded drawings and find nothing.

During my nearly two years on *The Sword in the Stone* I didn't have one falling out with the Disney Legend and working for Milt proved to be a delight As Bill [Peet]'s storyboards were approved by Walt and director Woolie Reitherman, they went straight into the music room [director]'s office and into production.

John Lounsbery was one of the first to begin animating the early scenes and he was followed by Milt Kahl. Bill had done some character designs but Kahl refined them. Milt was legendary for his temper tantrums. Kahl did not mince words when he felt you had done a shoddy job.

One of my most delightful assignments was cleaning up the wonderful character, Madam Mim. Actually, Mim was so much fun that I honestly wish there had been more of her in the movie. I think audiences agree with that feeling.

We had been working on the film for a number of months before we finally got around to this remarkable character that would be a scene stealer. Mim turned out to be a very engaging character that audiences loved.

While we had our fair share of fun sketching Merlin the Magician, Archimedes, Sir Ector, and Kay, this new character was a delightful change of pace. Working from Bill Peet's inspired story sketches, Milt Kahl embellished this zany female wizard in his own special way. The animated scenes were filled with zany fun and delightful bits of business.

In a final bit of animated fun, the less than attractive Madame Mim transforms herself into a sexy babe. It was no accident that the 'sexy Mim' bore a remarkable resemblance to a tall, leggy redhead who worked upstairs in the layout department on the second floor.

I seldom spent time with Milt going over his scenes on the Moviola, but the Mim scenes were an exception. Kahl actually seemed to get a kick out of viewing his own animation. He would run his animation of her over and over laughing his head off. Perhaps Milt was amused by his own special jokes and the personal stuff he added to his animation.

You had to admit, it was very funny stuff. During a song sequence in Mim's cottage, the female wizard turns herself into a tall, shapely young woman. Since I was cleaning up the scenes I couldn't help but be aware the sexy character reminded me of a co-worker.

Milt never said he based his drawing on the young woman on the second floor, however after drawing her remarkable attributes day after day it became pretty obvious. At least to me, anyway.

It was obvious it was inspired by layout artist Sylvia Roemer. Sylvia had started in Ink and Paint and worked her way up into layout. Others recognized the resemblance immediately as well but Sylvia either didn't notice or just never said anything.

Of course, grumpy Merlin was clearly based on Walt Disney himself and he never noticed or commented on the obvious similarities.

The home of Madam Mim is a stone cottage with a thatched roof that resembles the traditional witch's black pointed hat. The interior designed by Disney Legend Ken Anderson is organic, natural and sparse. Just one window lets in a little light and fresh air.

The only furnishings are a table and chairs, several cracked dishes, a dartboard, the standard witch's broom that Mim uses for flight and not for cleaning away the several cobwebs. An ash-covered chimney hearth has not been cleaned either.

The only real color in the surroundings is Mim herself. Her unkempt hair is purple and she is attired in a red and purple dress with pink bloomers. Her lone snaggle tooth indicates her lack of attention to dental care.

Mim likes playing games whether it be solitaire or cat-and-mouse with Wart and making rules but she loves breaking them more so she can win as she does immediately in the Wizard's Duel. She hates sunlight because it is too wholesome and takes delight if she thinks someone like Wart might be ill.

As a counterbalance to Merlin, she only uses her magical gifts for her own selfish ego or to cause harm to anything she thinks is good.

Most Disney fans and film critics agree that the highpoint of the film is the Wizard's Duel where animators created fifteen different animal personae for the battling sorcerers that still kept their individual personalities, visual characteristics and even distinctive color scheme.

Mim appears as a crocodile, fox, chicken, elephant, tiger, rattlesnake, rhinoceros and dragon (all of which had purple

hair, were colored pink and occasionally had purple stripes). Disney Legend Eric Larson animated on the dragon. Merlin transforms into a snapping turtle, rabbit, caterpillar, walrus, mouse, crab and a germ (all of which had his blue color).

Mim makes three rules prior to the duel: "No mineral or vegetable. Only animal"; "No make-believe things such as pink dragons" and "No disappearing".

Merlin's pet owl, Archimedes declares, "she only wants rules so she can break em!" but also to limit Merlin who is so honorable that he won't break rules. She breaks Merlin's only rule ("Rule four: No cheating") multiple times throughout their standoff and uses a loophole so that she turns into a purple dragon rather than a pink dragon.

Merlin's superior intellect allows him to win by transforming into a germ called Malignalitaloptereosis that gives Mim hot and cold flashes, sneezing fits as well as spots all over her body. Being a Disney film, the disease is not deadly and she will be able to recover with lots of rest and sunshine, something she hates.

Mim has appeared in several hundreds of comic book stories worldwide illustrated by Pete Alvardo, Tony Strobl, Al Hubbard, and others. She was frequently teamed with Disney villains like the Beagle Boys, Magica De Spell, Pete, Captain Hook and the Phantom Blot and in some European comic book stories lost her evil streak and became more like an Addams Family character.

Her first comic book appearance was in December 1963 in the comic book adaptation of the film and also from October to December in the Sunday newspaper strip adaptation.

In 2001, Madam Min showed off her magical skills once again in several cartoons as part of *Disney's House Of Mouse* including *Mickey and Minnie's Big Vacation, Goofy's Valentine Date* as well as the 2002 direct-to-video feature *Mickey's House of Villains*.

She appeared for the first time as a costumed character in the *Disney On Ice* show entitled *Mickey's Diamond Jubilee* that ran from 1988 to 1993. In the *World of Illusion Staring Mickey Mouse and Donald Duck* Sega Genesis video game released in 1992, she is the boss of the library/cookie jar level.

In the world of the *Descendents* franchise, Mim is trapped on the Isle of the Lost and has a granddaughter named Mad Maddy who used to be good friends with Mal.

Walt Disney Classics Collection recreated the Wizard's Duel for its 750 piece limited edition for its Gold Circle release in 2007, making Mim the first Villain to be the subject of a Gold Circle release. Merlin & Mim were sculpted by Bruce Lau and Archimedes & Wart sculpted by Jacqueline Perreault Gonzales.

Cunning, arrogant, bad-tempered and sadistic, Mim is obviously reckless (even destroying the interior of her cottage to show off her magic) and vain (even as she delights in her own ugliness). She hates Merlin and considers him a bungler even though he demonstrates greater magical skill than her. However, she remains a delightful character.

The Enchanting Magica De Spell

Magica De Spell is a Disney witch who is distinctly Italian and was created by Disney Legend Carl Barks in 1961. Today, she is a popular character on a variety of merchandise from pins to a Funko figure.

While Barks decided to make the character Italian to reference popular Italian movie actresses at the time like Gina Lollobrigida, Italy has had a long association with witchcraft from the Campanian myth of the Witches of Benevento to the enduring folklore at Christmastime of the old hag witch called La Befana with her broom.

In 1899, the American writer Charles Godfrey Leland published *Aradia, or The Gospel of the Witches*. It is a religious text, supposedly handed to him by a Florentine fortune-teller and witch informant called Maddalena that includes beliefs, spells, rituals and even recipes from a Tuscan witch cult that worshipped the Queen of Witches, the Goddess Aradia. Modern-day Wiccans celebrate her as a nature goddess.

This was the text that inspired the Italian-American pagan scholar Raven Grimassi, a descendant of a Neapolitan witch, to popularize his own ethnic Italian form of witchcraft, *Stregheria* or "the Old Religion" in the 1980s.

Italy imported Halloween festivities from the United States through films, television and pop culture around the 1980s. It all started as a way to entertain children with the famous tradition of trick-or-treat (a term that first appeared in print in the U.S. in 1939) but has grown over the years into a full-blown party celebration but with no substantial underlying meaning.

Italy has a long history of honoring the dead during All Saints Day (November first and a national holiday) and All Souls Day (November 2) so it wasn't much of a leap to include Halloween on October 31st as a sort of preamble event.

Among the most famous Halloween celebrations held in Italy is the one in Triora (Imperia), a village in Liguria known as "the town of witches". Triora was the site of a series of witch trials held from 1587 to 1589, when 200 local women were accused of being responsible for a number of different misfortunes. Triora hosts a number of other folklore- and horror-themed events through the year, such as the summer witchcraft festival in August.

In an interview with Klaus Strzyz in 1980, comic book artist Barks recalled:

> I thought at the time Disney has always had witches who were ugly and repulsive. Why shouldn't I draw one that's not ugly but outright sexy? That's why she's Italian and of course very popular with readers in Italy.

> She knows that if she took a barrel of Scrooge's money, why, in a little while it would be gone, but if she had that Old Number One Dime and made it into this very lucky amulet, she would have many barrels of her own money and would be the most powerful person in the world. She'd also be the richest.

The name, obviously, references a "magic spell". "Magico" is the Italian adjective for "magic" so adding the "a" at the end makes it feminine.

When Bruce Hamilton began reprinting Barks' stories, Barks told him that the physical appearance of Magica was modeled on the character of Morticia Addams, "the dark haired witch from the Charles Addams family cartoons in the *New Yorker* which I liked very much. She was downright sexy."

It was atypical for Barks to have a story with real magic. As a former Disney storyman, he was familiar with Walt Disney's philosophy of "The Plausible Impossible" meaning taking something that is against the laws of nature, basically impossible, and make it appear rational and acceptable or "plausible".

So when Barks introduced the character of Magica, her magic entailed devices like her "Foof" flash blinders (that were actually just chemical pellets) or a battery-powered gadget on her arm that generated a "stun ray—a power more stupefying than the evil eye" as well as being a master of disguise and hypnotism so that her so-called powers were all easily explained by science rather than sorcery.

Later, in *Uncle Scrooge #43* in the story *For Old Dime's Sake* (1964), he had Magica find a crypt beneath the oldest temple of Zeus, the cave of Circe and the ruined temples of Boreas, Juno and the Furies where she found recipes and herbs from these characters who "were more likely live sorcerers than figments of ancient dreams".

She dipped her wand into the horrendous mixture and was able to conjure fantastic powers. While the nephews broke it apart into little pieces, she was apparently able to repair it or replace it because she used it in later adventures.

Barks obviously felt he had limited his storytelling with a character who was not truly magical and was solely focused on getting hold of Scrooge McDuck's first dime. As he continued the stories, he shifted the approach so that Magica had real magic and in his last two stories with her shifted her attention to artifacts like golden eggs and a flying carpet that had somewhat magical properties.

Of course, Magica treats everyone in the same condescending, domineering manner and always speaks in a stilted, formal tone, rarely even using contractions in an elite-type of speech that at times seems almost operatic. She is the only recurring villainess in the Disney duck comics.

Here are the Barks' stories that featured Magica:

- *The Midas Touch* (*Uncle Scrooge #36* 1961) Magica is introduced and succeeds in getting Scrooge's first dime when he carelessly sells it to her for a dollar. When he realizes his mistake, he, Donald and the nephews give chase to Italy before she can melt it down into a lucky amulet.

- *Ten-Cent Valentine* (*Walt Disney Comics and Stories #258* 1962) Magica disguises herself as a secretary in order to get hold of the desirable dime but Scrooge has given it to Donald to protect it. At the end of the story Magica, seemingly, witnesses the destruction of the coin in a meat grinder. She storms off but the dime miraculously materializes from a special cake made for the desolated Scrooge because the nephews switched it with a phony dime.

- *The Unsafe Safe* (*Uncle Scrooge # 38* 1962) Scrooge has created an unbreakable glass safe in his Money Bin that

frustrates the Beagle Boys in their attempts to rob it. Feeling finally that his fortune is secure from robbers, Scrooge takes an around the world vacation with Donald and the nephews. Magica fails to break into the safe as well using a variety of musical objects to try to shatter the glass. In Africa, Scrooge discovers the Tanganyika Yeeker bird whose disagreeable cry shatters his glasses so could shatter his vault. Magica finds Scrooge and steals a Yeeker to take back to Duckburg with Scrooge and his relatives in pursuit. She does manage to steal the dime but her stunner weapon fails and Scrooge retrieves his prize.

- *Raven Mad* (*Walt Disney Comics and Stories #265* 1962) Magica hypnotizes Randolph the raven into stealing Scrooge's dime from an outdoor display and place it on the top of a rocket about to launch for the sun. Donald disguised as Magica hypnotizes the raven to save the coin at the last minute.

- *Oddball Odyssey* (*Uncle Scrooge # 40* 1963) Scrooge and the Ducks arrive at the Greek mythological enchantress Circe's island, where Magica in disguise tries to barter the dime for worthless junk. In the process, she happens to find Circe's ancient wand that can transform living beings into anything she likes. She transforms Scrooge into a mule, the nephews into pigs, and Donald into a goat and, next, a turtle in order to force Scrooge to part with his special dime.

- *For Old Dime's Sake* (*Uncle Scrooge #43* 1963) Scrooge's Money Bin is protected from lightning, cyclone and a meteor because his two spies watching Magica had discovered she has been able to create a formula to give her wand control over the weather. Failing to break into the Bin to get the dime, Magica disguises herself as Scrooge and gets the combination to the vault and steals the dime. She is thwarted by the nephews who see through her deception and destroy her wand.

- *Isle of Golden Geese* (*Uncle Scrooge # 45* 1963) Scrooge finds a golden goose egg in a regular egg carton. Scrooge discovers there are golden geese living on Featherbrain

Island, but Magica De Spell, who now lives temporarily in Duckburg to spy on him, tries to stop him with the Beagle Boys as her crew who she torments by throwing lightning bolts from her hands.

- *The Many Faces of Magica De Spell (Uncle Scrooge # 48 1964)* Magicia makes a potion she found in Circe's cave that can change a person's face into whoever they look at. She fools Scrooge's two detectives but Scrooge finds out about her scheme and flies with Donald and the nephews to an Unknown Valley in the Jungles of Nowhere where faceless people live in a maze of caves. She squirts Scrooge's face but thanks to the actions of the nephews she loses her own face while they restore their uncle's face.

- *Rug Riders in the Sky (Uncle Scrooge #50 1964)* Magicia tricks Scrooge into buying a flying magic carpet that will take her to a cave containing the treasure of Aladdin. She tries twice to steal the carpet but the ducks regain it and fly to the cave themselves.

Barks' stories found a new audience when they inspired the *DuckTales* animated syndicated television series produced by Walt Disney Television animation. It premiered on September 18,1987 and ran for four seasons and one hundred episodes until November 28,1990.

CEO Michael Eisner wanted to expand into the lucrative syndication market but not risk using top-of-the-line characters for fear of damanging their brand. However, he was not adverse to using "supporting" characters who might have a connection to one of Disney's major cartoon stars.

It was decided that the adventures of Scrooge McDuck from the popular comic books produced by writer and artist Carl Barks would provide some good adventure stories. Donald Duck would enlist in the Navy and Scrooge would become the guardian for Huey, Dewey and Louie.

Associate producer of the series Tom Ruzicka said in 1987, "Although the show was initially based on the concept of doing Scrooge McDuck and his nephews, Barks was never really consulted. We discovered that a lot of stuff that made wonderful

comics wouldn't translate into the 1980s or into animation, so we started evolving new characters and other things to contemporize the show. As we did that, the stories got further and further away from the comics, although a few episodes are lifted right out of them."

Many of Barks' characters were borrowed from the comic book pages including the Beagle Boys, Flintheart Glomgold, Gyro Gearloose and others including Magica De Spell who would appear in animation for the first time.

Her voice was provided by veteran voice actress June Foray using a pseudo-Slavic accent similar to the one she provided for the character of Natasha Fatale in the Jay Ward cartoons.

Magica was a prominent character in the first season of the show but as the show started developing its own characters, she disappeared except for one more episode based on a Barks's comic book story.

Her raven called Ratface who was her familiar in the comic books was re-christened as Poe in reference to Edgar Allan Poe who wrote a famous poem about a raven. He was now also her brother who was under a curse. In this television version Magica lives on her own unnamed volcanic island rather than on the slope of Mt. Vesuvius.

DuckTales episodes:

- *Send in the Clones* (9/21/87) Magica turns the Beagle Boys Bigtime, Babyface and Burger into look-alikes of Huey, Dewey and Louie to help her get Scrooge's lucky dime. Later she transforms herself into Mrs. Beakley. She gets the dime and takes Mrs. Beakley and Huey to her lair with her where they get into a potion fight with many transformations. Scrooge shows up and tricks her out of the dime and rescues her hostages.

- *Magica's Shadow War* (9/28/87) Magica brings her shadow to life to steal Scrooge's lucky dime but it takes on a personality of its own and wants to use the dime to free all the shadows in the world. Scrooge has to reluctantly team up with Magica to defeat this menace as it multiplies. Huey, Dewey and Louie destroy the extra shadows as well as the main super-shadow.

- *Raiders of the Lost Harp* (11/20/87) While uncovering the treasures of ancient Troy, Scrooge finds a golden harp with a carving of a beautiul female duck who can detect lies. Magica disguises herself as Helen of Troy to try to get the prize but the harp reveals her deception. A chase ensues. That night when Scrooge's Trojan Museum is to open, a fifty-foot stone minotaur who is the guardian of the harp invades Duckburg to retrieve it. Scrooge's foils Magica's last attempt and returns the harp to the minotaur.

- *Magica's Magic Mirror* (11/30/87) In disguise Magica gives Scrooge a mirror that will supposedly reveal the future but it is a trick. She stages future events broadcast over a second mirror to fool him but Huey, Dewey and Louie finally foil the sorcereress.

- *Duck to the Future* (12/1/87) Disguised as a fortune teller, Magica uses her "Sands of Time" to send Scrooge forty years in the future to Duckburg. There he finds that Magica has gotten rid of him, taken his dime and now runs Magica-McDuck Enterprises that controls everything. Scrooge retrieves the dime and journeys back to the past with Magica hot on his heels.

- *Dime Enough for Luck* (12/4/87) Magica hypnotizes Gladstone Gander to use his incredible luck to steal Scrooge's lucky dime. When he does, his luck turns bad since he used his good luck for a wicked purpose so he must journey to Magica's fortress and recover the dime to restore his luck. He does and both his and Scrooge's fortunes blossom.

- *Nothing to Fear* (12/14/87) Magica's gigantic "fear cloud" envelopes the McDuck mansion and everyone there is menaced by their worst fears. Scrooge and the nephews are even tormented by their nasty "opposites". It is only when they stop running and face their fears that they conquer them and turn the spell against Magica.

- *Till Nephews Do Us Part* (1/1/88) Magica has a short non-speaking cameo appearance at Scrooge's wedding along with almost three dozen other characters who had appeared at some time on the series.

- *The Unbreakable Bin* (11/15/89) based on the Barks' comic story *The UnSafe Safe* Gyro Gearloose invents a special unbreakable glass for Scrooge's Money Bin that is immune from Magica's spells. She gets a bird with a shriek that can shatter the glass and Gizmoduck must help protect the Bin.

A reboot of the *DuckTales* animated series premiered August 12, 2017 with some signifcant differences while maintaining the basic formula of the original show. Magica's voice was now portrayed by Catherine Tate who uses her own British accent.

Fifteen years before the start of the series, Magica De Spell was Scrooge McDuck's "bitterest" rival. During a battle between them atop Mount Vesuvius, Magica attempted to harness the power of the Lunar eclipse to trap Scrooge within his number one dime, however, Scrooge was able to turn the tables on her and imprisoned Magica in the dime instead.

Before she was sealed in the dime, Magica was able to create a living being from her shadow, to act as her spy. The shadow took on the form of a young girl named Lena, who took the source of Magica's power, an amulet she held within the head of her staff and worked to free her creator.

She became best friends with Webby but becomes progressively more under Magica's disembodied control as in *The Other Bin of Scrooge McDuck* (7/21/2018) where Magica directs her to steal the dime.

Magica first appeared in the form of a black shadow with red glowing eyes in *The Beagle Birthday Massacre!* (9/30/2017) and made her first speaking appearance in *Terror of the Terra-firmians!* (10/2/2017). In *The Shadow War!* (8/18/2018) a two-part episode, she regains her physical appearance: a tall green-feathered slender duck with yellow eyes and short black hair

Why does she looks like a snake with yellow eyes that have reptilian pupils? According to Frank Angones Co-Executive Producer and Story Editor of *DuckTales*, "The yellow and green is the corrupting effect of her magic. The slender, taller appearance harkens back to her first appearance in a Barks book. And the triangle pupils are like the opposite of the pie eyes that everyone else has. It makes her extra subliminally upsetting."

In *The Shadow War!*, once she has Scrooge's first dime in her possession, Magica's physical form is released from the dime with her shadow releasing Lena's body from her control. Magica reverts Lena back to her original form as a shadow and traps her within Magica's own shadow, while Scrooge is sucked into his own number one dime remaining trapped as Magica was for the past fifteen years.

Magica casts a spell upon all the citizens of Duckburg, with their shadows beginning to come alive and thus creating for herself an army of shadow puppets and swearing to Scrooge she will destroy everything he ever loved starting with Duckburg.

In the ensuing fights, Lena protects Webby, Magica's blast hits the dime freeing Scrooge who gets the upper hand and Donald's head breaks the magical ball on her staff causing her to lose her powers and shadow army.

Months later in *A Nightmare on Killmotor Hill* (9/5/2019), Magica begins hounding the dreams of Lena in an attempt to regain her magic powers and seduce Lena back to the dark side. Magica is using a telepathic helmet and drone to enter Lena's dreams and pressure her. Lena magically destroys the equipment and Magica is defeated.

In *Glom Tales* (9/10/2019), having lost her powers, Magica is stuck working at Funso's Fun Zone performing fake magic tricks for children's birthday parties. She teams with Scrooge's rival Flintheart Glomgold who is forming a group of Scrooge's enemies including the Beagle Boys and Mark Beaks to finally bring about the downfall of McDuck and his family.

Through some clever trickery, Louie defeats Glomgold and his allies turn on him. The wrong character model for Magica was sent to the overseas animation studio so in this episode her feathers are white rather than green.

Magica is a major character in Disney Italy comics, where she's called Amelia, "la fattucchiera che ammalia" (literally, "the bewitching witch") and interacts with family members.

Appearing in only one *DuckTales* comic book story "Dime After Dime" (*Disney Adventures* 1990), the character of Magica's young niece, Minima De Spell became so popular that she appeared in several Italian comic book stories and

was the inspiration for the character Lena in the rebooted animated series.

Granny De Spell (whose real name is Caraldina De Spell) was Magica's grandmother and taught her sorcery when she was a child. She first appeared in an Australian comic book story "A Lesson from Granny" (*Magica De Spell Giant Special* #381 1966) where she comes out of retirement to help Magica get Scrooge's dime.

The character was redesigned by artist Giorgio Cavazzano for a 1995 Italian comic book story "Magica De Spell and the Great Rock of Power-Plus" written by Francisco Artibani. Since then, Granny has appeared in several stories.

Magica makes a non-speaking cameo appearance in the *Darkwing Duck* animated series episode "In Like Blunt" (11/15/1991) where she along with the Beagle Boys and Flintheart Glomgold bid for the secret S.H.U.S.H. agent list at a criminal auction. She later appeared in the *Darkwing Duck* comic book series published by Boom! Studios.

Besides her many other comic book appearances by other writers and artists, she also appeared in videogames including *DuckTales/ DuckTales Remastered DuckTales: The Quest for Gold, DuckTales: Scrooge's Loot, Mickey's Racing Adventure, Donald Duck: The Lucky Dime Caper* and *Donald Duck: Goin' Quackers*.

TRICKS AND TREATS

In this section are a few "fun sized" trick-or-treat stories that couldn't be expanded to the length of the chapters that preceeded them.

In October 2005 until October 2011, the Disney Channel ran a nightly marathon of Halloween-related movies and television series episodes (like *Suite Life, Hannah Montana, Dog With a Blog, Jessie* and more) called Hauntober Fest and then Monstober.

The Yzma That Stole Kuzcoween first aired October 14, 2006 as an episode of the half hour animated series *The Emperor's New School*. Jealous Yzma can't stand that Kuzco is the star of the popular Kuzcoween festival, so she decides to ruin it in hopes of turning it into Yzmaween.

Over the decades, there have been several Disney Halloween television specials but they all seemed to include the exact same clips.

Disney's Halloween Treat is an hour Halloween-themed clip show which first aired on *The Wonderful World of Disney* on October 30, 1982 and featured a compilation of Disney animated shorts and feature films involving spooky or supernatural themes.

The special was narrated by a Jack O' Lantern puppet (voiced by Hal Douglas), which was also used in an eight minute educational short to talk about Halloween safety called *Disney's Haunted Halloween* where Hal Smith is the voice of the pumpkin explaining the history of the holiday and stranger danger to Goofy. The opening and closing credits feature an orange colorized version of the 1929 Silly Symphonies short *The Skeleton Dance,* as well as its own theme song, sung in the opening and closing credits. The lyrics were written by Galen R. Brandt with music by John Debney.

A Disney Halloween was a 90-minute Halloween-themed television special that first aired on *The Wonderful World of Disney* October 24, 1983 and included portions from *Disney's Halloween Treat* (1982) and *Disney's Greatest Villains* (1977) featuring classic short cartoons and excerpts from animated feature films.

It was hosted by an off screen narrator (Hal Douglas) and the Magic Mirror from Snow *White and the Seven Dwarfs* (voiced by Hans Conried). The opening and closing credits feature footage from *The Skeleton Dance* but the coloring this time on the skeletons has been changed to green. The special was shown in October the following years on ABC and the Disney Channel until the late 1990s.

DTV Monsters Hits aired on October 30, 1987. DTV was Disney making music videos (inspired by MTV) taking hit songs and pairing them with clips of Disney animation. The individual videos ran on the Disney Channel as filler between shows but three specials were put together for NBC. Jeffrey Jones voiced the Magic Mirror as the narrator host with Gary Owens as the announcer.

Voice actress June Foray recorded new lines for the character of Witch Hazel: "My favorite night is once a year, when spirits come from far and near to scare and terrify... any poor soul who happens by. I'd never been scared, never known fright, 'til I went trick-or-treating one Halloween night."

The music selections included: Michael Jackson: *Thriller*, Ray Parker: *Ghostbusters*, Creedence Clearwater Revival: *Bad Moon Rising*, Bobby "Boris" Pickett featuring The Crypt Kickers: *Monster Mash*, Rockwell: *Somebody's Watching Me*, The Electric Light Orchestra: *Evil Woman*, Stevie Wonder: *Superstition*, Pat Benatar: *You Better Run*, Spike Jones: *That Old Black Magic*, Daryll Hall: *Dreamtime,* From The Many Adventures of Winnie the Pooh: *Heffalumps & Woozles*, The Eurythmics: *Sweet Dreams (Are Made of This)*, Martha and the Vandellas: *In the Midnight Hour*, Cyndi Lauper: *All Through the Night*, Elton John: *It's Getting Dark in Here* and The Jackson 5: *The Boogie Man.*

Halloween Walt

Walt Disney was already an adult by the time the tradition of trick-or-treating became common practice in America. If he ever took his two daughters out for the activity, it was apparently so inconsequential that he never mentioned it and neither did they.

However, when I interviewed Disney Legend Ken Anderson, he told me that Walt probably loved Halloween because he was fond of reading stories about ghosts and witches. When he accompanied Walt on trips to New Orleans, he saw that Walt had a fascination with stories of voodoo queens who could communicate with "the other side" and felt it may have been one of the reasons Walt wanted to create a haunted house attraction for his theme park.

While living in Marceline, Missouri as young boys, Walt Disney and his older brother Roy loved exploring and playing in an old house that was rumored to be haunted. Some unknown incident happened on one of those visits and they never returned and Walt never talked about it.

Also while in Marceline, Walt and Roy earned some extra money by washing the funeral parlor's hearse. Actually, Roy did all the work. Walt spent the day laying in the back playing dead.

When an unsuspecting citizen walked by, Walt, with his unblinking eyes staring forward, would rise slowly from the waist with his arms crossed across his chest much to the consternation of the passerby. Apparently, Walt did it all day while an irritated Roy patiently did the job they were being paid to do.

Walt did have strong feelings about the spirit of Halloween. In his essay for Roland Gammon's book *Faith is a Star* (1963), Walt wrote:

> Children are people, and they should have to reach to learn about things, to understand things, just as adults have to

reach if they want to grow in mental stature. Life is composed of lights and shadows and we would be untruthful, insincere and saccharine if we tried to pretend there were no shadows.

Most things are good, and they are the strongest things, but there are evil things, too, and you are not doing a child a favor by trying to shield him from reality. The important thing is to teach a child that good can always triumph over evil, and that is what our pictures attempt to do.

In an interview with David Griffiths for *TV Times of London* in March 10, 1959, Walt said:

The world's fairytale literature has created its witches, its evil fairies, its hags, and its 'bad people'. Of course, they're repellent. They have to be. But in our movie versions of these venerable morality plays, we have tried to keep all the elements in proper balance of entertainment. We have often eliminated or greatly modified the 'horrific' material in the classic fairytale literature.

Since Walt's death in December 1966, there have been multiple sightings of his ghost almost always accompanied by the strong smell of his foul smelling French cigarettes he smoked later in life and visible puffs of smoke in the air.

These sightings have been reported in different places from the Disney Studio to Disneyland to places where Walt enjoyed eating like Club 33. Some claim to have even heard this phantasm speak. He is usually dressed in a grey suit or wearing a buttoned up sweater with a small tear much like he wore in life.

Lonesome Ghosts (1937)

In the 1930s and 1940s, American cinema was full of ghost chasers, ghost breakers, spook busters and more in comedy films starring Bob Hope, Abbott and Costello, the East Side Kids, the Three Stooges and more.

So it was not that unusual for Disney to delve into the topic with one of its most popular short cartoons that has been included in most Halloween compilations the studio has put together.

Lonesome Ghosts, which debuted on December 24, 1937 just three days after the premiere of Walt Disney's first full-length animated feature film, *Snow White and the Seven Dwarfs* was a co-starring vehicle for Mickey, Donald Duck and Goofy who were near the peak of their popularity.

That same year saw several other short cartoons that teamed the trio including *Moose Hunters, Mickey's Amateurs, Hawaiian Holiday* and *Clock Cleaners*. The following year would include *Boat Builders, Mickey's Trailer*, and *The Whalers*.

The seven minute short was directed by Burt Gillett and featured animation by Bob Wickersham, Clyde Geronimi, Dick Huemer, Milt Kahl, Art Babbitt and others. Gillett had joined the Disney Studio in 1929 and became one of its top directors helming both *Flowers and Trees* and *Three Little Pigs*.

As animation authority Steve Stanchfield has pointed out, "Burt Gillett must have had a hand in designing the ghosts in some capacity; they seem to have a kinship to some of the characters designed for *Bold King Cole* (that he had directed) over at Van Beuren a year before."

Mickey, Donald and Goofy own the Ajax Ghost Exterminators business and are hired over the phone by a female voice to drive four ghosts out of the McShiver mansion that is "full of ghosts". Although the outside of their office has a sign saying "Busy", the three are fast asleep when the phone

rings. A sign behind Mickey states that "We chase ghosts by the day, week or month. Phone."

Unknown to the heroes, they are being hired by four ghosts with bowler hats and bulbous noses who have gotten bored because no one comes around the abandoned house anymore and they wish to play their pranks. They are lonesome because no one visits.

They have seen the ad in the newspaper stating "Notice! We Exterminte All Kinds of Ghosts—Day and Night Service. Phone Gooseflesh 9000" and decide to scare the pants off of the "wise guys" who placed the advertisement in the classified section.

When the trio arrives carrying a double barreled shotgun, net, axe, rope, chain, mousetrap and more, the front door falls down when Mickey knocks on it. As they step on the door, it unexpectedly flies up and throws them in to the house and they hear ghostly sounds. Mickey decides they will separate and surround the ghosts.

Mickey is knocked on the head. A ghost puts its finger in Mickey's gun so it backfires and explodes. The ghost races upstairs and closes a door. Mickey tries to open the door and it falls down and ghosts playing a drum and fifes come marching out of it and go behind a set of double doors. Mickey opens those doors and a wave of water floods out with ghosts surfing across it on surf boards. The last one comes out on a motorboat and circles Mickey until it and the water disappears completely.

Donald is scared by a pile of dishes crashing behind him and then by a pile of chains thrown to the floor. He is whacked on his rear by a large board twice and then is mocked by a ghost imitating Donald's fighting stance. The ghost leaps into a pool of water on the floor and squirts Donald. The ghost then disappears along with the water and when Donald puts back on his hat, he finds it is filled with water that also disappears.

Holding an axe, Goofy is stalking a ghost but is frightened by a ghost banging a pan behind him and then playing a trombone behind him as Goofy tries to claw his way through a wall. Goofy chases the ghost into a set of dresser drawers and in the mirror on top of the dresser he and the ghost do a variation of the Marx Brothers' famous mirror scene from Duck Soup (1933).

Goofy becomes entangled in the dresser and thinking he sees the ghost sticks a pin in his own rear end to the amusement of all four ghosts. They push the dresser with Goofy in it down the stairs. At the bottom of the stairs, the runaway dresser pushes Mickey, Donald and Goofy into barrels of molasses and flour. As they struggle to free themselves from the goop, it makes them look like actual ghosts. That image frightens the four ghosts who rush through the house, breaking a window in the process and leaving their footprints in the snow outside as they run away. Donald laughs and calls them sissies.

One of the ghosts appears in the episode "When the Spirit Moves You" on the *Bonkers* television series where Bonkers and Miranda try to catch him. On *House of Mouse*, they appear in the episode "House Ghosts" where they scare Pete by pulling his underwear. They also appear in *Mickey's House of Villains* during the hostile takeover.

They appear in several videogames including *Mickey Mania: The Timeless Adventures of Mickey Mouse, Mickey's Wild Adventure, The Great Circus Mystery starring Mickey and Minnie, Disney Tsum Tsum, Search for the Secret Keys, Disney's Magical Quest 2 Starring Mickey and Minnie* and the *Epic Mickey* series (which features additional ghosts).

In 2009 the cartoon was shortened by approximately half its length for the *Disney Have-a-Laugh* series run on the Disney Channel.

Although unnamed in the original cartoon, the four ghosts have been given the names Jasper, Grubb, Boo and Moss. Jasper is considered the leader of the group and the smartest. Grubb is the smallest ghost and Billy Bletcher (Pete, Big Bad Wolf) provides his voice. Boo is the one who scared Donald and Moss is the one who tormented Goofy.

It has always been assumed that the cartoon helped inspire the live action movie *Ghostbusters* (1984) since it has a group of ghost hunters and at one point Goofy proclaims "I ain't a scared of no ghosts" which sounds like the phrase from the Ghostbusters theme song "I ain't afraid of no ghosts".

The cartoon inspired a storyline in the Mickey Mouse comic strip written by Ted Thwaites and drawn by Floyd Gottfredson.

Entitled *The Seven Ghosts*, it appeared in the Sunday comic section of newspapers from August 10 through November 28, 1936. Thwaites and Gottfredson had seen the animated short while it was in production and loved the idea of Mickey, Goofy and Donald Duck as ghost hunters but felt there could be a stronger story.

In a 1979 interview I did with Gottfredson, he recalled:

> We tried to follow the spirit of the Mickey animated cartoons but because we were doing adventure stories we had to go beyond them. The animated cartoons had just a loose story structure where there could be a lot of gags building to a conclusion.
>
> That isn't how stories are done in newspaper strips. We had to develop the characters more to help sustain the story. I loved doing these little adventures but keeping them as humorous as possible.
>
> Straight gags are too thin. Not enough meat to them. I think going back to gag-a-day was a step backwards and I think this was proved by the drop in popularity of the strip.

The Seven Ghosts tells the tale that Colonel Bassett's mansion seems to be the source of a series of ghost hauntings. Mickey, Goofy, and Donald decide to investigate. The ghosts have driven away the Colonel's family and staff so Mickey and his friends take the place of the servants and try to rid the place of the spirits.

The ghosts are actually smugglers who are scaring people away so they can use the hidden passageways in the mansion to seem to disappear and hide their illegal cargo. Mickey traps them and has them arrested and saves Bassett Mansion.

The story of the trio of ghostbusters was so beloved that it was incorporated into the 1993 marketing campaign, The Perils of Mickey. Images of Mickey as the ghostbuster was used on a plethora of merchandise including storybooks.

Ray Bradbury
Halloween Tree:
Disneyland Frontierland

Disney authority Tim O'Day told me in 2019:

> Ray and I actually came up with the idea of placing a Halloween Tree at Disneyland in late spring/early summer 2007 over lunch at Storyteller's Cafe at Disney's Grand Californian Hotel. We were joined by Duncan Wardle from Disney Parks Public Relations.
>
> I was unaware of Ray's book and when he mentioned that he had a "new" book coming out (an anniversary re-print) the proverbial light bulb went off in my head. The original idea for the Halloween Tree was to fabricate a large, 60-foot tall, gnarly oak tree in Town Square where the Christmas tree traditionally resides. The Oak tree would have been hung with hundreds of swinging, illuminated, jack-o-lanterns. It would have been quite the impressive sight!
>
> To be sure, Ray was VERY enthused about the idea and couldn't wait to see the concept become a reality. Duncan and I valiantly tried to move the idea forward but plans were already in place for the giant "Mickey" pumpkin to be placed in Town Square. Not letting a good idea die, I told Tony Baxter about the book release and the tree idea and he and Kim Irvine made it a reality.

On October 31, 2007, eighty-seven year old, wheelchair bound author Ray Bradbury attended the dedication of a Halloween Tree at Frontierland in Disneyland that was to be included as part of its annual park-wide Halloween decorations every year.

It followed a special, private dinner ceremony at Club 33 hosted by Imagineers Tony Baxter, Marty Sklar and Tim Delaney celebrating the 35th anniversary of Bradbury's book.

Bradbury told stories for about fifteen minutes about his love and connection with Disney.

The Halloween Tree is a 1972 fantasy novel by Bradbury, which traces the history of Samhain and Halloween. A group of eight boys (dressed in iconic costumes like a skeleton, grim reaper, mummy, Jack-O-Lantern, etc.) set out to go trick-or-treating on Halloween, only to discover that Pip, a ninth friend is on the verge of death.

Led by the mysterious Mr. Moundshroud, they must pursue their friend's spirit across time and space to rescue him. The kids travel on a giant patchwork kite, pieced together from the leftover scraps of a hundred carnival posters and powered by Moundshroud's magic.

Along the way, they learn the origins of the spooky holiday. The Halloween Tree itself, with its many branches laden with jack-o'-lanterns, serves as a metaphor for the historical connection of these many different traditions.

In October 1966, Ray Bradbury and his daughters sat down together to watch the Halloween special *It's the Great Pumpkin, Charlie Brown* and none of them liked it. They were all disappointed that The Great Pumpkin didn't show up and felt it wasn't a proper Halloween film at all.

Bradbury complained about it over lunch to his friend the animator and director Chuck Jones who agreed with him. He soon brought Jones an oil painting of a Halloween Tree Bradbury had made a few years before, a dark, haunting tree decorated with jack-o-lanterns swaying from its autumn branches.

Jones arranged for MGM to hire Bradbury to write a half hour animated special for Jones to produce and direct. However, soon afterwards MGM closed its animation department and the script was never done but Bradbury adapted it into a written story that became the book.

In 1993, Bradbury wrote another screenplay based on the novel but with some changes (like including a girl as one of the trick-or-treaters) for a feature length animated version for television for which he won an Emmy Award for outstanding writng of an animated program. He provided the narration for that Hanna-Barbera production as well.

After that special banquet at Club 33, Bradbury was taken outside with the rest of the attendees for an unexpected dedication. An oak tree near the Golden Horseshoe Saloon was designated to be the representation of Bradbury's Halloween Tree during the Halloween season and is decorated with nearly 1,500 glowing red and orange lights and roughly 50 different hand-painted jack-o-lanterns.

Bradbury, a long time Disney fan who knew Walt personally, had collaborated with the Imagineers on some Disney projects including Spaceship Earth at Epcot.

"I belong here in Disneyland, ever since I came here 50 years ago. I'm glad I'm going to be a permanent part of the spirit of Halloween and Disneyland," said Bradbury at the dedication as he pulled the stem of a lighted jack-o-lantern to light up the tree. He added "I know the ghost of Walt Disney is blessing me this very moment." He would visit the tree several times before he passed away in 2012

A plaque featuring some of the mask imagery from the book at the base of the tree commemorates the night of its dedication: "On the night of Halloween 2007, this stately oak officially became 'The Halloween Tree,' realizing famed author Ray Bradbury's dream of having his symbol for the holiday become a permanent part of Disneyland."

Brad Kaye, Creative Entertainment art director at Disneyland Resort, who helped decorate that very first Halloween Tree stated:

> As a fan of [Bradbury's] books, it was really an honor. For the first year, [Walt Disney Imagineers] Tony Baxter, Kim Irvine, and I sat in front of the Golden Horseshoe late one night and 'magic-markered' all the pumpkins. In the years following, park enhancement has done a wonderful job of keeping it up in all its Halloween glory.

"As the tree gets older and bigger, it will get more and more décor every year," said Baxter.

During Halloween, the Disney Cruise Line ships often put up a Pumpkin Tree in the lobby of its ships as an homage to Bradbury's Halloween Tree.

The Legend of the DCL Pumpkin Trees

Before the time of now, there was Halloween. Not the Halloween of today, filled with merriment and pranks, but a darker celebration. The night was filled with mystery. The moon seemed to shine a little bit brighter, and in every shadow lurked something unimaginable.

This was the time of the Pumpkin King who was the caretaker of the stories and the memories of Halloween. But as the years grew on, the Pumpkin King grew weary.

He needed someone to help him keep the history of his favorite, most beloved holiday. So he reached in his head and retrieved four pumpkin seeds, each one representing a different characteristic of his wicked personality.

He planted them around and watched as the seeds grew into beautifully morbid trees.

The trees bloom only once a year. Deep within its dark, gnarled branches hold the remnant spirits of Halloween memories gone past. According to the legend, once everyone has learned the who, the what, the why, the real and true spirit of Halloween, the Pumpkin King will bring the trees to life.

The trees which appear in September and October and each have distinctive facial features are located in the atriums of each ship and are named as follows:

- Grim – *Disney Dream*
- Mucklebones – *Disney Fantasy*
- Bog – *Disney Wonder*
- Reap – *Disney Magic*

Ben Cooper Disney Halloween Costumes

From 1937 to 1992, Ben Cooper Inc. was one of the largest Halloween costume manufacturers in the United States. The inexpensive plastic masks (made from "virgin vinyl") held on the face by a rubber band and sleeveless vinyl smocks were a part of most children's Halloween trick-or-treating rituals especially from the 1950s to the 1970s.

The company had originally begun as a vaudeville and masquerade costume company in Brooklyn, New York (even making costumes for the famous Cotton Club nightclub and the *Ziegfeld Follies*) founded by brothers Ben and Nat Cooper.

They soon saw the opportunity to become the kings of children's inexpensive Halloween (which started to rise in popularity in the 1930s) costumes because of their assumption that kids liked to dress up when they played and that parents in more urban cities often didn't have the time to make the costumes for their children.

The company had assumed control of A.S. Fishbach Inc. which had an existing license to produce costumes based on Disney characters like Mickey Mouse, Donald Duck and Snow White. They began selling Disney costumes under Fishbach's Spotlight brand and the two companies officially merged as Ben Cooper Inc. in December 1942. The first masks were made with gauze and later rubber.

While there were other children Halloween costume manufacturers like Collegeville and Halco, Ben Cooper Inc. rights to the Disney characters helped establish it as the largest and most prominent company and helped it to get other high profile properties like Superman.

Their costumes were sold through major retailers like J.C.Penney, Sears, and dime stores like Woolworth's in boxes for between one and three dollars.

As Nat's son Ira told writer Michael Eury:

> They got the existing Disney license when they purchased the other company. They would take trips to the West Coast to get approval for various new designs.

> For instance, Mickey was popular but he evolved as to his looks so that he became more and more kid friendly. There must have been five to six changes to Donald Duck over a ten year period. Snow White was next, and the prospect of success was not necessarily optimistic. But like Walt who they knew, Ben and Nat saw the value in the sheer quality of what Disney was producing and so they risked it.

> Superman approached Mickey Mouse in volume—but not overall, as Mickey sold to a wider age range of kids. In those days, Superman was strictly for boys ages eight and up.

As Ira told writer Matt Artz:

> I know one of their earliest visits to Walt Disney was when he was still at the Hyperion Studio. My sense of it is that Walt was a pretty busy man but always made time for them. There was a time in the early '60s, I must have been about 7 or 8 years old, where we had lunch in the Disney dining room, and they had previously met with him. So when he came into lunch, we were instructed not to go over and say 'hello'. But it was clear that everybody knew each other.

> I think in the early years, when *Snow White* and *Cinderella* and all those things were coming out, I think those were critical meetings, where there were real decisions made on what they were going to produce for the company. And there was always a difference of what was produced for sale in Disneyland, which came later, and what was going to be out in the marketplace.

> The walls of our early office were lined with original cels from *Snow White* signed by Walt to Ben and Nat.

To produce costumes in time for the Halloween season, the company had to begin production eight to ten months beforehand and it might take weeks to get final approval on a mask. At one point, Disney leaned on Ben Cooper Inc. to produce character costumes to promote the release of *The Black Hole* (1979) and those did not sell well.

In 1982, roughly a month before Halloween, several people including a child died after taking Tylenol that had been laced

with cyanide. It set off a nationwide panic that something could be so easily poisoned so parents worried that someone might attempt the same thing with Halloween candy. Sales of candy at grocery stores dropped almost fifty percent that year and many parents did not take their children trick-or-treating.

The holiday custom started to shift to indoor parties and more adults began participating demanding a higher quality cloth costume. While Ben Cooper Inc. did make cloth costumes, they were much costlier to produce. The company continued to hang on through the 1980s thanks to its many popular licenses but eventually was bought in 1992 by Rubie's Costume Company that dissolved the name and operations.

Some of the earlier costumes are considered highly collectible and can be priced at several hundred or even thousands of dollars because few survived in good shape or complete because they were meant to be worn by children. Even the Disney boxes are coveted because most were thrown away after the costume was removed.

Tim Burton's Disney Channel Halloween Special (1983)

When most Disney fans think of Tim Burton in connection with Disney, the first things that usually come to mind are *The Nightmare Before Christmas, Frankenweenie, Alice in Wonderland* and perhaps even the wonderful short *Vincent* about a boy who wanted to grow up to be Vincent Price.

Few if any Disney fans think of *Hansel and Gretel*, a thirty-five minute live action Disney television special of the famous story directed by Tim Burton and written by Julie Hickson that aired only once on the Disney Channel on Halloween night October 31, 1983 on the series *Walt Disney Studio Showcase*.

A recently discovered and restored version has only been shown a handful of other times over the decades at Tim Burton retrospective film shows around the world.

The Disney Channel Magazine indicated another airing was scheduled for October 29, 1983 but there is no confirmation that it was shown at that time. Supposedly Burton was embarrassed by the final production and Disney executives found it too dark and disturbing.

To promote the show on April 26th 1983 the Walt Disney Studio Showcase had an episode entitled *Backstage at Disney* with animation historian John Culhane. The show included a three minute segment of Burton and production designer Rick Henrichs discussing their films *Vincent* and *Hansel and Gretel*.

Costing $116,000 and filmed on 16mm film, the live-action *Hansel and Gretel* special featured a cast of Asian amateur actors, Japanese toys and kung fu fights blended with Burton's distinctive designs working with Heinrichs who made the three-dimensional models.

It reflected Burton's interest in Japanese toys (which is why he made the father a toymaker rather than the traditional

woodsman) and the Godzilla movies and featured highly stylized, surrealistic sets familiar to fans of Burton's work. The production incorporated puppets, forced perspective and some stop motion animation.

It had a short, live introduction by actor Vincent Price because the showing also included the Burton stop-motion animated short *Vincent* narrated by Price so that the entire program would be forty-five minutes long. The music for the special was done by John Costa who was the music director for the television series *Mr. Rogers' Neighborhood* for approximately thirty years.

The story follows the traditional tale with unexpected Burton twists.

A poor toymaker (Jim Ishida) and his son and daughter (Andy Lee and Allison Hong) suffer under the toymaker's wicked new wife (Michael Yama) who hates Hansel and Gretel. During an altercation at dinner, the two children are sent to their dark attic bedroom where their father later comes and tries to cheer them up with a performance by a small clown puppet named Jocko and a few cookies. He also leaves a small toy swan to watch over them.

The next morning, the stepmother tries to lose the children in the forest but they find their way home thanks to some small stones Hansel has dropped along the way. The next day while the father is in town trying to sell his toys, the stepmother again tries to lose them in the forest. She gives them a toy duck that eats the trail of stones they leave behind them to help find their way home.

While they are sleeping at night in the forest, the toy duck transforms into a small toy robot that leads them to a house made of gingerbread and candy that oozes out of its walls. The witch with a curved candy cane nose (also played by Michael Yama who played the stepmother) who lives there lures them inside with promises of sweet treats. She tells them the furniture like the chairs and table are real candy and the two children greedily enjoy devouring them completely.

Tired, they are led by the witch to two marshmallow beds that capture them with candy cane arms. The bed drops Hansel into a large room with a huge mobile of Dan Dan, the

gingerbread man, (a puppet voiced by David Koenigsberg) who insists Hansel eat him so that Hansel will be fattened up for the witch's meal. Hansel does eat some of the gingerbread man but comes to his senses and shatters the creepy clown's head into pieces.

Meanwhile, the witch has taken Gretel down to the kitchen to help heating the oven to bake Hansel. Two long candy cane arms drop from the mobile above Hansel and bring him to the kitchen. Before he can be put into the oven, Gretel grabs the fire iron and hits the witch with it. The witch and Gretel engage in a kung fu style battle using cookie cutters, candy cane nunchucks and throwing star cookies. Hansel breaks free to join the fight.

When the witch makes a flying kick, the children duck out of the way and she flies into her own oven and is trapped. The house begins to melt into a pool of colored frosting while Hansel and Gretel escape just in time.

A toy swan their father had given them earlier appears out of the melted candy and enlarges into the form of a boat and takes the children back home. The father explains that their wicked stepmother is mysteriously gone for good which is why it is so quiet now. The swan boat begins to spout gold coins from its mouth providing the money the poor family needed to live happily ever after.

At best, the film is an interesting curiosity but the pacing is very slow and uneven and the acting is very amateurish. It is very much as if someone made a home movie or even a student film but did not have the professional expertise to make its ideas come to life. It may be a scary Halloween treat but for all the wrong reasons.

The film was shot off the Disney lot in a small Hollywood studio to avoid conflicts with the studio unions. Following the tradition of classic Japanese theater where women were not allowed on stage, Burton cast the two female roles with the same male, Michael Yama, and as the stepmother had him appear in full traditional Kabuki attire.

When Tim Burton's *The Nightmare Before Christmas* was released on DVD, Disney chose to include Burton's short films Vincent and Frankenweenie but purposely omitted *Hansel and Gretel*.

Burton recalled:

> I had a bunch of drawings and Disney let me do it. I had a room filled with these drawings and I think that was the thing that made them feel comfortable that I could do it to some degree. I have always been drawn to the Japanese sense of design.

> It was pretty amateurish but that was more to do with me. I learned a lot from it. It's funny, if you've never made a movie with actual people you think you can do it. It looks very easy. But there is something about it that's abstract. So it was a good learning experience for me.

> Being an animator, I rarely spoke to people. I was not a good communicator but in live action filmmaking you have to learn to communicate what you are thinking to a large number of people. I learned a lot of stuff from *Hansel and Gretel* in terms of how to communicate with people.

> The film is weirdly ambitious on the one hand and on the other it's really chessy and cheap. There was no money to make it, less than it cost to make *Vincent*. There are little moments in it that I like. It was like one of those scary children's shows I grew up watching.

Twitches (2005)

On Halloween night, in the magical dimension of Coventry, the royal witch Miranda gives birth to identical twin daughters that she names Apolla (for the sun) and Artemis (for the moon). Their father apparently dies protecting them from an evil being called the Darkness.

The girls are taken to the non-magical Earth for safe-keeping and given up for adoption so they grow up in different families not knowing of each other's existence.

On their 21st birthday, on Halloween, the twins are reunited because they are the only ones capable of saving Coventry from the Darkness but must work together. The girls call themselves "twitches" as a combination of "twin" and "witches".

That is the premise for the Disney Channel Original Movie *Twitches* (2005) starring real life twins Tia and Tamera Mowry and based of the popular book series published by Scholastic Press. The two actresses had previously appeared in the sitcom *Sister Sister* (1994 -1999) where they played twin sisters seperated at birth who were reunited.

Originally, Tia was supposed to play Camryn and Tamera was supposed to play Alex, but the two wanted their roles to be switched. For the first few days of filming, the cast and crew had a hard time telling the two girls apart so it made it easy for Tia to fill in for Tamera's character during the party scene.

When the movie first aired on Disney Channel on October 14, 2005, it attracted seven million viewers. In four subsequent airings during its first weekend, the movie drew a total of 21.5 million viewers and was the week's most popular cable program.

That popularity was enough to inspire a sequel *Twitches Too* (2007) where the twins are attending a university and are able to bring their father back from the Shadowlands and finally defeat Thantos who was the Darkness. The film premiered as part of the Disney Channel Hauntober Fest in October.

The film has an alternate ending where during the final celebration, it turns out that the biological mother of the twins, Miranda, has an evil, long-lost sister named Minerva who has comes back to get revenge. Apparently, she has evil intentions for her nieces. This ending which was cut from the final film was to set up a third installment of the franchise.

Twitches Too racked up 6.96 million total viewers in its 90-minute Friday premiere, making it the most-watched program on basic cable for the night—beating out the National League Championship Series on TBS. More than one-third of all kids 6-11 and tweens 9-14 watching TV were tuned in to *Twitches Too*.

Haunted Mansion Holiday

A Disney press release proclaimed: "Pumpkin King Jack Skellington has been busy decorating the Haunted Mansion with frightfully festive touches inspired by *Tim Burton's The Nightmare Before Christmas*. Experience some of your favorite sights, special seasonal surprises—and scare-aracters from the movie. Sally, Oogie Boogie and other Nightmare nasties will be on hand to wish you 'Season's Screamings!'"

With the ongoing popularity of *Tim Burton's The Nightmare Before Christmas* (1993), Disney looked at possible ways to integrate Burton's vision into the Disney theme park experience. In 1996, Imagineer Chris Merritt submitted a proposal for a traditional Disney dark ride that was inspired by *Nightmare*.

Visitors would enter through the tree/portal to Halloween Town, and board a coffin sleigh for a trip that would take them through the land of Halloween, into the Professor's laboratory and through Oogie Boogie's lair, resulting in a whirlwind trip through a familiar snow-covered graveyard where Jack finally gets his girl before the sleighs return to the world of the living.

While that concept never got off the drawing board, another one about combining the Haunted Mansion attraction with an overlay of elements from the *Nightmare* film took almost three years to get approval.

The original concept had been to theme the iconic Haunted Mansion to Dickens' *Christmas Carol* and its Christmas ghosts but the idea of using *Nightmare* supplanted it because it could be used for both Halloween and Christmas because it represents a time when "the two holidays collide".

On October 3, 2001, Haunted Mansion Holiday opened and quickly became popular with many guests. The storyline is that this experience takes place after the events in the film. Jack Skellington discovers the home of the Happy Haunts

and to spread some holiday joy, he shares some of his original "dark" Christmas presents and decorations.

By 1997 Garner Holt Productions was being invited to be one of the bidders that the Disneyland Purchasing Department called in for their periodic new project bidder's conferences.

In 2001, GHP produced over two dozen audio-animatronics including Jack Skellington for Disneyland's Haunted Mansion Holiday overlay that has been running for nearly twenty years. GHP was the first outside vendor to provide audio-animatronics for Disney.

GHP creative director Bill Butler said:

> Guests don't realize that ninety percent of what you see of that overlay is actually stored inside the ride during the rest of the year. If the lights were on and you could see around corners, it would be obvious. It's a huge space with lots of places to hide."

Sally, the rag doll from The Nightmare Before Christmas, joined the vast menagerie of characters at Disneyland in September 2016. She was positioned behind a graveyard tombstone.

The animatronics version of Sally is a little cleaner and simpler than the one in the movie. She doesn't quite have the clay skin and baggy eyes of a girl held prisoner by an evil duck doctor.

"We also created the animatronics Oogie Boogie," said Bill Butler, Holt's creative director. "And a second version of the show at Tokyo Disneyland."

Spooks and Magic: Mouse Factory (1972)

A syndicated television series entitled *The Mouse Factory* that was produced and directed by Disney Legend Ward Kimball debuted in January 1972. It was a half hour show that included clips of Disney cartoons interspesed with live action comedy with a guest host who was always billed as "Mickey's Friend".

The hosts included Annette Funicello, Kurt Russell, Don Knotts, Jonathan Winters and others. It was intended to be a zany, fast-paced show in the spirit of the popular *Laugh-In*. It ran for almost two seasons from 1972 to 1973.

The animated closing sequence during season one featured Mickey Mouse in a biplane getting swallowed by King Kong who is hanging on to the outside of the Empire State Building.

The fourth episode that ran the week of February 16, 1972 was entitled *Spooks and Magic* and featured comedienne Phyllis Dillwer as the host. Diller is a wacky witch who is celebrating Halloween at her house. Perhaps it was delayed for some reason from an October airing which is why it popped up in mid-season long after the holiday was over.

Diller used her well-known comedic schtick (even mentioning her husband "Fang") to play the affable "Ghost Host." She claimed her favorite relative was her "Auntie Mim" from whom she inherited her hair. She wore a purple dress with white stars and a pointed purple hat with white stars while holding her long cigarette holder (but no cigarette). When she entertained her guests, she wore a long red sparkly dress.

The episode gave viewers brief glimpses inside Disneyland's Haunted Mansion, which stood in as Diller's Midnight Manor, that Diller describes as "a rooming house for worn-out witches, ghosts, goblins, and similar 'death of the party' types where every night is Halloween!"

At the end of the cartoon *Lonesome Ghosts* (1937) Diller frightens live-action Mickey, Donald and Goofy costumed as their characters from the short. The show included *Trick or Treat* (1952), as well as the Wizard's Duel from *The Sword in the Stone* (1963).

For the Wizard's Duel sequence, live action costume characters Goofy as Count Goofula and Donald Duck as Duckenstein make a brief appearance as Diller's friends joining The Big Bad Wolf (the Wolfman) and Brer Bear (the Hunchback) to watch television on a crystal ball with rabbit ears.

The show was written by Jack Hanrahan, Tom Dagenais and Ted Berman.

Associate producer was Lou Debney and Music supervisor was George Bruns. Set decoration was done by John A. Kuri with costumes by Chuck Keehne. Assistant director was Michael Messinger.

The closing of the episode has a live costumed Snow White show up at the door as a trick-or-treater. Diller offers her a shiny red apple as a treat but Snow White wisely refuses. Diller then says she will give her a trick by turning her into a toad but when she points her wand at the young princess it changes her into Donald Duck, Goofy, King Louie, Witch Hazel and finally Mickey Mouse.

Diller taps the "wigged out wand" on her arm and changes into Snow White and laughs in an echoey voice "That's better!"

This silly installment had some unexpected treats including a costumed Witch Hazel stirring a cauldron in Diller's kitchen and quips by Diller that in the old days witches were tossed into water to see if they would sink (proving their innocence) or float: "If they didn't sink, they were still sunk. Some test."

Barks Halloween Stories

Disney Legend Carl Barks is renowned for his writing and drawing comic book stories featuring the Disney ducks, in particular Scrooge, Donald and his nephews.

He did several memorable Christmas stories of the ducks but only a handful of Halloween stories. It wasn't his lack of affection for the holiday that prevented him. As he told Klaus Stryzyz in 1980, "I think that the idea behind Hallowe'en, namely getting into costume and mischief is actually quite universal and can be understood in other countries."

However, he felt limited by the subject matter of the holiday. As he told historian Michael Barrier, "Always there were decisions to make. Could a loup garou be a real werewolf? Could a witch be a real witch? How far can I stretch the ridiculous without getting into trouble with the office?"

Of course, his most famous Halloween comic book story was *Trick or Treat* in *Donald Duck* #26 where using Photostats of the storyboard for the animated short of the same name, he drew a story that was later censored by nine pages when it veered from the original cartoon by adding additional scenes and an entirely new character.

With those pages censored, he had to make up the difference in page count in that same issue with an additional story entitled "Hobblin' Goblins". According to inventor Gyro Gearloose, "All troubles are caused by goblins—and on Halloween they work overtime!"

So he has developed an invention in a horseshoe shape to foil their schemes by reading their thoughts and giving advice. It is much like the traditional Magic 8-Ball that dispensed random advice to questions. No goblins appear in the story.

He gives the device to Huey, Dewey and Louie who use it to try to escape a party given by Daisy because they will have to dance with little girls. They agree to help Donald stack

pumpkins in order to get out of the party but their uncle warns them not to carve any jack-o-lanterns. Of course, an accident results in that happening to three of the pumpkins so the nephews have to attend the party for two hours of dancing.

In addition to the two stories, the comic book had two one page gag sequences in the inside covers of the book. On the inside cover, Donald and the nephews in costume take a stranger's suggestion to do a typical prank by taking apart a buckboard and reassembling it up on the roof. It turns out the stranger is the owner of an antique shop and they save him a costly installation job of putting the object on his roof.

On the inside back cover, Daisy is nervous about masks at Halloween so Donald volunteers to toughen her up by jumping out at her wearing scary masks but to no effect. Then Donald appears without a mask and says "Boo!" and Daisy screams and faints. The gag was a teaser for the back cover that featured a cut-out mask of Donald Duck.

The cover of *Walt Disney Comics and Stories* #158 has Donald and Daisy trying to take a bite out of an apple suspended from a string without using their hands. In the background is a large jack-o-lantern and the nephews in Halloween costumes. They are smiling because a worm has come out of the side of the apple in front of Donald.

The cover of *Walt Disney Comics and Stories* #134 has Donald in a chef's hat holding a rolling pin and standing behind a counter that has a pumpkin pie that has been carved into a jack-o-lantern face by the nephews who are happily eating the missing pieces.

In the 1961 story "Jet Witch" (*Walt Disney Comics & Stories* #254) the story opens with Donald Duck at a Duckburg town meeting loudly denouncing the mischief of children on Halloween. After Donald leaves, the town council does come up with a plan for a safe and orderly Halloween as done in some other cities.

On Halloween, seeing his nephews in costume leaving the house, he quickly buys treats for any visitors but only one tiny child shows up at his door. He notices all the other houses and the streets are empty. Gyro Gearloose shows up dressed as a

witch riding a flying broom. Gyro was testing his new jet stick that is so top secret he needed to wear a disguise.

Donald takes the disguise and the ionic ejector to search for everyone else and finds they are holding an outdoor party in the park. Donald's appearance scares them and the zoo animals who all run away because they think he is a real witch. An exhausted Donald slinks home just in time for the nephews to arrive excited about the fun they had at the big party.

Barks did three oil paintings with Halloween themes. The first was "Halloween in Duckburg" in 1973 that took its inspiration from the *Trick or Treat* story in *Donald Duck* #26. A frightened Donald Duck opens his front door to be confronted by Witch Hazel hovering on a broom, the nephews in costumes and several humorous but terrifying creatures.

Then in 1974, he repainted the same scene labeling it "Trick or Treat" with the same composition but a different color scheme and different creatures. Also in 1974, he painted "Student Witch" where an attractive, young brunette sorceress in a skin-tight red dress showing lots of cleavage conjures some amusing animal-like demons while being watched by Witch Hazel's pet orge named Smorgasbord the Bad.

Halloween Hall o' Fame: The Wonderful World of Disney (1977)

Halloween Hall o' Fame is a 1977 sixty minute Halloween themed episode of *The Wonderful World of Disney* which originally aired on October 30, 1977. Directed by Arthur J. Viarelli and written by George Petlowany.

Comedian Jonathan Winters stars as a night watchman working late doing his rounds on Halloween night at the Disney Studios. He is accompanied by his dog, Peanuts, who is a beagle so this is probably a clever reference to Charlie Brown and his beagle Snoopy.

The watchman isn't happy about working on Halloween. When he checks the inside of the prop room, in the type of comedy he was famous for, Winters begins doing prop comedy with some of the items.

He gives an award trophy to a tiny baseball team whose players are the same size as the trophy. Finding a basket, he becomes an Indian fakir who charms the snake, gets bitten and then bites the snake. A small town fire chief rallies his crew to put out a doghouse fire. As a doctor he chides a hanging skeleton for not eating enough vegetables.

He finds an object covered by a cloth and when he removes it, he finds a crystal ball and inside the spirit of John O'Lantern better known by the nickname Jack O'Lantern.

That talking pumpkin head is also played by Winters. It is a highly effective transformation by Disney's make-up team. Unlike some actors, Winters claimed to *Time* magazine (October 3, 1977) that he loved being in the elaborate make-up, "I was secure with my head. I knew I was a pumpkin mentally. There's a lot of seeds up there; some gone." Publicity photos show him smiling during the extensive process.

Jack O'Lantern is hiding out from Halloween because it's no longer scary like it was back in "the olden days". He complains, "The only thing scary about Halloween these days is the cavities the kids are going to get from eatin' all that candy."

He threatens to "turn the place into a vacant lot" if Winters doesn't let him hide out until midnight when Halloween will be over. The jack-o-lantern claims that Halloween is "just the dumbest thing I ever saw....there's nothin' scary about it." In the old days, he claims, they had REAL ghosts and goblins.

The night watchman disagrees and feels that Jack should be ashamed of himself for hiding out on Halloween. While the two debate the situation, there are clips shown in the crystal ball from the following Disney cartoons: *Trick or Treat* (1952), *Lonesome Ghosts* (1937), *Pluto's Judgement Day* (1935) and *The Legend of Sleepy Hollow* (1949).

The watchman provokes Jack to come out of hiding and he does so by switching heads with the watchman. He is going to use the body to go out and mix with the trick-or-treaters since he doesn't have one of his own.

The watchman is actually happy because he gets the night off and got Jack to enjoy the celebration. He tells the viewers that if they see "Mr. Pumpkin Head" on their block to remind him he has to get back to the prop room before midnight or else.

Winters ends by saying:

> And it was always said of him, that he knew how to keep Halloween well, if any man alive possessed the knowledge. May that be truly said of us, and all of us! And so, as Tiny Tim observed, Happy Halloween, Every One!

The *TV Guide* ad said:

> Jonathan Winters in a pumpkin head. Disney's Halloween Fright Night. The madcap master of make-believe presents zany comedy and classic cartoons!

Once Upon a Halloween (2005)

Once Upon a Halloween is a fifty-three minute 2005 direct-to video film made by Walt Disney Studios Home Entertainment only released in the U.K. It features The Wicked Witch from *Snow White and the Seven Dwarfs* and features clips from Disney animated movies of classic Disney villains as well as shorts and songs.

On the night before Halloween, the Evil Queen in her persona as the Wicked Witch plans to conquer Halloween so she peers into her magic cauldron to have it show her several villains who might be able to help her with her plan which prompts clips from various Disney animated films.

Those villains include Pete (from *Officer Duck*), Ursula (*The Little Mermaid*), Captain Hook (*Peter Pan*), Yzma (*The Emperor's New Groove*), Ratigan and Fidget (*The Great Mouse Detective*), Alameda Slim and the Willie Brothers (*Home on the Range*) and Judge Frollo (*The Hunchback of Notre Dame*).

The cauldron explains its origins and The Horned King (*The Black Cauldron*) to affirm it is not the cauldron from *Snow White and the Seven Dwarfs* but the mystical Black Cauldron from the the 1985 film of the same name.

> I am but one of many magic cauldrons, all forged in hate, by the witches of Morva. The villains you seek may be summoned from within my depths, O Queen. For it is within me that all dark things reside.

Susanne Blakeslee provides the voice for the Evil Queen and Corey Burton voices the cauldron. The two banter back and forth during the bridging sequences:

> The Evil Queen: Is there anything more laughable than great suffering, cauldron?
>
> Cauldron: [*muttering*] Your plans, dear queen.
>
> The Evil Queen: What?
>
> Cauldron: Oh—nothing.

While the box cover art shows the Evil Queen, only the Wicked Witch appears in the video and only as a threatening shadow. The bridging animation between clips was all done in CGI.

The Disney description was:

> Every heroic story must have a villain, and Disney villains are the best to ever appear on the screen. Join the evil queen from *Snow White And The Seven Dwarfs* as she scares up some of the most memorable villains and villainous moments in Disney history—including Ursula from *The Little Mermaid*, Yzma from *The Emperor's New Groove*, Cruella DeVil from *101 Dalmatians* and Captain Hook from *Peter Pan*.
>
> This special collection features clips from your favorite Disney movies plus shorts, songs and interactive games. It's frightful fun for the whole family that only Disney can conjure up.

A game in the DVD allows the player to go into the Evil Queen's Castle searching for three villains. Players can visit the Magic Mirror room, a unknown area with a useful carpet, some containers and a door as well as the queen's laboratory with her potions, dungeons, a garden and a swampy forest area where she floated away to find Snow White.

Ursula voiced by Pat Carroll who provided the character's voice in the original film sings *Sidekicks and Henchmen* by Marty Panzer and Dan Grady.

> As you sit on the bomb,
> who sounds the first alarm
> and rescues you from harm?
> Sidekicks and henchmen.

At the end, the cauldron turns against the Evil Queen and makes her vanish into nothingness, foiling her plans to take over Halloween.

> Cauldron: But where these villains all reside, for all eternity, is such a place as you've never seen, would never wish to be. For when you live your sorry life as if evil were your friend, you soon enough learn a final truth: all bad things must come to an end.

Donald's Halloween Scare: House of Mouse (2000)

Donald's Halloween Scare is a seven minute short cartoon made by Walt Disney Television Animation and originally aired May 20, 2000 as an episode of *Mickey Mouse Works*. It was later shown as part of the *House of Mouse* episode *Halloween With Hades* (October 2003).

It was also used in the direct-to-video feature *Mickey's House of Villains* (September 2002) that opened with "Oooo, it's a Houseketeer Halloween! So grab your garlic and get set for America's most haunted. He's Count Mickey Mouse."

On Halloween, Huey, Dewey and Louie go trick-or-treating in similar devil costumes but each in a different solid color (red, blue, green). They get treats from Minnie Mouse disguised as a witch stirring a cauldron who is with her black cat Figaro. Next they go to Mickey Mouse pretending to be a vampire laying in a candy filled coffin. Finally, they meet Goofy dressed as the Easter Bunny giving them colored eggs. He thinks it is Easter and his house is decorated appropriately for that holiday. The nephews tell him it is time for candy not eggs which puzzles Goofy.

When they visit Uncle Donald's house, they peer inside and think they see him sitting watching television. However they are confronted with a figure in a hockey mask and with a huge hook for a hand and they drop their bags of candy and run away in terror to hide behind a tree.

They soon discover that it was Donald disguised as the menancing figure. He had propped up a dummy on the chair in his house and scared the nephews so he could get their candy and gorge himself on all of it. They sneak into his house with the background music playing *Hall of the Mountain King* and put glue inside his mask and hook glove.

When Donald hears another knock at the door, thinking it is more kids he can frighten, he puts back on the mask and

hook. However, at the door it is Police Chief O'Hara with a wanted poster for a person dressed exactly the same as Donald's costume who is wanted since "three young duck have gone a-missing". Donald struggles to remove his mask or hook but can't so runs away.

It turns out it was really Huey, Dewey and Loue standing on each other's shoulders and wearing a rubber mask and raincoat pretending to be the police officer. Donald runs into Mickey, Minnie and Goofy who believe he is really the culprit since they have copies of the fake wanted poster and try to capture or attack him.

Sight gags ensue until Donald hides in Minnie's cauldron and is rolled into a graveyard where a tombstone shatters his mask.

He sees three tombsotnes with his nephews' names on them and Huey, Dewey and Louie crawl out of their graves as zombies. They tell him that he scared them to death. They chase him across the graveyard and he falls into a grave where it looks like they will bury him alive.

A tearful and very scared Donald promises to get all their candy back. They make him wear a costume of their own making as they go trick-or-treating. At one house, a shadowy figure appears at the door with apparently a hook for a hand and they all run away terrified. It is Goofy now dressed as Santa Claus holding a hooked candy cane in his hand. He laughs and licks the cane.

The two creative forces behind *Mickey's Mouse Works* were Tony Craig and Robert Gannaway. Their goal was to create Disney cartoon shorts for a new generation with the popular characters while honoring the spirit of the classic shorts. When the show was replaced by *Disney's House of Mouse* in January 2001, most of the *Mouse Work* segments were repeated there.

Witches of Morva:
The Black Cauldron (1985)

A trio of often forgotten Disney witches appeared in the animated feature film, *The Black Cauldron* (1985). Unlike some of the other Disney witches they never appeared outside the film and its related merchandise.

Deep in the dreary marshes of Morva, surrounded by sickly mist and twisted, decaying landscaping, sits the ramshackle cottage of the three powerful witches of Morva who live alone in this forsaken place. The cluttered interior is in dusty disarray but hides many of the dark secrets of these sinister sisters.

Concealed among a towering pile of rusty kettles and battered pots is the terrifying Black Cauldron. When evil Arawan broke his pledge to return it after creating his army of zombie warriors, he paid a severe price: the angry enchantresses reclaimed it themselves and once again secured it safely in their forest hovel.

In the original book by author Lloyd Alexander, the hideous threesome had an age-worn loom and were meant to resemble the famous Fates of Greek mythology who controlled the destiny of every person alive with the tattered threads on their ancient loom. As one of the Fair Folk says to the heroic Taran, "It's more a question of what they are, not who they are."

"We're neither good nor evil. We are simply interested in things as they are. Care isn't really a feeling we can have," claims the ugly Orddu in the book.

Forceful Orddu, with her straggly crimson hair frantically seeking escape from the prison of her small simple headband, is the dominating leader of this terrible trio. Physically, she is the tallest with a plump torso, but oddly scrawny arms and bony legs that flail wildly as she talks. Her long pointed nose protrudes outward like a warty spike above her toothless grin. She passionately craves Taran's powerful sword and furiously

sulks at the end of the film when the other two witches offer it back to the disheartened Taran.

Hunched over Orgorch, wearing the traditional pointed witch's hat, is the most disagreeable of the three mystical hags, constantly at odds with the desires of her siblings. Half as tall as Orddu, Orgorch has the same spiky defined features and unkempt fire red hair, but her physical appearance seems even more evil when combined with her aggressively threatening personality. It is quickly apparent that she has no patience with idle chatter when there is something to be transformed and eaten. With her sharp, pointed teeth, she is ravenously hungry for her favorite snack—fresh juicy tender frog legs.

The voice for Orgorch was actress Billie Hayes, who played a funny but fearful witch character who desperately schemed to steal a magic flute on a popular children's television show nearly a decade earlier when production on the animated feature originally began, and was a favorite of some of the young Disney animators.

That show was Sid and Marty Krofft's *H.R. Pufnstuf* where she played Witchiepoo. At the age of 85, she still continues to do voice over work for cartoons.

Orddu was voiced by Eda Reiss Merin and Orwen by late Adele Malis-Morey.

Girlishly plump Orwen, with her huge rolls of flesh cascading over her large body and her annoying giggle, appears to be the youngest of the group. She is the only one to wear make-up, but overdoes the pinkish cheek rouge and blood red lipstick so that it distracts from any natural attractiveness. She is the only sister to wear jewelry, a necklace of oddly shaped asymmetrical blue stones, and frilly purple pantaloons under her dress. Unlike her fellow witches, this flirtatious sorceress is hopelessly and constantly lovestruck and decides her perfect mate is the hapless Fflewddur Fflam, the aged minstrel who is visibly repulsed by her too-abundant charms.

However, like her magical companions, Orwen should be greatly feared. The three of them have turned all humans who have unknowingly offended them into frightened little green frogs, and intend to do the same with the brave Taran and his compatriots for inadvertently releasing dozens of the

imprisoned amphibians from a creaky old brown chest in the living room. The three barefooted sisters, clad in loose, bluish colored garments, chatter quite jovially and casually about the most dreadful things—like dining on the transformed frogs—that frightens and unnerves the heroic band.

While the wicked inhabitants of the scary home retain some of the horrible whimsy of their literary counterparts, the adapted story in the animated feature, according to animation historian Brian Sibley, allowed "little or no time for them to be adequately established, let alone fully developed...it results in an almost lack of involvement [by the audience] with these delightful characters."

One of the most important aspects that remained about these Morvaian mystics was their love of negotiating. Crafty Orddu pridefully exclaims, "We never give anything away. What we do is bargain. Trade." The two trades they arrange for the Black Cauldron are key pivotal moments in the final animated feature and, strangely, favor the heroes and what they need to live happily ever after.

Being supernatural, the trio also inhabit an ethereal plane high in the clouds where they casually lounge while observing the affairs of humans. They await the proper moment to exercise their mischief by projecting crackling blue light magical sparkles from their tapered white fingertips.

In the original book, the witches could transform themselves into beautiful maidens and, in fact, trade identities with each other—although none of them ever wanted to transform into disgusting Orgorch, who always had intestinal problems from eating too many toads.

The energetic sorcery of these exuberant crones supplies an element of dark humor that reminds audiences of the overwhelming forces that ill-equipped Taran and his friends will ultimately confront in their final battle with the Horned King. The model sheets were done by Andreas Deja. Tim Burton had done some concept art of the witches connected together in one dress and moving as one. Of course their arms had the traditional Burton black and white stripes.

Girl vs. Monster (2012)

Premiering on the Disney Channel on October 12, 2012, this ninety minute film begins one day before Halloween. Fifteen year old Skylar Lewis (Olivia Holt) is preparing for a big Halloween party with her two nerdy best friends Sadie (Kerris Dorsey) and Henry (Brendan Meyer). She is planning on singing at the event with a dreamy classmate even though she has stage fright but is crushed when her parents make her stay home and activate an alarm system to keep her there.

Trying to cut the electricity to deactivate the system unleashes an immortal monster named Deimata (Tracy Dawson) and other monsters from a containment unit in the basement who intend to go out and feed on people's fears.

Skylar learns that she is actually the fifth generation of a monster hunting family. Her parents wear welding masks and black trench coats and have wrist proton packs that trap a monster in a CD discman player. Skylar was totally unaware of their real job and thought they were mold experts.

Deimata's two companions are Theadosia (Anna Galvan), an evil school teacher, who is Sadie's fear monster and Bobb (Stefano Giulianetti), an evil scarecrow who is Henry's fear monster.

Filled with fear, Skylar and her friends go armed with her parents' monster hunting equipment to the party but fear strikes her friend Henry and he is frozen and must be rescued by Cobb (Adam Chambers) who has been training with Skylar's parents. Deimata lures Skylar's parents into a trap by pretending that Skylar is in trouble.

Deimata possesses Skylar's rival, Myra, and sings at the party inside of Skylar. Afterwards Deimata leaves Myra's body and Myra warns Skylar how Deimata can possess people.

Henry learns that letting go of his fears will cause monsters to disintegrate and returns to the party to tell Skylar. Skylar

faces her fear by singing in front of everyone and the monsters vanish. Deimata reveals she cannot be destroyed that way and she still is holding Skylar's parents captive.

Skylar realizes that Deimata is feeding off the fears of her parents about her safety. Once she convinces them that she is fine, they capture Deimata. However, at the end credits, Deimata blows on the glass in her unit and cracks it and her laugh is heard one last time suggesting there will be a sequel.

The film is filled with minor scares like trees that spring to life, floating heads that appear out of nowhere, and the maniacal, redhaired Deimata. The fears may seem simple things like being made fun of but for a teenager that is huge and that was the target audience for this film.

Girl vs. Monster was filmed in Vancouver, British Columbia, Canada. The story was written by Annie DeYoung ("Princess Protection Program" "Return to Halloweentown") and the teleplay by DeYoung and Ron McGee ("The Nine Lives of Chloe King" "Atomic Twister").

The movie was directed by DGA winner and Emmy Award nominee Stuart Gillard ("Scream Team" "Twitches") and executive-produced by Sheri Singer ("Good Luck Charlie, It's Christmas"), with Tracey Jeffrey ("The Suite Life Movie") as producer. *Girl vs. Monster* is a production of Bad Angel Productions, Ltd.

Roughly 4.9 million viewers watched the premiere. Olivia Holt performed three of the movie's songs that included *Fearless, Had Me at Hello, Nothing's Gonna Stop Us, I Got My Scream On*, and *Superstar. Had Me at Hello* won the Best Crush Song at the 2013 Radio Disney Awards.

The Scariest Story Ever: A Mickey Mouse Halloween Spooktacular! (2017)

The Scariest Story Ever: A Mickey Mouse Halloween Spooktacular! is a roughly half hour animated Halloween special that premiered on November 15, 2017.

The special is an extension of the new series of Disney Channel Mickey Mouse cartoons that premiered in 2013 with Chris Diamantopoulos voicing Mickey Mouse. He was nominated for an Annie Award for Outstanding Voice Acting in an Animated Television / Broadcast Production for this Halloween special.

The popular series with a more modern design was created by Paul Rudish for Disney Television Animation to introduce a new generation of kids to the character while still being faithful to Mickey's original cartoons that were broadly physical.

This is the second thirty-minute special of the series, following *Duck the Halls: A Mickey Mouse Christmas Special* (2016). Both half hour specials have been released together on DVD as *Mickey Mouse: Merry & Scary* DVD on September 26, 2017.

The special was written by Darrick Bachman, Alonso Ramirez Ramos, Paul Rudish, Eddie Trigueros and Dave Wasson.

It was directed by Alonso Ramirez Ramos, Eddie Trigueros and Dave Wasson. They won an Annie Award for Outstanding Achievement for Directing in an Animated Television / Broadcast Production for this special.

The show's musical composer was Christopher Willis who worked on all the seasons of the television show as well as writing a new song for the Mickey & Minnie's Runaway Railway theme park attraction. He won an Annie award for Outstanding Achievement for Music in an Animated Television / Broadcast Production for his work on this special.

About the Halloween show, Willis said:

> I think it's very much what you would hope. It feels very spooky and festive in that particular Halloween way. The Halloween special has two more songs than the Christmas special; one is in the end credits and the other one happens in the middle of the action.
>
> Mickey is trying to keep Huey, Dewey, and Louie entertained with scary stories and he's not doing very well. What that means for me, musically, is that for each of the stories we go into a different stylistic world so I have to completely change gears, which is huge fun. There's some old-fashioned 1930s song music and then there's some very 1980s music, and then there's some creepy Disney music, which provides more scares than one would expect.

Donald's nephews Huey, Dewey and Louie along with Mickey's nephews Morty and Ferdie have had a fun evening trick-or-treating together. When they return to Mickey's home, Mickey decides to tell the kids a scary story as part of the festivities. The three classic tales are parodies of Frankenstein, Dracula and a variation of Hansel and Gretel.

Mickey begins his first story by stepping in front of a curtain and warning his audience of how scary it is. This is a reference to the original film version of *Frankenstein* (1931) starring Boris Karloff that began with a similar warning.

At the castle of "Dr. Goofenstein" (Goofy as Dr. Frankenstein), "Duckgor" (Donald Duck as assistant Igor) finds the body parts needed for Dr. Goofenstein's experiment. They bring to life a giant Frankenstein Monster (with Mickey's head) who promptly comes to life and begins happily singing and dancing to a Broadway/disco number. The kids are unimpressed and not scared.

Goofy feels that what was missing was "visual aids" so he tells a story about a swamp monster using a sock puppet. However, he gets scared of his own puppet and hides under the couch. Donald using a flashlight to create spooky lighting tries to tell a story but the kids can not understand anything he is saying.

Mickey tries again with a story about the Prince of the Vampires. The only people who can stop him are "Van

Mousing" (Mickey as a parody of Van Helsing from Bram Stoker's *Dracula*) and his partners "Dipworth Goofington III" and "Drake McQuack".

The three make their way through the skeleton labyrinth and past two werewolves where they face the Prince of Vampires. Van Mousing finally uses sunlight to defeat him but during the battle has been bitten and turns into a vampire himself.

Goofy and Donald tell Mickey he is incapable of telling a really scary story because he is such a nice guy. When they return to the kids, they have become rowdy and wild. Mickey decides to tell one final scary story.

Five children (represented as Huey, Dewey, Louie, Morty and Ferdie wearing lederhosen) are constantly stealing pies in a nearby village. One day, they steal an unusually tasty pie from an old lady.

They find the old lady's house and split up to look for more pies. Within the house, Dewey, Louie, Morty and Ferdie are all captured while Huey finds the pie. He is discovered by the old lady who reveals that her secret ingredient are "the most snot-nosed, rotten little boys" she could find and intends to use Huey and his friends in her next one. She transforms into a green-skinned witch.

The story really scares the kids, Donald and Goofy, who all run upstairs and hide under the blankets in bed. Mickey hears trick-or-treaters at the door and when he opens it he sees the witch from his story with a pie. Mickey screams and runs upstairs to join the rest. The witch turns out to be Minnie, who is just wearing a costume and has arrived with Daisy.

Daisy asks what kind of pie Minnie had that scared Mickey. Minnie says that it's just pumpkin and a couple of jack-o'-lanterns scream in terror and pass out with their lantern smoke spelling out "The End".

There are many "hidden" references in the cartoon.

Mickey's lederhosen costume is the same one he wears in the *Mickey Mouse* series episode "Yodelberg" (2013). Goofy wears a Super Goof costume, a character from the Disney comic books who also appeared in the *House of Mouse* (2002). Donald is dressed as...a sailor.

Huey, Dewey and Louie's costumes (a devil, a witch, a ghost) are the same as the ones they wore in the short *Trick or Treat* (1952). Morty and Ferdie are dressed as a pirate and a dragon.

Furniture from the Haunted Mansion appears in Mickey's house as Halloween decorations such as the Demon Clock, the pipe organ from the ballroom scene and one of the busts.

The six children who are trick-or-treating in the beginning at the special were dressed up as the Lost Boys from Peter Pan.

Chernabog from the "Night on Bald Mountain" segment of Fantasia makes a cameo as well as the Headless Horseman

After the kids settle in and start eating their Halloween candy, Goofy expresses his fear of goblins. Donald responds in reference to the nephews, "They're the only goblins I know. I don't think we should feed them after midnight." It is a reference to same warning in the horror-comedy film *Gremlins* (1984)

When Mickey says he doesn't want to "toot his own horn," a steamboat out the window toots its horn. This is the same steamboat from Mickey's debut short, *Steamboat Willie* (1928).

The special won an Annie Award for Outstanding Achievement for Production Design in an Animated Television / Broadcast Production.

About the Author

Jim Korkis is an internationally respected Disney historian who has written hundreds of articles and thirty books about all things Disney over the last forty years. Jim grew up in Glendale, California where starting at the young age of fifteen, he was able to meet and interview some of Walt's original team of animators and Imagineers.

Jim was a writer, designer and performer at Six Flags Magic Mountain's yearly Haunted Mountain promotion during the Halloween season. He has learned through experience to only buy the good candy that he enjoys to hand out to trick-or-treaters.

He knows that most children today do not go door-to-door anymore but attend events at churches, theme parks and elsewhere for safety reasons. So Jim can happily enjoy the bowl of sugary treats himself as he watches Halloween related entertainment on television. He even eats candy corn but only at Halloween.

In 1995, Jim relocated to Orlando, Florida where he worked for Walt Disney World in a variety of capacities including Entertainment, Animation, Disney Institute, Disney University, College and International Programs, Disney Cruise Line, Disney Design Group, Disney Vacation Club, Disney Learning Center, Yellow Shoes Marketing and more.

His original research on Disney history has been used often by the Disney Company as well as other organizations including the Disney Family Museum.

Several websites currently frequently feature Jim's articles about Disney history:

- MousePlanet.com
- AllEars.net
- Yesterland.com

- CartoonResearch.com
- YourFirstVisit.net

In addition, Jim is a frequent guest on multiple podcasts as well as a consultant and keynote speaker to various businesses, schools and groups.

Jim is not currently an employee of the Disney Company.

To read more stories by Jim Korkis about Disney history, please check out his other books, all available from ThemeParkPress.com:

- *Extinct Disneyland (2020)*
- *The Vault of Walt: Volume 8, Outer Space Edition* (2019)
- *The Unofficial Walt Disney World Companion 1971 (2019)*
- *The Vault of Walt: Volume 7, Christmas Edition* (2018)
- *Secret Stories of Mickey Mouse* (2018)
- *More Secret Stories of Disneyland* (2018)
- *Extra Secret Stories of Walt Disney World* (2018)
- *Call Me Walt* (2017)
- *Walt's Words* (2017)
- *Other Secret Stories of Walt Disney World* (2017)
- *Secret Stories of Disneyland* (2017)
- *The Vault of Walt: Volume 6* (2017)
- *Gremlin Trouble* (2017)
- *Donald Duck's Daddy* (2017)
- *More Secret Stories of Walt Disney World* (2016)
- *The Vault of Walt: Volume 5* (2016)
- *The Unofficial Disneyland 1955 Companion* (2016)
- *How to Be a Disney Historian* (2016)
- *Secret Stories of Walt Disney World* (2015)
- *The Vault of Walt: Volume 4* (2015)
- *Everything I Know I Learned from Disney Animated Features* (2015)
- *The Vault of Walt: Volume 3* (2014)

- *Animation Anecdotes* (2014)
- *Who's the Leader of the Club? Walt Disney's Leadership Lessons* (2014)
- *The Book of Mouse* (2013)
- *The Vault of Walt: Volume 2* (2013)
- *Who's Afraid of the Song of the South?* (2012)
- *The Revised Vault of Walt* (2012)

ABOUT THEME PARK PRESS

Theme Park Press publishes books primarily about the Disney company, its history, culture, films, animation, and theme parks, as well as theme parks in general.

Our authors include noted historians, animators, Imagineers, and experts in the theme park industry.

We also publish many books by first-time authors, with topics ranging from fiction to theme park guides.

And we're always looking for new talent. If you'd like to write for us, or if you're interested in the many other titles in our catalog, please visit:

www.ThemeParkPress.com

· ·

Theme Park Press Newsletter

Subscribe to our free email newsletter and enjoy:

- ◆ Free book downloads and giveaways
- ◆ Access to excerpts from our many books
- ◆ Announcements of forthcoming releases
- ◆ Exclusive additional content and chapters
- ◆ And more good stuff available nowhere else

To subscribe, visit www.ThemeParkPress.com, or send email to newsletter@themeparkpress.com.

CW01511722